# SPECIAL OPERATIONS EXECUTIVE: POLISH SECTION

## The Death of the Second Polish Republic

### Wiesław Rogalski

*Tell the people in Poland that, here in England,
the Poles have faithful friends who will never abandon them…*

Lieutenant Colonel Harold Perkins,
Head of SOE Polish Section 1943

For Jude and Theo

Helion & Company Limited
Unit 8 Amherst Business Centre
Budbrooke Road
Warwick
CV34 5WE
England
Tel. 01926 499 619
Email: info@helion.co.uk
Website: www.helion.co.uk
Twitter: @helionbooks
Visit our blog at blog.helion.co.uk

Published by Helion & Company 2022
Designed and typeset by Mach 3 Solutions (www.mach3solutions.co.uk)
Cover designed by Paul Hewitt, Battlefield Design (www.battlefield-design.co.uk)

Text © Wiesław Rogalski 2022
Images © Polish Institute and Sikorski Museum, London
Maps drawn by George Anderson © Helion & Company Ltd 2022

Every reasonable effort has been made to trace copyright holders and to obtain their permission for the use of copyright material. The author and publisher apologize for any errors or omissions in this work and would be grateful if notified of any corrections that should be incorporated in future reprints or editions of this book.

ISBN 978-1-915113-74-0

British Library Cataloguing-in-Publication Data.
A catalogue record for this book is available from the British Library.

All rights reserved. No part of this publication may be reproduced, stored in a retrieval system, or transmitted, in any form, or by any means, electronic, mechanical, photocopying, recording or otherwise, without the express written consent of Helion & Company Limited.

For details of other military history titles published by Helion & Company Limited contact the above address or visit our website: http://www.helion.co.uk.

We always welcome receipt of book proposals from prospective authors.

*As soon as any man says of his affairs of the State, what does it matter to me? The State may be given up for lost.*

Rousseau, *Social Contract*, III, 15

Emblem of the
Second Republic of Poland
1918–1947

Emblem of the
People's Republic of Poland
1947–1989

# Contents

| | | |
|---|---|---|
| Abbreviations | | vii |
| Staff List | | viii |
| Preface | | ix |
| Prologue | | x |
| Lines of Command – Overview | | xvi |
| 1 | British Military Mission to Poland 1939 | 17 |
| 2 | The Polish Army | 29 |
| 3 | The September 1939 Campaign | 35 |
| 4 | Republican Forces in France | 46 |
| 5 | Republican Forces in Britain | 54 |
| 6 | The Polish Resistance | 57 |
| 7 | Special Operations Executive (SOE) | 63 |
| 8 | SOE Polish Section | 70 |
| 9 | The 'Silent and Invisible' (Cichociemni) Polish Special Forces | 80 |
| 10 | Trial Flight | 91 |
| 11 | Planning Air Corridors to Occupied Poland | 99 |
| 12 | In Pursuit of Freedom | 111 |
| 13 | Why Can't Life be Simple? | 125 |
| 14 | Allies at War | 134 |
| 15 | Transfer to Italy | 137 |
| 16 | Wildhorn Operations | 143 |
| 17 | A Shortage of Trust | 150 |
| 18 | The Soviet Push to the West | 155 |
| 19 | Sixty-Six Days (Warsaw Rises) | 160 |
| 20 | The 'American Armada' | 178 |
| 21 | Surrender | 183 |
| 22 | Death of the Second Polish Republic | 190 |
| 23 | Postscript | 195 |

Appendices
I  Maps                                                                  203
II  Aircraft Employed in Operations to Poland (not to scale)              237
III  List of Polish Special Forces Dropped into Poland (pseudonyms inclusive)  239
IV  Details of RAF Flights to Poland Procured by SOE                     243
V  Drop sites in occupied Poland                                         246
VI  SOE locations employed by Poles                                      247

Bibliography                                                             248
Index                                                                    252

# Abbreviations

| | |
|---|---|
| AI | Army Intelligence |
| CAS | Chief of the Air Staff |
| CIGS | Chief of the Imperial General Staff |
| COS | Chiefs of Staff |
| FO | Foreign Office |
| F/O | Flight Officer |
| GOC | General Officer Command |
| JIC | Joint Intelligence Committee |
| JPS | Joint Planning Staff |
| MAAF | Mediterranean Allied Air Force |
| MIR | Military Intelligence Research |
| P/O | Pilot Officer |
| PRP | People's Republic of Poland |
| SAAF | South African Airforce |
| SHAEF | Supreme Headquarters of the Allied Expeditionary Force |
| SIS | Secret Intelligence Services |
| STS | Special Training School |
| SRP | Second Republic of Poland |
| USAF | United States Air Force |
| WO | War Office |
| W/T | Wireless Telephony |

# Staff List

| | |
|---|---|
| Hugh Dalton | Minister for SOE until February 1942 |
| Earl of Selborne | Minister for SOE from February 1942 |
| Frank Nelson | Executive Director of SOE August 1940–May 1942 |
| Charles Hambro | Executive Director of SOE May 1942–September 1943 |
| Colin Gubbins | Executive Director of SOE from September 1943 |
| Bickam Sweet-Escott | Head of Polish Section |
| Harold Perkins | Head of Polish Section |
| Major Pickles | Head of Polish Section |
| Richard Barry | Director of Plans until 1942 |
| Alan Boxer | Commander 161 Squadron 1944 onwards |
| Archie Boyle | Air Commander RAF |
| Victor Cavendish-Bentinck | Chairman of the JIC |
| John Corby | Wing Commander RAF Tempsford |
| Wilfred Dunderdale | British Intelligence Liaison Officer with Polish Secret Service |
| James Easton | Director of Intelligence Research |
| Colin Grierson | Replaced Barry 1942 |
| Ron Hazell | Head of Minorities Section |
| George Hill | SOE Moscow |
| David Keswick | Director Mediterranean Group 43 |
| Moray McLaren | Head of Polish Section (Political Welfare Executive) |
| Steward Menzies | Head of SIS |
| John Palmer | Commander of Tempsford Airfield after Fielding |
| Alan Ritchie | Air Advisor – took over from Grierson |
| Stawell | Director of Cairo Group 1943–1945 |
| Henry Thornton | Air Commander and SOE Officer at Tempsford |
| Henry Threlfall | SOE Mediterranean |
| John Venner | Finance Director |

# Preface

On 20 June 1983 a memorial was unveiled in the grounds of Audley End House at Saffron Walden in Essex. During the Second World War the country mansion and estate had been requisitioned by the Special Operations Executive (SOE) and used as a special training school for secret missions to occupied Poland. The memorial is dedicated to the 'Silent and Invisible', an elite group of special operations forces of the Polish Allied Army in exile, who had trained in Britain and had lost their lives in the service of the SOE Polish Project. The monument, still standing today, consists of a memorial urn on a plinth. On the front of the plinth there is an oval tablet depicting the badge of the 'Silent and Invisible', a swooping eagle paying homage to the Polish Eagle. The eagle carries a wreath in its talons with the letters 'PW', which stand for *Polska Walcząca* and translated as 'Fighting Poland'. On another face is an inscription, which read:

> 'Between 1942 and 1944 Polish members of the SOE trained in this house for missions in their homeland. This memorial commemorates the achievement of those who parachuted into enemy occupied Poland and lost their lives for the freedom of this and their own country.'

Although the Poles had fought from the first day of the war to the last, Britain's Polish ally lost everything. The Government of the Polish Second Republic, exiled in London for most of the war, were left without a nation to govern at the end of the conflict. The Polish Forces, under British operational command, ended the war without a territory to defend and, uniquely, were demobilised in exile by the British Government – displaced Polish persons ended up without a homeland to return to. This was nothing more than total loss and was partly due to the Republic's allies. The ordeal of SOE Polish Section in this history deserves to be better known for posterity.

316 Special Forces were parachuted into Poland. 103 Lost their lives.

# Prologue

According to the one-time Polish Chief of State, Marshal Józef Piłsudski (1867–1935),[1] each Polish generation has to demonstrate in blood that Poland still exists, is alive and is not reconciled to foreign slavery.[2] He stated that if any generation fails to do this, it would have shown itself to be an unworthy successor to previous generations that had risen against the Russian Tsars and the Prussian Kings. Such startling sentiments find their roots in Poland's tormented history. For over 120 years during the 18th, 19th and 20th centuries, the country was partitioned and occupied by her neighbours the three great European powers: Tsarist Russia, Germany (Prussia)[3] and the Austro-Hungarian Empire. Barely a century after her armies had saved Christendom at the gates of Vienna, which were besieged by the Ottomans in 1683, Poland vanished from the European map.[4] This condemned the Poles to years of protests and uprisings in an attempt to resist complete national annihilation, for example, Polish legions joined Napoleon's army in 1812 in the hope that this would bring about some relief from growing Russian suppression. This strategy failed when the French were defeated and had to reteat. As punishment for joining Napoleon's forces, many Poles were deported into the depths of Siberia[5] whilst others escaped into exile. Another attempt at preserving national identity occurred in 1846, when the Poles in Austrian occupied Kraków rose to demand autonomy. This rising was crushed by Austrian and Prussian Forces. Such cycles of

---

1   A scion of a Polish noble family from Lithuania. He was inspired with patriotism in a politically charged home. In 1886 he was arrested by the Russian police on an alleged charge of plotting the assassination of Tsar Alexander III and was exiled in Eastern Siberia for five years. In 1892 he returned to Wilno and joined the newly founded Polish Socialist Party. He took part in clandestine activities designed to realize Polish independence. Many believe Pilsudski to be the most outstanding Polish politician of the twentieth century and the chief restorer of Poland's independence after World War One.
2   E.D.R. Harrison, 'The British Special Operation Executive and Poland', *The Historical Journal*, Vol 43, No 4, December 2000, pp. 1071-1091.
3   The Kingdom of Prussia was a German Kingdom that formed part of the state of Prussia between 1701-1918. It was the driving force behind the unification of Germany in 1871.
4   On the 12 September 1683, Polish King Sobieski, at the head of Polish-Lithuanian army, defeated an Ottoman Army hence breaking the siege of Vienna. Considered by historians as one of Europe's most important battles it cleared central Europe of Ottoman Forces. Roger Moorhouse, *First to Fight, The Polish War 1939* (London: Bodley Head, 2019), p.39.
5   Moorhouse, *First to Fight, The Polish War 1939*, p.40.

risings followed by suppression and then risings again, repeated themselves like the medieval wheel of fortune. This sequence, however, was broken early in the twentieth century when the occupying powers floundered during the Great War and Poland regained her independence at the Versailles peace negotiations[6] to become the Second Republic of Poland (SRP). According to the victorious powers, (primarily Britain, America and France), reborn Poland was to act as a bulwark between Russia and Germany and so contribute to peace in Europe. However, this situation was short lived as both the Germans and the Russians returned in 1939, causing the country's subsequent partition. When the young Second Republic was invaded in 1939, it was barely twenty years old, having emerged in 1918. The Republic's modern history, that is between the wars, was one long struggle of uniting the previously partitioned population into one coherent nation which included, rebuilding political cohesion, revitalising social and cultural identity, and realising stability and national security. The region which had previously been under German occupation was perhaps the most advanced compared to the territories occupied by the Russians and Austrians. Despite attempts to 'Germanise' them the Poles never allowed thier culture to be eradicated which permitted Polish technical and commercial knowledge to grow and a middle class to emerge. The Polish region which had been under Russian partition was perhaps the most backward. Russia did more than any other occupier to keep its Polish population at a humble level of existence and so the Polish community here was mostly agrarian. The Austrian sector was perhaps the most politically liberal and therefore Kraków and Lwów[7] became flourishing centres of Polish learning, with the Poles even being permitted to take part in the governance of the Hapsburg empire. This divided history meant that the leaders of modern Poland had their work cut out uniting the three Polish populations into one coherent whole when the country from partition re-emerged after the Great War.[8] In order to understand Polish history during the Second World War, it is important to appreciate the legacy of the country's eradication and the various difficulties it was still facing when she came under attack in 1939. For example, during the 1920s the new Polish state had six different currencies, four separate legal systems and no integrate transport system to speak of. In spite of this, it is also necessary to recognise that despite the significant shortcomings in military equipment and strategic knowhow, the Polish Second Republic was making great strides in overcoming these difficulties by mobilising all national resources, including the people. In 1939 and during the Second World War the Poles were required to fight for their cultural existence once again. This was unique during the conflict, as the Nazi *drang nach osten,* was to destroy Polish culture and people in

---

6   Versailles Treaty signed June 1919. Peace treaty between Germany and the Allies at the end of the First World War where territory was given back to Poland among other newly formed states.
7   Old Polish name for the Ukrainian city of Lviv.
8   Poland regained her independence in 1918 after the Great War. Independence lasted until 1939 and the invasion of Nazi Germany and the Soviet Union marking the beginning of the Second World War.

order to create *lebensraum*[9] whereas in countries such as France, Belgium, Denmark and Holland, among others, also under German occupation, the intention was not to destroy these cultures, but to subjugate and dominate them. Therefore, schools, universities, theatres and art galleries and so on in these countries remained open whereas in Poland the intention was to erase all symbols of the Polish way of life except for some vocational schools which were kept open in order to train up slaves for the Reich. The Russian objective in invading the east of Poland was not too dissimilar to that of Nazi Germany though it was based on class war rather than on territory and so it was primarily political. The aim was to eradicate the Polish bourgeoisie and to annexe the Polish territory which had passed to Poland following the Treaty of Riga and the Russo-Polish war of 1920 when the Bolshevik army under Kamieniev had been pushed back by Piłsudski. Given Poland's unfortunate history and geography it is perhaps unsurprising that in 1939 following defeat in the Polish War, clandestine resistance groups appeared spontaneously and immediately. Initially, these were grass root movements set up by various social groups such as the peasantry, the intelligentsia, industrialists, students and army officers, who had fought in the failed September Campaign[10] and managed to avoid the German and Soviet round-ups. Once again, the Poles had their backs to the wall and were forced to demonstrate the existence of their country, even though it was under tyrannical occupation. Eventually, most of these individual underground formations were brought together to form the clandestine Home Army finally comprising some 400,000 recruits.

\* \* \*

Polish resistance during occupation was both civilian and military in nature, for it had to embrace all spheres of national life. Cultural preservation was ensured through a clandestine judiciary, an underground press, theatres, publishing houses and secret education institutions. These cultural organisations were collectively known as 'The Underground State'. As the term suggests, military resistance comprised of acts of defiance against the occupiers using armaments and explosives. The Home Army[11] (Armia Krajowa) became the main conspiratorial movement in the country which spearheaded resistance in the name of the Government of the Second Republic. It was supplied with arms, money and officers procured by the SOE under the guidance of the Republic's Government exiled in London and led by Premier, General Władysław Sikorski.[12] Sikorski arrived in Britain together with the remnants of the Republic's

---

9  German word for 'living space'. Hitler's reason for starting the Second World War was the search for more living space for the Germans.
10  The defence war of Poland in 1939.
11  The National Archives (TNA) HS4/147: Polish Secret Army, Polish planning for the reoccupation of Poland.
12  Sikorski left Poland on the 17-18 September 1939 and went to France where he was appointed Commander of Polish Forces. On the 30 September he became Premier of the Polish Government in exile and its Minister of Defence. He mobilised about 100,000 troops under French command. On the fall of France in 1940, he decamped to London and began

Forces which had evacuated mainland Europe (France) alongside the British expeditionary force during the humiliating Dunkirk retreat. On arrival in Britain, Sikorski, who was a hostage to his ambitins, promised Churchill that the Poles would continue to fight on for as long as it takes to realies Allied victory. Winston Churchill, the British Prime Minister, was pleased to hear these words for at that time he believed Britain was isolated and vulnerable and will be Hitler's next target. The two men ended up forging a mutual respect for each other and a close working relationship ensued. However, as the war progressed, the political influence and importance of the Polish exiled government in the allied camp was eclipsed by the Soviet Union, which had changed sides in the war in 1941 to become part of the Western Alliance. This dramatic change in Soviet Russian fortunes eventually resulted in the dismantling of the Second Republic of Poland in favour of the communist People's Republic of Poland (PRP) which occurred in 1947.[13] The Polish clandestine resistance army fighting for this change during the occupation was the People's Army (Armia Ludowa) which was supported and financed by the Soviet NKVD and fought in opposition to the Second Republic's Home Army. According to best estimates the People's Army comprised 10,000 recruits.

\* \* \*

The Special Operations Executive (SOE), was a British Intelligence Service organisation which grew out of SIS[14] and was established in July 1940, just a few weeks after the Dunkirk evacuation. It was disbanded in 1946. According to its founding charter, its function was to wage secret warfare behind enemy lines in occupied Europe. Its 'big bangs' approach is often contrasted to the 'silent and quiet approach' of the SIS which was considered by some to be more sophisticated and gentlemanly. The Executive comprised a number of departments called Sections, each taking responsibility for a particular country or region on the continent. The Polish Section was set up in November 1940 and was initially run by Bickam Sweet-Escott. Subsequently he was replaced by Captain Harold Perkins, whose commander was Brigadier Gubbins (later knighted) who was a close confidant of General Sikorski.[15] The Section liaised with the Polish Sixth Bureau (Intelligence) of the Polish General Staff, previously known as the Liaison Bureau of the Polish General Staff based in London, and started operating on 26 June, 1940.[16] The legislative framework for SOE's involvement in Poland was the Anglo-Polish Agreement signed in 1939, which assured mutual assistance in case of Poland being invaded. The setting up of SOE was a response to feelings of despondency and vulnerability in London following a number of military

---

    rebuilding the Polish Forces once again. He signed the Polish-Soviet Agreement on July 30 1941. Sikorski was killed in an air accident off Gibraltar in July 1943.
13   Founded 1947. Dissolved 1989.
14   Secret Intelligence Service
15   Jonathan Walker, *Poland Alone* (Stroud: The History Press 2008), p.148.
16   Jozef Garliński, *Poland, SOE and the Allies,* (London: George Allen and Unwin, 1969), p.39.

setbacks in the war such as the BEF's[17] retreat from France and Belgium and the failed Battle of Narvik.[18] As a result Churchill investigated the use of clandestine forces thinking that the establishment of a secret organisation such as the SOE would take the fight behind German lines and facilitate conventional armies to prevail. The Special Operations Executive could only work effectively within the politics and policies of the British Government and her Allies. Consequently, it seems prudent to remember the political conditions that prevailed at the time when discussing SOE operations, particularly in Poland. This work is not a history of SOE's Polish Section, more a rumination on its work between 1940 and 1945. The reader may be helped by the realisation that during this period Poland was ruled by three distinct regimes, each in opposition to the other.[19] The years between 1918 and 1939 (that is the end of the Polish Defence War of 1939) the Second Republic of Poland was ruled by the Piłsudskiite Sanationist Regime. This regime crumbled with Poland's defeat by the binary invasion of Nazi Germany and Soviet Union in September 1939. The subsequent regime, which governed from exile between 1939 and 1945, was the Sikorskiite Regime under the leadership of Wladislaw Sikorski, the exiled Prime Minister and Commander-in-Chief of Polish Forces. The Sikorskiite Regime worked first from France, but then on the capitulation of the French, from Britain. This regime was betrayed and then disenfranchised by London at the end of the war in favour of the third and final regime: the Regime of the Polish Workers' Party, which was installed in Warsaw by the Soviet Union and finally accepted by London as the post-war government of Poland. At this point in time the Second Republic of Poland ceased to exist being replaced by the socialist People's Republic of Poland, which existed between 1947 and 1989.

This work is an attempt to redress the lack of attention given to SOE's Polish Section in literature. The failure of historians to comprehensively discuss this historiography is a serious omission and compromises our understanding of the Second World War and its immediate aftermath in Europe. This topic, therefore, warrants further consideration. It is not as if the activities of the SOE in other European countries have been ignored, far from it, for much discussion on SOE's activities in countries such as Italy, Romania, the Low Countries and France exist–see for example SOE in France: *An account of the Work of SOE in France 1940 – 1944*, by M.R.D. Foot or *They Fought Alone: The True Story of SOE's Agents in Wartime France*, by M. Buckmuster, are numerous. There may be a number of reasons why the SOE's Polish Section has been largely ignored in literature, one being the relegation by the COS of Polish resistance operations to a secondary level of importance as the war continued and the view that the support provided by SOE Polish Section to Polish resistance fighters was disappointing with some even arguing that it did more harm than good.

---

17  British Expeditionary Force.
18  Battle of Narvik, April-June 1940, was part of the Norwegian Campaign. The campaign failed due to the Royal Navy's lack of radar control and high-performance fighters.
19  See Wiesław Rogalski, *Divided Loyalty: Britain's Polish Ally* (Solihull: Helion and Company, 2017).

Is this true? Clearly, the topic requires further examination so that its history is much better known to posterity.

* * *

Frank's diary provides much valuable information about what life was like on the home front. He includes many newspaper cutting of the day (not included here) and descriptions of his life as a Post Office manager in the south of England. Frank Leslie Balmforth was born in Leeds on 25 April, 1898. He regarded his home town to be Oswestry in Shropshire where he attended Oswestry National School later called Oswestry Church of England School. In 1912 Frank moved to a school in Leeds where he lived with his grandparents. He soon became homesick and returned to Oswestry where he attended a school in Welshpool. In 1914 he passed a Post Office Leadership Examination and joined the PO staff at Oswestry. In 1922 Frank married Gerty at St Oswald's Parish Church and after requesting a transfer to a position in a main Post Office moved to Staines, Southern England. Frank started writing his diary just as the Second World was beginning. The diary gives us a picture of the Home Front. Despite several attempts to get involved in the war effort Frank was retained in the Post Office as a protected profession where he was needed to supervise the new intake of staff (mainly female) which had been recruited into the postal service to replace the men that had been called up. The original diary entries were written in longhand in quarto exercise books and cover the period 1939–1945. Later entries were written on loose leaf paper and bound in quarto ring binders.

# Lines of Command – Overview

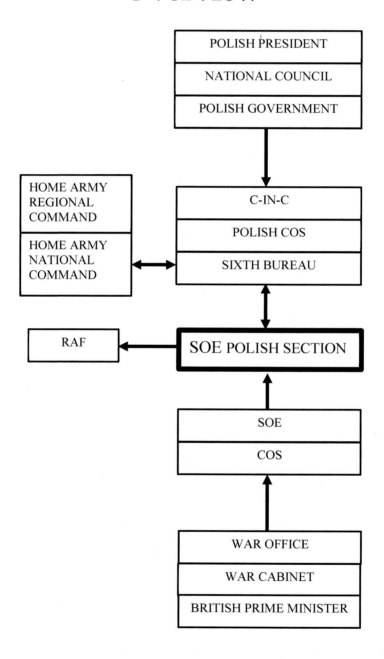

# 1

# British Military Mission to Poland 1939

*Because the friendship of comrades originates through their own choice, love of this kind takes precedence of the love of kindred in matters where we are free to do as we choose, for instance in matters of action.*

Aquinas, *Summa Theologica*, II-II, 26,8

On 2 September, 1939, one day after the invasion of Poland by Nazi Germany, Gerty and Frank Balmforth were returning from holiday in Oswestry. The train they were travelling in was very full and extra carriages had to be attached at Wolverhampton in the midlands. Frank engaged an RAF Gunnery Officer in conversation, who was travelling to Rouen following a detour to his home in Oxford. The officer did not talk about the reason for his travelling but informed Frank that the RAF had priced in a loss of a staggering 1000 men per day in RAF operations over Europe. As the train snaked through Birmingham city centre towards Paddington in London, Frank saw his first barrage balloons flying above the city. When they arrived in Paddington, he noticed that the station was abnormally busy and outgoing trains were exceedingly crowded. They boarded their train for Staines which arrived two hours late. When they alighted, they saw a busy high street with people crowding into shops, panic buying goods of various kind. Shopkeepers were hurriedly preparing makeshift blackout blinds from off-cuts of fabric. On 3 September Frank simply wrote in his diary, 'At war 11a.m.'[1]

Meanwhile, back in London once it was realised that Hitler's latest ultimatum concerning central European countries would also involve the Second Republic of Poland making changes to her territorial integrity and independence, it dawned on people in Whitehall that appeasement was an inappropriate strategy to adopt

---

1   Minett, Peter (ed.), *Franks Wartime Diary* (Gloucestershire: Self Published, 2014) p.1.

against an expansive Nazi Germany. Experience with the treatment of Austria[2] and Czechoslovakia, had proven the point. By 1939 the word 'resistance' rather than 'appeasement' become the new by-word in Whitehall. Chamberlain wrote to his sister Hilda, 'it is perfectly evident that force is the only argument Germany understands and that collective security cannot offer any prospect of preventing such events until it can show a visible force of overwhelming strength backed by determination to use it'.[3] Of course, the word 'resistance', in this particular context, meant war. However, there were those in the highest reaches of power who were terrified of the prospect of conflict with Germany so soon after the Great War,[4] who called for London to come to some sort of understanding with Berlin. Others had the view that to resist the German Chancellor would be a justified and moral crusade. Baldwin was to observe:

> The worst of it is we none of us know what goes on in that strange man's mind; I am referring to Hitler. We all know the German desire, and he has come out with it in his book, to move east, and if he should move east, I should not break my heart, but that is another thing. I do not believe she (Germany) wants to move West because West would be a difficult programme for her, and if she does before we are ready I quite agree the picture is perfectly awful.[5]

But whilst dismantling the Versailles Treaty remained a German objective, something which threatened to undermine the status quo on the European continent and endanger Britain's position in the European balance of power, there seemed no other options but to oppose and confront the Germans. As far as Hitler was concerned Poland had to be erased from the European map, for it was on territory that a future German empire would be based. In order to justify aggression against Poland in 1939, the Germans contrived a fictitious Polish attack on the country using three German corpses dressed in Polish military uniforms. Berlin, claimed that these were the bodies of three Polish soldiers sent to take over Gleiwitz radio station in order to broadcast anti-German propaganda[6] and had been caught and killed. Hitler demanded that the free city of Gdańsk (Danzig)[7] be returned to the Reich (which in reality was a League of Nation matter) and for free and unfettered access across Polish territory (the Polish Corridor)[8] to East Prussia. No one knew whether these demands, which some considered quite reasonable, would be Hitler's last but his rush to war certainly suggested otherwise. The Soviet Union's attitude to the Second Republic in 1939 was not too dissimilar to that of Germany's, for it also included the annexation of Polish territory;

---

2   See the forced annexation of Austria by Adolf Hitler, March 1938
3   Tim Bouverie, *Appeasing Hitler* (London: Vintage, 2019), p.187.
4   The First World War 1914-1918.
5   Bouverie, *Appeasing Hitler*, p.103.
6   Gleiwitz Operation
7   Polish name Gdańsk, German name Danzig
8   A strip of Polish territory providing Polish trade with access to the Baltic Sea. The strip was known as the 'corridor' and crossed pre-war Germany. Verified by the Versailles Conference 1920

although, this time in the east of the country, the so called borderlands (*Kresy* to the Poles). Soviet policy was to liquidate the Polish bourgeoisie, who the Russians called the enemies of the people, and sovietise the territory which it considered to have been 'snatched' from her at the Treaty of Riga in 1921.[9] In order to prevent both countries clashing over their respective foreign policies concerning Poland, Berlin and Moscow signed the Molotov-Ribbentrop Alliance of mutual understanding which ensured the amicable sharing out of Polish territory between the two signatories following military conquest. The alliance, which was signed in August 1939, freed both countries to pursue their own political aims, knowing that neither would interfere with the other. The rapid collapse of the Second Republic of Poland in the face of the dual invasion in 1939 resulted in the fourth and most recent partition of the country. The Republic's authorities, both political and military, escaped the invasion and regrouped in France, which was the country's nearest ally. Although Germany and the Soviet Union shared Polish territory cordially, each harboured a secret desire to annex the whole country just as soon as conditions allowed. The Soviet Union's secret aim was to attack the Germans and continue spreading communism deep into central and if possible to western Europe. The secret German objective was to occupy the whole of the Republic of Poland and use it as a spring board to conquer Soviet Russia (Operation Barbarossa) and gather up her huge reservoir of natural resources particularly wheat and oil found in the Ukraine. In the meantime both countries agreed to defer and conceal their latent long term objectives.

\* \* \*

Britain in 1939 felt isolated and vulnerable which had resulted in her returning to the policy of 'collective security' and she looked for allies in Europe. Relations with France went back to 1840 so an alliance with her seemed obvious, but Britain's defensive alliance with Poland was something new. Britain extended her guarantee on 31 March 1939. There had never been a close relationship between London and Warsaw until the destabilising foreign policies of Nazi Germany. The signing of their defence pact, which many regretted in Whitehall including Churchill, could be considered to be the brainchild of Neville Chamberlain, who sought an ally in the East in order to surround and neutralise troublesome Germany. Hitler flew into a rage when he heard of the British 'checkmate' and growled, 'I'll brew them a devil's potion'. [10] Churchill, was never an enthusiastic supporter of the alliance arguing that the Soviet Union would have been a far better eastern ally for Britain not Poland. This view was to influence his decision making throughout the war and when the Soviet Union changed sides joining the Western Allies after Operation Barbarossa, he believed that with Russia on Britain's side, the war against Hitler was all but won. Churchill said, 'We are moving through reverses and defeats to complete a final victory … Now we are not alone; we have mighty Allies … There can only be one end…we may stride

---

9   See the Russo-Polish War
10  Moorhouse Roger, *The Devils' Alliance* (London: The Bodley Head, 2014) p. 23.

forward into the unknown with growing confidence.'[11] With this change in Soviet fortune, the Second Republic of Poland's position as Britain's ally was irretrievably damaged as London's attitude to Poland grew to be ambivalent. This had significant and serious repercussions for SOE's Polish Section, for resources earmarked for Poland from this point in time would have to be vetted to ensure its delivery to the Poles did not offend Moscow.[12] But why would the Soviet Union be annoyed with SOE activity in Poland? Surely, helping an ally is something positive and a legal requirement? This is one of the questions this work attempts to address.

\* \* \*

After the signing of the pact between London and Warsaw in May 1939, Colonel Colin Gubbins of the Military Intelligence Research Group (MIR) met with members of Polish General Staff in Warsaw in order to discuss possible consequences of German aggression. The pact between the two countries was designed in such a way as to surround troublesome Germany with allied countries and make her forces fight on two fronts, if she decided to move against her neighbours. In reality it was a warning to Hitler to desist from destabilising Europe. Gubbins, sometimes described as a 'dapper little fellow' who 'wore smooth suede gloves and walked with a silver-topped cane in London' in that foppish way, was considered to be a luminary on irregular warfare and this was the main topic of conversation in the Polish capital.[13] Known for his flexible and sharp mind, Gubbins had just written a booklet titled, 'The Art of Guerrilla Warfare', which was translated into various languages including Polish prior to his arrival in the country. Gubbins was born in Scotland in 1896 and saw service in the First World War where he won the Military Cross. In 1919, Gubbins served under General Edmund Ironside on the side of the White Army[14] in Russia, but returned to England when the communist Red Army (Bolshevik Army) won the civil war.[15] Ironside, who was Chief of the Imperial General Staff at the outbreak of World War Two, was promoted to Field-Marshal in 1940 and placed in command of the Home Defence Force. The 'Ironside' light armoured vehicle, was named after him. The first Baron Ironside, was a large man and rather cruelly given the nickname 'Tiny' by his colleagues although he was never called this to his face. Ironside spoke many languages and was said to be the original for John Buchan's hero Richard Hannay in his book, The Thirty-Nine Steps. His entry in the Dictionary of National Biography reports that he was warm, sensitive, impetuous, mercurial and blunt. He had virtually no appreciation of music or poetry, little of theatre, none of dance…

---

11  Fennel Jonathan, *Fighting the People's War* ( Cambridge: Cambridge University Press, 2019) p.159.
12  Walker *Poland Alone*, p.148.
13  Milton Giles, *Churchill's Ministry of Ungentlemanly Warfare* (London: John Murray, 2017), p.15.
14  Non-Communist forces in the Russian Revolution.
15  The Russian Revolution 1917.

Certain of British superiority, he professed special dislike of the Irish, Jews, Latins and 'lessor races.'

\* \* \*

When in 1939 Nazi Germany demanded the undoing of the Versailles Treaty, Gubbins made two visits to Poland, the first in May and the second in August. On 14th August he met with Colonel Józef Smoleński[16], who after the war and the communist take over of Poland, ended up in English exile washing dirty dishes in a Hounslow hotel for the airline TWA . There were two fundamental views circulating in Whitehall at the time: that Poland would ally with Hitler or be Germany's target for occupation. In fact the British guarantee to Warsaw was designed to prevent the former possibility. The two men discussed Gubbins' booklet, vibro-switch devices designed for sabotage work on railway tracks and the possible military consequences of a Polish withdrawal to Romania, if a German attack could not be held. Smoleński, a dynamic individual, was born September 18, 1894 in Gostków, Poland and died January 19, 1978 in London. He studied at the technical university in Liege, Belgium, and later at the School of Advanced Rural Economics in Warsaw.[17] After a series of appointments, he ended up as Head of the Second Department of the Polish General Staff concerned with intelligence.[18] Given his engineering background he was made responsible for the preparation of operational plans for an uprising if the German's occupied Poland. At the seminal meeting, Smoleński spoke very highly of Gubbins' book and assessed that the vibro-switches[19] he was presented with to be more useful to regular troops, rather than guerrilla fighters, but promised to order a confinement once they had been suitably modified. As the men talked, Gubbins impressed on Smoleński the vital necessity to Germany of Romanian oil[20] and therefore the importance of the Aniołowo-Kraków railway line between the two countries. Smoleński reassured Gubbins that in the event of a forced Polish withdrawal, the rail line would be rendered unusable, and the primary target of Polish sabotage work would then be switched on hitting oil and petrol refineries in Romania. However, he did express Warsaw's anxiety about oil transports on the river Danube. Gubbins replied that the Danube was a long, meandering and wide river where barges slowed in order to navigate the twists, turns and strong currents, and consequently, could easily be bombed when necessary. When Smoleński was asked about the possibility of a simultaneous

---

16  Director of Polish Intelligence later Head of Sixth Bureau
17  Szkoła Glowna Gospodarstwa Wiejeskiego
18  In 1940, Prime Minister Sikorski appointed him Deputy Commander of the underground army called the 'Union of Armed Struggle', the precursor to the secret Home Army.
19  A switch which made contact when vibrated, such as when a train passed over the device. Usually, used in sabotage work on the railways.
20  Romania was the largest producer of oil in Europe. During the war much of the oil extracted was used by the axis powers. Germany bought 1,072,402 metric tons in 1936, 435,281 in 1937 and 703,732 in 1938. During same period Britain bought 846,276 tons, 580,182 and 549,227. Source, *Picture Post* 9.12.39.

German attack on Romania and Poland, the Polish colonel replied that according to Polish assessments this was highly unlikely given what was known about the current state of German deployment and the estimated number of divisions that would have to be redeployed for such an operation. Gubbins returned to London in a jolly mood having been flattered by the positive feedback his book had received.

* * *

The Warsaw meetings were followed hotfoot by similar meetings held in London. During the middle of July, for example, the War Office entertained two Polish technical specialists, Lieutenant Colonel Gano and Engineer Mieczyslaw Frankowski, both of the Polish II Bureau (Technical Intelligence). During these meetings the Poles were shown the latest British devices designed for guerrilla warfare, and methods used to avoid problems associated with railway demolition. The British demonstrated their latest equipment and discussed future engineering projects on sabotage work, which the War Office at the time was willing to share. A subsequent meeting in late July involved Major Edmund Charaszkiewicz, who like Gubbins, specialised in clandestine warfare, and was in personal charge of all arrangements concerning para-military activity in the Second Republic. Edmund Charaszkiewicz was born in October 1895 and died on 22 December, 1975. Between 1931 and the start of the Second World War he served in Bureau II of the General Staff and was charged by Warsaw with the planning, preparation and execution of clandestine warfare. As war loomed in 1938, he was ordered to oversee the establishment of a secret network of training schools for civil-defence training including schooling in cryptology, intelligence microphotography, toxicology, railway sabotage, hand to hand combat, weaponry and explosives. By chance this agenda was very similar to SOE's Mission Statement. The Major informed the British that he had only just started working on his plans in May, owing to the abrogation of the Polish-German Pact which did not permit such activity. Nevertheless, he informed the British that he had recruited a number of 'cells' of fighters comprising anything between 3 to 7 fighters, mostly men, who would make secret incursions into German held territory and across the Slovakian frontier as far east as Nowy Sącz. He envisaged that each group would undertake approximately 25 patrols per month and would operate from safe houses under strict regional control. The Major continued that arms and explosives would be cached and objectives for their use considered. Also, the plans to form larger cells comprising 15 men, who would work alongside the smaller groups and operate across the German-Slovakian frontier, were also underway. The Major continued that this number of men was chosen as experience had shown that it was the optimum number of personnel that could be effectively controlled under the pertaining occupation conditions. These groups would operate on the East Prussian front and along the Carpathians[21] from Kraków to the Romanian border. The Poles had rejected such operations taking place

---

21 Carpathians Mountains, a range of mountains stretching from Czechoslovakia, passing through Poland, Hungary, Ukraine, Serbia and Romania

along the country's Western border with Germany on account of the terrain there being flat, agricultural land offering no possibility of concealment or evasion. Up to the time of the meeting, the formation of these groups was more or less complete as far east as the village of Jasło, about halfway to the Romanian border. According to Charaszkiewicz, the task of forming cells in these areas was relatively simple, as the inhabitants living in these districts were from what he called 'pure Polish stock'; whereas, on territory east of Jasło, the process slowed owing to the presence of less reliable minorities, such as Jews and Ukrainians. The discussion then turned to the nature of the training programmes he envisaged using in training schools. The Polish Major declared that schools for instruction were already in existence and had been operating successfully for at least three months. He made it known that the emphasis in early training sessions was on methods of disrupting German communication lines and that, up to July, approximately 800 men had already completed the course. He explained that the Poles envisaged that their radio transmissions under occupation would be severely disrupted and as a consequence, they were now concentrating on developing other methods of communication, for example, face to face contacts, liaison patrols of runners, and freelance officers who would be dispatched across the lines. These officers would be answerable to a central High Command. No conclusions had yet been reached on the setting up of new reliable wireless networks in the country, although it was agreed that they were sorely needed. The methodology described by Charaszkiewicz, was a clear inspiration for what later became Section D's [22] standard practice and was the pattern used in Norway, Britain, France and Romania. Section D was a top-secret Whitehall department, which had been tasked to conceive a wholly new form of warfare behind enemy lines. The 'D' stood for 'destruction' which employed such methods as murder, sabotage and subversion.[23]

\* \* \*

Following the meetings between London and the Poles in 1939, the War Office was reassured that the Polish officers it had met were frank and open to sharing information known only to a handful of their own staff. It noted that Major Charaszkiewicz was indeed the actual head of para-organisations in the Republic and was responsible for every aspect of planning sabotage, with a few highly trusted individuals working alongside him. It was acknowledged that the nature of the guerrilla organisation being set up by Charaszkiewicz was based on his own concepts and ideas which, according to his own admission, was 'work in progress'. A special flattering note was made in official files that the tactical and administrative doctrines the General was intending to employ were very similar to those described in British and French training manuals. In conclusion, the War Office noted that it was obvious that, in the stress of hasty preparation for a situation that appeared imminent, it was not possible for the Poles to make a serious study of the means of continuing sabotage

---

22  Forerunner of SOE
23  Giles, *Churchill's Ministry of Ungentlemanly Warfare,* p. 13.

and guerrilla activities if the war turned out to be prolonged; nor for the coordination of their activities between territorial sectors and the operations of the main armies.[24] The British conclusion was that what had been achieved by the Poles so far was a carefully prepared plan almost ready for execution timed to start at zero hour, and recommended that a higher national organisational structure be organised to oversee and coordinate operations throughout the country. An important British recommendation was to develop a wireless network which could be used to coordinate resistance activity with the Polish HQ in Britain as quickly as possible. The view in London was that the Poles had not considered this aspect for want of time and funds, and possibly the lack of specialist apparatus. Consquently, the initial intention of the British was to supply such devices which would allow the Poles to make inroads into establishing effective radio communications with London. Meanwhile, Section D started organising supply lines to Poland via Scandinavia. This involved Walter Wren's mission to set up direct communication lines for the supply of propaganda and sabotage material via Sweden using Alfred Rickman's dental supply company as a cover. The COS agreed to make the latest wireless equipment available for assessment by technical staff in Poland and then to await a sizeable order to come forth. It was also decided to press the Polish central authorities to make arrangements for facilities to control sabotage activities, which could then be employed behind German lines, and to encourage the continued organisation of partisan bands particularly in the Carpathian region. London also recommended that the appointment of group leaders be completed as quickly as possible so that coordination of effort could be realised. Finally, the British advised the Poles to consider the use of mounted guerrilla bands in view of their undoubted advantages and to consider the usefulness of a British Military Mission which could be sent to Poland. As the major nations of Europe were squaring up for a fight, it was decided to send a Military Mission to Warsaw. The Mission was headed up by General Adrian Carton de Wiart VC, who was born of Belgian and Irish parents. He had had a long and distinguished military career by the time of his appointment and was living in Poland in a picturesque hunting lodge provided for him by Prince Charles Nicholas Radziwiłł (1886-1968).[25] Carton De Wiart wrote how the Prince proposed that the residence called *Prostyn* was to be rent free and completely at Carton's disposal. 'When Prince Charles told me that my proposed estate was forty miles away, and could be approached only by water, I was already fascinated by the sound of it. It took us nearly a whole day to get there, with four men paddling the boat, and we arrived to find another little wooden house sitting quite alone on a small island, surrounded by water and forest. My mind was made at once, I knew it was exactly what I wanted…'[26] The Poles were pleased with Britain's assessment of Poland's preparations for clandestine warfare and accepted the

---

24  The National Archives (TNA) HS4/163: Sabotage and Guerrilla Warfare in Poland.
25  The Radziwiłł family was an influential noble magnate family with origins in the Grand Duchy of Lithuania and later the Crown of the Kingdom of Poland.
26  Adrian Carton De Wiart, *Happy Odyssey* (Great Britain, Jonathan Cape Ltd. 1950,) pp. 123-124,

recommendations readily. However, they noted that London had failed to mention the situation in Gdańsk, which the Poles had included in their planning or sabotage action in the Czech Republic or in Slovakia. Furthermore, it surprised the Poles that discussions in London did not consider the situation in the eastern territories of Poland and the Soviet Union position in the crisis.

\* \* \*

The British Mission to Poland brought together a number of distinguished personnel notably Colin Gubbins, amongst others, who was appointed General Adrian Carton de Wiart's Chief of Staff and leader of the MIR[27] contingent, and Harold Perkins, who later became a leading figure in SOE Polish Section. The Mission comprised of two types of personnel, those already serving secretly in Poland and those who were sent out from Britain when the German emergency arose. The first group consisted of two language officers and others from of the OER. The contingent, which had travelled from Britain with Gubbins, included reserve officers with language qualifications, signals personnel under the command of an officer from the Royal Corps of Signals and a group of regular officers. Prior to leaving for Poland, Lieutenant Colonel Gubbins reported to the War Office in order to receive final instructions including details of joint plans, the latest intelligence information and a list of points which required further elucidation by the Poles. Military Intelligence supplied him with maps and summaries dealing with the areas of operations and included final instructions for despatch overseas. It was envisaged that the main supply route for the Mission would be via Russia and, if Italy remained neutral, through the Mediterranean.[28] In the end neither was possible because Russia and Italy had allied with Nazi Germany[29]. Gubbins' group was to travel (under War Office authority) in plain clothes. Once in Poland, Gubbins was informed that he could expect General Adrian Carton de Wiart to have provided six motorcycles of adequate capacity and power for use by the Mission. In addition, the War Office understood that Warsaw would supply six motorcars with drivers. It was hoped that these drivers would be British subjects who could speak Polish, but if this was not possible, Polish drivers who could speak English. Warsaw was also to obtain the services of three bilingual British male clerks resident in Poland, who had shorthand typing skills. If British subjects were not available, then Polish clerks could be recruited, so long as they spoke good English. Finally, suitable manservants could be hired, but only after they had been vetted by the Polish Security Service and agreed a wage at the rate usual for such personnel in Poland. In conclusion Gubbins was instructed to take supplementary papers referring to operational matters for passing to General Adrian Carton de Wiart. These included a statement on Britain's bombing policy, the feasibility of operating British planes over Poland, cooperation with Romania, and the

---

27 Military Intelligence Research.
28 TNA: HS4/148: Liaison with Poland by means of air.
29 The Molotov-Ribbentrop Pact 1939.

precise nature of allied action in the West to relieve pressure on Poland. Britain's mobilisation instructions stated that in view of the difficulties of rendering direct military support by British armed forces the question of inspiring confidence in the Poles was of primary importance. Gubbins was informed that any allied action was dependant on developments after the outbreak of war, as well as on French policy. In fact, the French Mission to the Republic had not even been despatched and details could only be communicated once its composition was known. On leaving the War Office, Gubbins was reminded that the Mission's first objective was to ensure that the programme of cooperation between the Polish Army and the combined plan of the allies was in step. Secondly it was to keep the War Office fully informed of military developments in the country. Related to this duty the French Mission was instructed to keep in close contact with the British Military Missions in Romania and Turkey. However, the War Office acknowledged that the means of communication available would be limited, since issuing high-grade ciphers was unfeasible because their safe keeping in Poland was not guaranteed. Consequently, the Mission was instructed to use 'bag resources' [30] available at the British Embassy in Warsaw were to be used. London was fully aware of the difficulties of rendering direct military support to the Poles therefore the primary objective was to inspire confidence in Polish leaders through personal contact with staff.

\* \* \*

The Mission was to use two RAF aircraft and an Imperial Airways[31] airliner (under special government charter) to get to Poland. The first leg of the journey was to take the men to Alexandria and then onto Athens. The leg beyond Athens would depend on whether the Turkish Government would agree to RAF aircraft flying over its territory. If such permission was not received then only the civilian Imperial Airways airliner would be used as an airbridge to Constanza it ferrying the contents of the RAF planes. After unloading, would return to Alexandria. On the other hand if Ankara agreed to RAF planes flying through Turkish airspace, the three aircraft would proceed to Istanbul, where the Imperial Airways aircraft would ferry the party to Constanza. The RAF planes would return to Alexandria after unloading. If the Romanians agreed to the RAF overflying their territory then all three aircraft would proceed to Bucharest. Communication with the party in transit was planned to take place through Imperial Airways wireless; RAF wireless and British Military representatives. The progress of the party would be reported to H.M. Embassy in Alexandria, followed by RAF HQ Middle East then Military HQ in the Middle East, and then onto London. Prior to departure Gubbins was informed that the senior RAF officer on each aircraft would take responsibility for all matters connected with safety on the aircraft and his orders in this connection were to be obeyed by all personnel

---

30  Diplomatic Bags.
31  Imperial Airways, the early British commercial long-range airline operating from Croydon Airport. Operated from 1924 to 1939.

on board. A similar principle to be followed in the case of the Imperial Airways aircraft. In the event Gubbins and his party departed London on the 25 August, initially flying to Alexandria then on to Athens, followed by Bucharest. The final leg to Warsaw was completed on a hired bus arriving in the Polish capital on 3September, three days after the German invasion. On arrival General Adrian Carton de Wiart signalled London that the journey was completed successfully, despite considerable diplomatic difficulties through Greece and Turkey. He added that the difficulties were surmounted very largely through the good offices, determination and forceful character of Polish diplomatic representatives to whom appeal had been made when other resources failed. In the final analysis fifteen people made up the Mission and included the naval and air attaches: Captain N.L. Wharton, RN, and Group Captain A.P. Davidson, RAF. Also included were five language officers from the Baltic States, ordered to Warsaw to avoid internment as well as staff from the British central passport office in Warsaw. Gubbins managed to meet up with Stanisław Gano,[32] Head of the Polish Second Bureau, and members of Polish resistance. Many of the exchanges between the British and the Polish remain secret, but one thing we do know is that Gubbins had been given a leather holdall encasing a machine which resembled a typewriter. In fact, it was the German encryption machine known as 'Enigma'. On return to London, it was quickly despatched to Bletchley Park along with Polish instructions on how it worked.[33] Gano and Gubbins' paths crossed again in 1939 in France. The Polish officer discussed how the secret army in the Republic was struggling to initiate action, as it was being hampered by lack of equipment. Gubbins promised to help and contacted London. The response was nothing but discouraging. All that was on offer were old revolvers. What seemed to have happened was that Gubbins' request was blocked by the Secret Intelligence Services. The alliance between Britain and Poland was a new arrangement, as neither country had ever had a formal military agreement with each other. Historically, Britain had never considered Poland as a potential ally until 1939. Conversely, the relationship between France and Poland was long and deep, ever since the Napoleonic times.

\* \* \*

Both Britain and Poland had different expectations regarding their alliance. For Britain the pact was more of a signal to Hitler to refrain from threatening the status quo in Europe, rather than necessarily saving the Second Republic of Poland. Consequently, had London never seriously contemplated military intervention to assist the Poles in September 1939. Moreover, the objective of Britain and France

---

32  Gano was born in May 1895 and studied at the Institute of Technology, Moscow. Served as a commissioned officer in the Imperial Russian Army and then in the Fourth Polish Rifle Division. Following Polish independence graduated from the Higher Military School. In May 1933 military attaché in the Polish Legation in Helsinki. February 1939 returned to the Second Department of the Staff of the Commander-in-Chief. Files from the Second Bureau passed to the British in 1945. After demobilisations he settled in Morocco.
33  The Poles broke the Enigma code in 1932 and passed their methodology onto Bletchley.

was to encourage Poland to fight whilst they rearmed – in other words, during 1939 and 1940 Poland was a 'sacrificial lamb', something well demonstrated during the so called 'phoney war.' There were no troop movements in the West against the Germans until much later in the conflict, by which time the Second Republic of Poland had been lost.[34] As far as Poland's attitude to the Anglo-Polish alliance was concerned, the agreement was considered to be the best complement to Poland's alliance with France, which was already in existence. In Warsaw the view was that the trilateral pact between France Britain and Poland was such a formidable combination that a victory over Germany was a mere formality. There was ecstasy in Warsaw when the pact with Britain was announced but it proved of little value in the face of the allied betrayal in 1939.

---

34  See Tom Shachtman, *Phoney War, 1939-1940* (New York: Harper Collins, 1982).

# 2

# The Polish Army

*There is justice in the claim that steadfastness in his country's battles should be as a cloak to cover a man's other imperfections; since the good action has blotted out the bad, and his merits as a citizen more than outweigh his demerits as an individual.*
Thucydides, *Peloponnesian War*, II, 42

Whilst Gubbins was travelling to Warsaw with his retinue, a feeling of foreboding regarding Hitler's intentions gripped the Second Republic of Poland. Government propaganda emanating from Warsaw was whipping up the dispirited population in order to prime the Polish people for confrontation and to rally them to the flag; however, in government circles in Warsaw, there was a real feeling of optimism, for it was believed that the Polish Army together with Poland's allies, France and Britain, would easily deal with the troublesome Germans. Meanwhile, the German Army was gathering ominously on the Polish border. The British Embassy in Warsaw continued to monitor the situation closely with regular updates being sent to London. One of the earliest reports concerned the situation in East Prussia where four active German divisions, three to six reserve divisions, heavy artillery, armoured SS units and one cavalry brigade were massing. In the vicinity of the Free City of Danzig (Gdańsk),[1] German military strength amounted to between 20,000 and 25,000 men, estimated to be the equivalent of 2 divisions. The reports pertaining to Pomerania were more detailed and stated that the 23rd Infantry Division was in the Lauenburg-Buton area, the 3rd Infantry Division was in the Schlochan area, the 32nd Infantry Division was south of the 3rd Infantry Division and the 2nd Motorised Division was in the Schneidemuhl region. However, the report on the whereabouts of the 1st Light Infantry Division was not clear, although it had described the presence of an armoured train at Jastror (now Jastrowie). Secret sources were also suggesting that there was a reserve division in the Frankfurt area

---

1 'Free City' not belonging to any one nation. In Gdansk this meant that it was neutral and shared Polish and German jurisdiction.

together with three fortress regiments. Confirmation was also received on the presence of 5 infantry divisions, three light divisions, three armoured divisions and three motorized divisions in Silesia. The 10th Division was also known to be in this area, but its exact location had not been established. It was also believed that the 8th, 16th, and 28th Divisions had been reinforced with infantry and motorised units from Breslau (Wroclaw) and Oppelin (now Opole). The 7th, 27th, 44th and 45th Infantry Divisions were confirmed as being in Moravia and Slovakia, whilst units of the 1st Mountain Division had been identified in the Prorer area. On 27 August, 44 infantry and 6 armoured divisions were reported to be in the Morawska-Ostrawa area, while the 71st Infantry Division and possibly the 45th were believed to be in the Zilina district.[2]

The German troop movements on the Polish border had been evident for a considerable amount of time prior to the outbreak of conflict. The Polish Chief of Staff, General Stachiewicz, estimated that 30 German divisions had already gathered on the border by 26 August.[3] On 24 August he had informed General Adrian Carton de Wiart that two thirds of the total number of peacetime formations/units had been placed on a war footing.[4] As incidents carried out by German authorities in Danzig (*Gdańsk*) became more and more provocative, for instance on 10 June, Alexander Kakol, a Polish port official together with his wife and 16-year-old son were wrongly arrested by Danzig Police.[5] Meanwhile, the Polish Government decided to bring up to strength three quarters of the normal peacetime units including the navy and air force. The garrison at Westerplatte[6] was also strengthened with extra men and materials. The Polish forces prepared for possible battle. These consisted of 20 infantry divisions, as well as cavalry brigades, armoured units and other unspecified formations; however, the British had warned the Poles not to mobilise fully in case this provoked Berlin into aggression. On 27 August an additional seven German reserve divisions were within easy reach of the Polish frontier. The Military Mission to Poland also received definite indications of a general mobilisation occurring within Germany. This was accompanied by a restriction of civilian traffic in the border regions and saw the requisition of war material on a large scale. It was also evident that frontier guards were in position on Germany's Western border in case France and Britain responded to the German action in Poland.

\* \* \*

2    City in North West Slovakia.
3    Elizabeth Turnbull and Andrzej Suchcitz (eds.) *Lieutenant Colonel E.R. Sword, British Military Attaché in Warsaw Diary January-September 1939*, in *The Diary and Despatches of a Military Attaché in Warsaw 1938–1939* (London: Polish Cultural Foundation, 2001) p. 52.
4    Lieutenant Colonel. E.R. Sword, *The Diary and Despatches of a Military Attaché in Warsaw 1938–1939* (London: Polish Cultural Foundation, 2001), p. 52.
5    Lieutenant Colonel E.R. Sword, *The Diary and Despatches of a Military Attaché in Warsaw 1938–1939*, p. 44.
6    Westerplatte, Polish garrison set up to protect Polish interests in the Gdansk region.

On 28 August the Polish General Staff decided that, in addition to the measures already taken, the following units were to complete their mobilisation: eleven cavalry brigades, all non-divisional units (including medium and heavy artillery, anti-aircraft artillery and armoured units), and the equivalent of 30 infantry divisions and 40 independent infantry battalions. On the 29th the General Staff expected German readiness on the Polish frontier would be complete by 3 September although this did not mean that Germany would hold back its attack to this date. On British recommendation complete Polish mobilisation was to be avoided in case it was interpreted as provocative. In a military sense, Polish general mobilisation was abundantly justified, it was done in secret. Announcements to the Polish population by means of posters regarding the possibility of war were postponed until midnight on 30 August. The British Military Mission, however, approved the policy of moving some Polish destroyers to join the British fleet in Scotland, knowing that a small flotilla would be no match for the German Navy.

\* \* \*

On 30 August the number of German divisions estimated to be amassed on the Polish frontier was 50. Thus, on the day before the outbreak of war approximately 50 magnificently equipped divisions were facing 30 poorly equipped Polish divisions while the remaining 10 had only commenced mobilisation. The British Military Mission lamented the fact that the poorly equipped Polish Army was not yet in possession of the war materials promised by Britain. The need for these materials had been so urgently underlined during early meetings in London. According to the Mission the most urgent need was for fighter aircraft, but unfortunately these were still languishing in their packing cases on the high seas and would never be delivered. Shortages of artillery (especially of anti-aircraft equipment), together with administrative weaknesses and the low level of mechanisation (to which attention had previously been so frequently drawn), were offset by Polish determination and bravery. Alas the Poles were called to defend a defenceless border. The German ability to paralyse armies from the air together with a prolonged drought in 1939 had turned normally boggy tracks into broad dusty highways would prove vital factors. The subsequent Soviet invasion on 17 September rendered the situation for the Poles completely hopeless.

\* \* \*

In January 1939, eight months before the start of open conflict, the British Military Attaché to Warsaw, Lieutenant Colonel Edward Roland Sword, gave a lecture at Sandhurst Military Academy in England on the Polish Army and the prevailing situation in the Second Republic. He began by saying that the Republic was fundamentally different from other European countries, in that it had only emerged from partition and occupation 20 years earlier. As a result, Sword continued, the country was facing a variety of unique problems and suggested that from the time of her independence in 1918 the country had made great strides in correcting these problems right but 'there was still a long way to go.' In a comprehensive presentation, Sword continued to analyse Poland's systematic preparedness for war, whilst putting his points into a useful historical context. For example, he discussed Poland's topography and attempted to explain the consequences for invasion. According to the Military Attaché, the country's northern frontier faced strong German forces based in East Prussia. However, when it came to Polish defences in the northern region, these were dependent on old forts the main ones being at Grudziadz, Ostroleka, Lomza and Grodno. During the 1930s the Polish Government had scheduled work for their modernisation and strengthening, but this work had only just begun. According to Sword, North East Poland was protected by natural features such as belts of forest, lakes and marshes. It was only possible to cross this region via two passes, one in the Molodeczno region and one at the Baranowicze district. These passes were protected by two old German forts built during the partition, which were being modernised by Warsaw. The Pripet Marshes at Bialowieza were a serious natural obstacle to invading forces, which would have to be bypassed in any attack. The Republic's southern frontier was protected by the geographical barrier of the Carpathian and Tatra mountain ranges. The Carpathians were heavily wooded and had a few crossing places similar to the Ardennes Forest in France. The Upper Silesian industrial region centred on Katowice, which made this region vital for the Poles but unfortunately it was only protected by a thin defensive line. The Poznan salient consisted of open country and was, as a result, difficult to defend. The Polish corridor and the port city of Gdynia, according to Sword, was indefensible.

\* \* \*

He continued to say that, as with any country, efficient internal communications was crucial in the time of war. This was particularly important in Poland as Polish forces were widely dispersed throughout the Republic and the new industrial quarter was a long way away from its raw material suppliers in the West. Following the partition the country's rail system was of varying quality. The most developed was found in Western Poland in the former German occupation zone. The least developed rail lines were found in the East in the previous Russian zone of occupation. There were too many rail lines concentrated on Warsaw in central Poland and so the Poles were addressing this issue by building new rail tracks, towards Kraków in the south and towards Gdyna in the north. The road system in Poland was poor compared to Britain's, but then again the highways in the west were superior to those in the east. All these factors were to play a significant role in the Polish War.

The supply of war material would always be a struggle; however, on the acquisition of the industrial Teschen region[7] by Poland, output increased significantly. The mines at Karwina Orlowa contained good quality coke and the steel works at Trzyniec,

---

7    A region in Czechoslovakia occupied by Polish Forces after the First World War.

where 5,000 men were employed, manufactured metals to world class standards.[8] Unfortunately, all these industrial complexes were situated near the German border and so the Polish Goverment had started to build new production sites south of Warsaw including in Radom, Sandomierz and Rzeszow. The enegy used for the build was natural gas which was carried in overland pipes. A 40,000 kilowatt generating station was in production at Nisko and new power stations were on the drawing board ready for development. The country's main armament factories were also found in the Nisko region. The factory at Starachowice, produced medium sized artillery field guns and anti-aircraft guns of Polish design. The production of six-ton tanks also started here and were based on the British Vickers model. Such new ventures were a sign that the Poles were committed to urgent industrial and military modernisation and if this proved to be inadequate during wartime, all private enterprises were liable to requisitioning. Finance and the supply of raw material was under strict state control. The chief difficulty was the availability of cash and raw material. To make good the shortages in military equipment the Ministry of War had set up a National Defence Fund, which encouraged citizens to donate treasures and valuables for the war effort. By the mid-1930s the fund was valued at 2,000,000 zlotys[9], 400,000 US Dollars in today's money. Also, the fund had access to 6,000 tons of scrap metal, 36 aircraft and 600 machines guns. Taxation was used to raise further funds.

According to Sword,[10] the organisational structure of the army was problematic. The army was primarily the responsibility of the Ministry of War, but the ministry was in a separate building to the General Staff and the General Inspectorate of Forces. The General Staff, together with the Inspectorate, was responsible for military planning, whilst the Ministry responsible for the realisation of plans was yet in another building. This unwieldy and complex arrangement resulted in confusion leading to tactical errors being made. The General Inspector of Military Forces was General Smigly-Rydz.[11] He took precedence over the country's President and, although an experienced General his political ability was allegedly limited. The requirements of the military in the country took precedence over other state interests, although this did not solve the various shortages that continued to exist. There were only 500 fighter aircraft in the front line, which was clearly inadequate for a country the size of Poland. Other shortages included heavy and medium artillery pieces, tanks and lorries. Cavalry regiments still used horses as only two had been mechanised. Despite these shortcomings, morale in the Polish Forces was high. The influence of French methods of combat were apparent in Polish operational plans since many Polish Officers were trained in French Staff Colleges. However, German military thinking was also a growing influence as German publications were starting to appear on

---

8    Elizabeth Turnbull and Andrzej Suchcitz (eds.), *The Diary of a Military Attaché in Warsaw 1938–1939*, p. 64.
9    Name of Polish currency.
10   British Military Attache in Warsaw 1938-1939.
11   Sometimes called 'Rydz-Smigly. Faithful follower of Pilsudski. Served as an officer in the Polish Legions and was Commander of the Polish Military Organisation. After Pilsudski's death he became General Inspector of the Polish Armed Forces.

military library shelves. Sword considered the intelligence of the Polish rank and file soldier to be low but praised the physical fitness and commitment of the men. Sword finished his presentation by summarising the strength of Polish Forces: 54 infantry divisions, one cavalry division, 12 cavalry brigades, 12 armoured battalions and six frontier defence corps. On completing his presentation, he stepped down from the lectern. Also at this time General Ironside, who had just returned from a visit to Poland, was giving Churchill a most favourable report on the Polish Army. He had witnessed Army manoeuvres under a live barrage and told the British Prime Minister that Polish military morale was high.

# 3

# The September 1939 Campaign

*As it is necessary for kings and nations to take up arms for the infliction of such public vengeance, the same reason will lead us to infer the lawfulness of wars which are undertaken for this end. For if they have been instructed with power to preserve the tranquillity of their own territory, to suppress the seditious tumults of disturbers, to succour the victims of oppression, and to punish crimes, —can they exert this power for better purpose, than to repel the violence of him who disturbs both private repose of individuals and the general tranquillity of the nation; who excites insurrections, and perpetrates act of oppression, cruelty, and every species of crime? If they ought to be the guardians and defenders of the laws, it is incumbent upon them to defeat the efforts of all by whose injustice the discipline of the laws is corrupted. And if they justly punish those robbers, whose injuries have only extended to a few people, shall they suffer a whole district to be plundered and devastated with impunity? For there is no difference, whether he, in a hostile manner invades, disturbs, and plunders the territory of another to which he has no right, be a king, or one of the meanest of mankind: all persons of this description are equally to be considered as robbers, and ought to be punished as such. It is the dictate both of natural equity, and of the nature of the office, therefore, that princes are armed, not only to restrain the crimes of private individuals by judicial punishment, but also to defend the territories committed to their charge by going to war against any hostile aggression.*
Calvin, *Institutes of the Christian Religion*, IV, 20

The British Military Mission confirmed that German troops had crossed the frontier of the Second Republic at 0500 hours on 1 September 1939. At first, German progress appeared to be slow, but it subsequently became clear that the first military objective was to establish complete air superiority in order to paralyse Polish mobilisation and troop concentrations. 2,000 German sorties took place over Polish territory on the first day of conflict with extensive bombardment of aerodromes and other military objectives throughout the Republic. 50 percent of Polish aircraft were destroyed by 6 September.[1] Reports were soon coming in that open towns and unarmed civilians were being strafed although air attacks were mainly confined to military targets. The first shots of the war to be fired in anger came from the German battleship, SMS Schleswig-Holstein[2] which had sailed into Gdańsk harbour on an alleged courtesy visit. Early in the morning of the first of September she slipped her moorings, took aim at the Polish garrison at Westerplatt and opened fire at point blank range. Despite the area of Gdańsk being a demilitarised zone under the Versailles Treaty, it was the first example of German military aggression against the Second Republic. During the inter-war years Poland had established a small garrison on the Westerplatte peninsula, which was Polish territory, in order to protect her interests in the Gdańsk (Danzig) region. The depot, which was at the head of the Polish Corridor, was protected by a contingent of 182 men with heavy infantry equipment. On 1 September, a Polish infantry battalion commanded by Major H. Sucharski[3] defended the peninsula against overwhelming German forces for seven days before surrendering. The Polish losses comprised fifteen killed and 40 wounded, whilst the Germans suffered 400 killed. The battle of Westerplatte[4] became a symbol of Polish courage and determination and was the first battle to be completed in the Second World War.

\* \* \*

The invading German land forces established the first contact with the Polish army in a town called Myszyniec (See map 1. Polish Campaign September 1939 A). A weak and unsuccessful attack accompanied by aerial bombardment was delivered to the bridge at Tczew (see map 2. Polish Campaign September 1939 B) and the whole of the Danzig free state territory, with the exception of the Polish garrison at Westerplatte (see map 2. Polish Campaign September 1939 B) was soon overrun. An attack in the direction of Gdynia, Poland's pre-eminent port, was held up (see map 3. Polish Campaign September 1939 C). The Germans were pressing from East Prussia[5] Pomerania[6] and Silesia.[7] On the Pomeranian front the main attack was delivered between Chojnice (see map 4. Polish Campaign September 1939 D) and the river Notec in the direction of Bydgoszcz (see map 4. Polish Campaign September 1939 D). The attack on Chojnice was planned as a surprise attack employing an armoured

---

1   Halik Kochański, *The Eagle Unbowed* (London: Allen Layne, 2012), p. 85.
2   *Kriegsmarine* vessel *Schleswig-Holstein*. A *Deutschland* class battleship built by the *Kaiserliche Marine*. Named after the province of Schleswig-Holstein, laid down in Kiel August 1905.
3   Henryk Sucharski was a Polish military officer and a major in the Polish Army. At the outbreak of World War II, he was the commander of the Westerplatte garrison in Gdansk. His troops defended the garrison for seven days against overwhelming odds. Sucharski survived the war.
4   Sometimes called the Battle of Danzig.
5   Wschodnie Prusy.
6   Pomorze.
7   Slask.

train[8] called 'Panzerzug 3', which was one of four such armoured trains used by the Germans. It was engaged by Polish artillery at Chojnice Station and was destroyed by Polish fire when it became trapped on a bridge, which had been demolished earlier. The attack on Chojnice itself failed. It was also noted that gangs of individuals of German extraction living in pre-war Poland were active in the area, but they were severely suppressed by the Poles. There was little activity on the Poznan front but Rawicz and Zbaczyn (see map 5. Polish Campaign September 1939 E) were captured. On the Silesian front the attack consisted of two infantry thrusts supported by tanks and motorised units. One was directed at Czestochowa (see map 6. Polish Campaign September 1939 F) and the other towards Pszczyna (see map 6. Polish Campaign September 1939 F). The German advance was so rapid that the barracks of the 11 Uhlan Regiment was overrun on 3 September, while the men ate their morning meal in the mess.[9] On the Slovakian front, attacks by armoured units erupted on Nowy Targ (see map 7. Polish Campaign September 1939 G) and Nowy Sącz (see map 7. Polish Campaign September 1939 G). For example, the 18th German Corps swept down the valleys of the Tatra Mountains in a north easterly direction. They were held for two days by a valiant Polish defence.[10] When the line could not be held any longer the Poles carried out a fighting withdrawal.

\* \* \*

The 2 September, saw little activity on the East Prussian front. An attack in the direction of Przasnysz was held up at Mława and Grudziadz (see map 8. Polish Campaign September 1939 H). Recalling his participation at Mława a German tank driver recalled the drumming of Polish bullets against his tank's armoured turret.[11] From Grudziadz the main line of resistance ran north of Koronowa and Budzyn (see map 9. Polish Campaign September 1939 I). The Polish front north of this line was retired. In Pomerania the defensive line ran West of Ryczywol, Wronki, Nowy Tomysł, Rakoniewicz and Leszno (see map 10. Polish Campaign September 1939 J). On the Breslau (now Wrocław) front Grabów, Dzialoszyn and Częstochowa were held, but a gap was made by armoured troops in the direction of Boronow (see map 11. Polish Campaign September 1939 K). The German 2nd Light Division reached the neighbourhood of Zarki whilst Zawiercin was held. South of Katowice the 5th Armoured Division was held up at Oswiencim (see map 11. Polish Campaign September 1939 K). The line ran south of Bielsko, north of Żywiec through Jordanow (see map 12. Polish Campaign September 1939 L) which had been taken by the 2nd Armoured Division. 60 tanks were reported to have been destroyed by anti-tank fire near Częstochowo and 30 tanks in the Morawska, Ostrawa area (see map 13. Polish Campaign September 1939 M). Meanwhile, air bombing of towns and aerodromes

8   Moorhouse *First to Fight*, p. 30.
9   Moorhouse, p.86.
10  Moorhouse, p. 88.
11  Moorhouse, p. 28.

continued. Four Germans were reported to have been parachuted near Radom (see map 14. Polish Campaign September 1939 N) .

\* \* \*

Meantime, Frank erected his ARP shelter in his back yard covering it with garden soil. He wondered whether it would ever be used in an air raid. That evening he went alone to the cinema to see the screen version of the Mikado. In his diary he records that the colouring of the scenery conjured up memories of the real thing. He writes, 'Wars may come and wars may go, but Gilbert and Sullivan go on for ever'.[12]

On 3 September, a strong attack occurred against Przasnysz (see map 14. Polish Campaign September 1939 N) on the northern front, which was captured from the Mazowiecki Cavalry Brigade. Grudziadz (see map 14. Polish Campaign September 1939 N) was also taken in the evening and at Gdynia (see map 14. Polish Campaign September 1939 N) the destroyer *Wicher* and minesweeper *Gryf* were sunk. On the Poznan front, Rawicz (see map 5. Polish Campaign September 1939 E) was taken. On the Pomeranian front the Germans delivered three attacks on Bydgoszcz and despite an attack in their rear by the 9th Polish Division retiring south from Swiecie, Bydgoszcz (see map 15. Polish Campaign September 1939 O) fell that evening. During the battle ethnic Germans who lived in the region had risen against their neighbours but were crushed by the Poles. The German propaganda machine vowed that this would be avenged.[13] On the Silesian front the Polish Army of Lodz was withdrawn to a defensive line Blaszki-Szczercow-Lekawa (see map 16. Polish Campaign September 1939 P). Czestochowa (see map 17. Polish Campaign September 1939 Q) was taken, when the seven Infantry Division withdrew, by the 3rd Armoured Division, which continued its advance towards Radomsko. The fall of Czestochowa precipitated great anxiety in Poland and Christendom as a whole, concerning the safety of the famed icon, the Black Madonna, which was housed in the city's Jasna Góra Monastery. The icon had been associated with the Polish state for seven hundred years and it was feared that it would be desecrated by invading German forces; however, the Poles needn't have worried for the Black Madonna had been hidden by the monastery's friars and replaced by a copy, thereby surviving the war undamaged.[14] Katowice was also taken and the Poles fell back to a line running north and south through Oswięcim, with clashes breaking out between Polish and German irregulars. Neighbours, friends and even family members came into conflict with each other according to whether they held Polish or German allegiance.[15] On the Slovakian front Nowy Targ (see map 17. Polish Campaign September 1939 Q) fell and the Germans continued to Ochotnica and Mszana Dolna (see map 18. Polish Campaign September 1939 R). German

---

12 Minett (ed.), *Frank's Wartime Diary*, p. 8.
13 Moorhouse, *First to Fight*, p. 98.
14 Moorhouse, p.106.
15 Moorhouse, p. 99.

assault units were joined by the Slovakian 'Hlinka Guard'[16] who were involved in the burning of small villages and towns on behalf of the Germans. Around mid-day on the 3rd, Colonel Gubbins arrived in Warsaw. Air activity continued against aerodromes all over Poland, almost all of which by now were out of action.

On 4 September, the Germans passed through Ciechanów continuing towards Płonsk (see map 19. Polish Campaign September 1939 S) on the northern front. Ciechanów was 30 kilometres to the south of Mława and its defence was spearheaded by a Polish armoured train; however, this was not enough to prevent the Germans from taking the town. The Polish retreat was hurried and frenzied and maps with military orders were abandoned along with equipment, ammunition and guns.[17] The Poles held out west of Płonsk and on the Lidzbark-Brodnica-Wąbrzeżno-Chełmno line (see map 20. Polish Campaign September 1939 T). Przasnysz was retaken by the Mazowiecki Cavalry Brigade and went onto hold the hills to the East. The Suwalki Cavalry Brigade was reported to have made a successful raid into East Prussia from the direction of Suwalki (see map 21. Polish Campaign September 1939 U). In the Polish port of Gdynia, ORP General Haller was sunk and the floating dock damaged. By this time nearly all of the Polish planes had been destroyed. On the Silesian front there was no enemy activity approaching Łódź and troops were being transferred to the south. In the Radomsko region (see map 22. Polish Campaign September 1939 V), mechanised units made up of at least 3 divisions reached and occupied the Gorzkowicz-Włoszczowa-Siedzów line (see map 23. Polish Campaign September 1939 W) by late morning. This formation included the 3rd Armoured and 2nd Light Divisions. By late evening the mechanised units had taken Jędrzejów and Kielce (see map 24. Polish Campaign September 1939 X). Reports had also come in stating that Kraków had been bombed and the civilian population machine gunned from the air. On the Slovakian front the Germans had advanced to Nowy Sącz whilst Warsaw had been bombed.

\* \* \*

On 5 September the advance on the Nasielsk-Płońsk-Lidzbark-Brodnica line (see map 25. Polish Campaign September 1939 Y), but it was delayed by the Poles. The Military Mission also recorded that the garrison at Poznań was being withdrawn. On 6 September, the Poles were holding the line stretching from the river Narew to the river Wistula (Wisła) (see map 26. Polish Campaign September 1939 Z). Information was also coming in that the axis of the German advance had swung from the south of Warsaw to the south-east towards Pułtusk (see map 27. Polish Campaign September

---

16   The Hilinka Guard was the paramilitary unit created by Catholic Priest Andrej Hlinka and controlled by the Slovak People's Party or HSSP. The Guard was officially established on 8 October, 1938 but its roots can be traced back as early as the 1920s to the 'Rodobrana' a strong-arm group that styled itself along the lines of Mussolini's' Black shirts, and the Nazi SA.

17   Moorhouse, *First to Fight*, p. 86.

1939 A(a)), in order to cross the river Narew and to outflank the Warsaw defenders. Pressure to the south, towards Modlin was relaxed and German units reached the neighbourhood of Serock. On the Poznań front Army Poznań withdrew as rapidly as possible in the direction of Warsaw (see map 27. Polish Campaign September 1939 A(a)). The withdrawal was heavily bombed. On the Silesian front Army Łódź temporarily delayed the German advance on the Sieradz-Piotrków line (see map 28. Polish Campaign September 1939 B(b)).

\* \* \*

Meanwhile, Frank Balmforth was busy working in his Post Office in artificial light. At the same time, Twickenham Girls' County School and Hampton Grammar School were shut until further notice. Frank had been on duty behind the counter on Sunday from 8:30 a.m. for five hours and this arrangement was to continue indefinitely on alternative Sundays. Gerty had gone with Michael to Kingston (Bentalls) to buy him a new raincoat (navy blue: 33/6d) and a pair of grey knickers (5/11d). Frank had made an itineray of food reserves and noted that the family had an emergency supply of sugar, Trex, tinned herrings, cocoa, dried beans as well baked beans, cake flour, corned beef, Ideal milk, Golden Syrup, matches, pears and flour.[18]

In Poland the Germans were advancing on three axes: Sieradz-Łódź, Piotrków-Rawa Mazowiecka and Kielce-Radom (see map 28. Polish Campaign September 1939 B(b)). Polish General Staff reported that considerable reserves were in position from the Kielce area, south-east along the high ground to Sandomierz. Army Kraków was withdrawing to the Dunajec line and was being threatened by a German motorised group advancing from Slovakia on Jasło (see map 29. Polish Campaign September 1939 C(c)). On the Slovakian front the Head of the German 2nd Armoured Division had reached Lipnica, south-west of Tarnów and was moving east (see map 30. Polish Campaign September 1939 D(d)). An armoured train was reported to be at Presow (Slovakia) and two artillery regiments and one motorised regiment were spotted at Bardejour. On the northern front the Poles withdrew to the river Bug on the Ostrów Mazowiecki-Wyszków-Nowy Dwór line (see map 31. Polish Campaign September 1939 R(e)). On the Pomeranian front the light divisions of the Pomorze and Poznan armies were withdrawn to Warsaw as rapidly as possible (see map 32. Polish Campaign September 1939 F(f)). The three divisions and two cavalry brigades of Army Łódź were withdrawn to Otwock, south east of Warsaw (see map 32). Two German armoured divisions were reported marching on Warsaw from the south-west, one on the axis Łódź -Skiermiewice and the other on the axis Rawa Mazowiecka-Mszcznów. Three Polish divisions in the vicinity of Tomaszow Mazowiecka, were retiring on Maciejownice. A new group of three divisions were formed south of Radom to cover the withdrawal of the army group near Jędrzejów. These were to retire in turn to the river Wistula in the direction of Opole. The crossings on the Wistula were damaged by air bombardment and the river itself was

---

18  Peter Minett, (ed.)., *Frank's Wartime Diary*, p. 2.

only held by a small reserve detachment. On the same day, on the Silesian front, the situation was grave. Two divisions of Army Kraków suffered murderous losses during their retirement through Dąbrowa and another was hit by the Germans at Tuchow. Nevertheless, the Poles continued to fall back to the river San. The main feature of the German campaign to date had been the air campaign and rapidly moving motorised units. Air bombardment of aerodromes, railway junctions and bridges completely disorientated the Polish Airforce and dislocated the mobilisation and concentration of Polish Forces. 12 infantry divisions, intended for general reserve, were still not concentrated or even mobilised. Targets for air bombardment by the Germans were military although on 7 September, the open towns of Siedlice and Lukow were bombed indiscriminately with explosive and incendiary devices with considerable loss of civilian life. The lack of anti-aircraft artillery and fighting aircraft enabled the German bombers to attack targets at leisure and from a low height. Dive bombing was employed in many cases behind the Polish lines. On 7 September, fine weather enabled mechanised forces to achieve great progress. The rate of the German advance had rendered demolition programmes ineffective in most sectors.

\* \* \*

The armies of Pomorze, Poznań and Łódź continued their retirement on Warsaw although they were harassed by air attacks. The collapse of the front at Łódź, highlighted one of the major problems faced by the Poles. Aside from the acute military challenge, Polish forces struggled with failing communications.[19] German motorised columns advanced on Warsaw from the south west, where some units had crossed the river Wistula. However, they were unable to hold a bridgehead owing to lack of infantry support. The general Polish retirement continued along the Silesian front. At a conference on the evening of 8 September, Marshal Smigly-Rydz decided to fall back on the Nalkowic-Brześć- Demblin-Jaroslaw- Przemysl line. The Chief of the Military Mission reminded the Marshal for the need to establish a 'firm line' on the rivers Wistula and San, covering Lwów and Lublin, so as to maintain communication with Romania. This move in effect ceded western Poland to the enemy. The Military Mission moved to Włodawa.

\* \* \*

On the 9th, Marshal Smigly-Rydz, ordered a general retreat to the Pinsk-Brzesc-Deblin-Rzeszow line and instructed the Polish right flank to fall back towards Brześć. The Marshal was uncertain where the right flank would finally rest but thought it would probably be somewhere south of Pinsk. He also ordered the forces in Warsaw to fight it out and sent eight divisions as reinforcements. The Marshal informed the British Mission that he was determined to fight to the very end on Polish soil,

---

19  Moorhouse, *First to Fight*, p. 110.

however small the area he held might be. In reports to London the Mission noted that, during German campaigns, infantry attacks were accompanied by heavy air bombardment of rear echelons and flanking tank attacks. It was also noted that tank units appeared to be attached to divisions and generally grouped on the flanks. Such mobile formations operated independently in order to disorganise reserve lines, communications and rearward services. On the northern front, Polish dispositions remained unchanged, but on the 9th, it was reported that German armoured cars were seen in Ostrow Mazowiecki. On the Pomeranian front the Pomorze and Poznan Armies were amalgamated and put under the command of General Kutrzeba. He was a veteran of the Austro-Hungarian Army, during the partition and saw action on the Balkan and Russian fronts in the Great War.[20] He was given orders to fight his way through to Warsaw. Elements of the Northern Army Piotrków managed to cross the Wistula river and concentrate about Maciejowice. In the south west sector, a German armoured division was reported about Tyczen. Unconfirmed reports were also coming in that Slovakian troops had crossed into southern Poland in support of German forces.

\* \* \*

On the 10th, German troops reached Malkinia and Wyszków on the river Bug, but they were unable to cross. The Military Mission was now able to identify all German mobile divisions on the Polish front, amounting to 15 in all, including the recently formed 10th Division. According to the Polish II Bureau a reorganisation of German light divisions had taken place. These now amounted to two armoured divisions each comprising of four to five hundred tanks. The Military Mission moved to Tarnopol. On the 11th, Polish G.H.Q. moved to Włodzimierz (see map 36). On the northern front the line ran along the river Narew to Ostrolska and thence to Wyszków. German troops were also reported to have reached the river Wistula opposite Deblin and taken Rzeszów.

\* \* \*

On 12 September in the north, a battle was in progress at Łódź, in which the Polish divisions cut off in Poznań, were fighting their way back in the direction of Radom. In response the Germans directed forces south of Warsaw to deal with this movement, although the Poles reported that a successful action against them had taken place near Kutno. Marshal Śmigly-Rydz hoped that this diversion might give him time to form his troops on the line of Pinsk and Deblin and the Wistula and San rivers. However, being astutely aware of the shortage of armaments, he urged London to put the RAF into action in the west against German military targets so as to relieve the pressure on Poland. The request was not answered. At 12.00 hours German reconnaissance divisions reached Rudki

---

20  Moorhouse, *First to Fight*, p. 139.

whilst a German Light Division was approaching Jawor. General Kazimierz Fabrycy hoped to delay the German advance on lake Gródek Jagielloński. According to the assessments of the Military Mission, Marshal Śmigly-Rydz had no knowledge of the extent to which this threat was developing on his left flank, a symptom of the shortcomings in communications between the Polish GHQ and army commanders in the field.

\* \* \*

On 13 September, Polish troops withdrew from the line of the river Bug to Minsk Mazowiecki. Heavy attacks forced the Polish Northern Army to withdraw to Łuków-Latowicz line. The Poznań-Toruń Armies, under General Tadeusz Kutrzeba, reported a successful action in a south easterly direction against the rear of the German motorised columns directed against Warsaw which were reported to be retiring. In the south the 2nd German Armoured Division continued to advance from Rudki and, on meeting opposition on the line of the Gródek Jagiellowski lakes swung south to Mikołajów and then onto Lwów, where again they met opposition. They circled the town to the West and met artillery fire from the town. In view of the deteriorating situation the Polish Command structure was reorganised. General Sosnkowski[21] flew to Przemysl with General Fabrycy's Chief of Staff[22] to take personal command of the 11th, 24th and 39th Infantry Divisions, with the intention of moving on Lwów and attacking the German 2nd Armoured division from behind. General Fabrycy was relieved of his duties. The British Military Mission understood that by 10.00 hours all streets in Lwów were barricaded and that two battalions were in anti-tank work.

On 14 September, Polish GHQ moved to Młynów. Heavy German attacks delivered on Siedlice resulted in the virtual collapse of the Northern Front. Pressure on Army Kraków, commanded by General Tadeusz Piskor, continued until it was surrounded forcing the General to surrender. Piskor was held in Colditz. The situation was becoming so grave that a strategic withdrawal made increasing sense and the order was given to retire as soon as possible to the Romanian border and take up a defensive line along the rivers Dniestr and Stryj with such forces that could be

---

21 During the September Campaign he was in charge of the Southern Front. In October 1939, he went to France and was appointed Commander of Polish resistance operations. After General W. Sikorski's death, he became the Commander-in-Chief of Polish Forces on 8 July 1943. He was relieved of his duties under British pressure on 30 November, 1944 and retired to Canada.
22 Kazimierz Fabrycy was born on 3 March 1888 in Odessa, in the Kherson Governorate of the Russian Empire. Upon graduating from school in Niemirów he enrolled for a year-long military service in the Imperial Russian Army. He followed this with enrolment at Polytechnic School of Lwow (Lviv) and then later at the Technical University of Munich. From this latter institution he was conferred a degree in engineering. Even as a student Kazimierz flung himself into activities of the Polish independence movement. Between 1908 and 1910 he co-founded first the Union of Armed Struggle and then the Rifle Association.

withdrawn. Garrisons were left to defend Warsaw, Lublin and Lwów. Meanwhile, the Military Mission informed London of Polish resentment at the apparent lack of British activity when their factories, communication and aerodromes had been reduced to rubble by German bombing. Meanwhile, German troops, probably under the influence of the drug Pervitia, a member of the metham phetamine family of drugs, behaved with wanton, murderous cruelty towards Polish civilians. Meanwhile, Frank wrote in his diary, 'enjoyed a walk across the fields (nice, sunny morning) my first since returning from holiday on the 2nd instant'.[23]

\* \* \*

On the 15th the British Military Mission moved to Kosów now Kosiv. On the 16th German detachments had advanced towards Suwalki, Augustów and Osowiec. Only weak Polish units remained to oppose this advance since the main body of troops in this area were by now withdrawing southwards, leaving garrisons in Grodno and Białystok. Two German armoured divisions, which had been operating in the Siedlice area, were temporarily out of action owing to absence of diesel, but advantage could not be taken due to lack of aircraft. General Sosnkowski's advance south of Lwów met with success and resulted in the destruction of 100 German tanks and the taking of 1,000 prisoners. The situation on the 16th eased somewhat and the Polish Chief of Staff planned for a counter offensive, once the Polish withdrawal had been completed and organisation and equipment prepared. However, early in the morning of 17 September, Soviet troops crossed Poland's eastern frontier at many points, executing the classic 'stab in the back'. At 2.15 a.m. the Polish Ambassador was summoned to the Soviet Foreign Office to meet Wladimira Potkiomkina. The Polish Ambassador, Wacław Grzybowski, was prepared for the worst. When he arrived Potkiomkina read out a letter from Molotov. The German ally had written that the war between Germany and Poland had demonstrated the bankruptcy of the Polish state. In 10 days, Poland had lost all of its industrial and cultural centres. Warsaw, as Poland's capital, was no longer in existence. The Polish Government was in disarray. All this meant was that Poland as a state had ceased to exist. Consequently, all agreements and pacts between the Polish State and Soviet Russia became null and void. The Soviet Government could no longer stand idly by as fellow Slavs were left with no defence. On account of this the Red Army was ordered to enter Polish territory. Facing the Red Army was a Border Defence Corps, protecting a frontier of 1,400 kilometres. The Corps comprised 12,000 lightly armed men supplemented by 300,000 regular troops who had been withdrawn from the German front, as well as recruits being made ready for combat. By 10.00 hours a column of 100 Soviet tanks was approaching Uszieczko. Soviet commanders proclaimed that their intention was to support their 'Slav brothers' against German aggression and they attempted to fraternise with Polish border guards. However, this proved to be a ruse, which resulted in the Polish Government

---

23   Minett, (ed.), *Frank's Wartime Diary*, p. 2.

crossing the frontier into Romania, rather than declaring war on Russia. Polish troops were ordered not to fire on the Russians unless attacked. Soon panic spread when rumours surfaced about the behaviour of the Soviet troops. Polish troops withdrawing from the east called on the people to flee and hide, because the Russians were showing no mercy. In one village a small child was 'frozen to the ground' by fear, as a Russian tank approached him down the road. The tank simply gunned him down.[24] The Military Mission called on Marshal Śmigly-Rydz and requested information pertaining to his probable movements, as these would determine the action taken by the Mission. The Marshal gave his intention of awaiting developments but wished the Military Mission to move to Kuty. He subsequently requested that it should cross into Romania, which it did on 16 September. The Marshal himself crossed the frontier on the morning of the 18th. Poland had an agreement with the Romanians which guaranteed safe passage for Poles entering its territory in time of a national emergency. However, when Berlin threatened reprisals on Bucharest for harbouring an enemy of the Reich the Polish Government and troops were systematically interned on arrival in the country. However, security here was on such a casual level that many Poles were able to escape to France where the Polish government in exile was being formed.

Frank wrote in his diary, 'News of Russia's intervention in Poland: possible developments give food for thought. ARP shelters being distributed in alphabetical order of roads, etc. ... Decided where to put the ARP shelter when it comes ... Commenced to take weekly readings of electricity meter and try various wattage lamps in order to keep an eye on consumption of electricity... Received our Identity Cards under the National Registration scheme.'[25]

24  Moorhouse, *First to Fight,* p. 168.
25  Peter Minett (ed.), *Frank's Wartime Diary,* pp. 3-4.

# 4
# Republican Forces in France

*No one is so foolish as to prefer war, to peace, in which, instead of sons burying their fathers, fathers bury their sons.*

Herodotus, *History*, I, 87

On September 16 1939, the day before leaving for the Romanian border, the British Military Mission began to write a report on the Polish defeat. The final version was signed by Colin Gubbins and dispatched to Colonel Holland, Head of MIR in London. Gubbins, who was about to leave Polish territory, had just paid a final visit to the Polish Chief of Staff where he expressed in French, Britain's sympathy for the Polish predicament. On leaving he reassured the Poles that Britain will stand by the Second Republic until it was free. According to Gubbins, there were three main reasons for the September defeat; the absolute superiority of the German Air Force, the role of German armoured and mechanised divisions and the exceptionally dry weather conditions. It is still unclear why he failed to mention the unannounced Soviet attack on Eastern Poland which took place on September 17, which obviously must have had a major influence on Polish strategic decision making and good fortune. Gubbins stated in his report that Polish industry, aerodromes and most of the Polish Airforce was destroyed in the first few days of conflict and added that Polish anti-aircraft batteries were hopelessly inadequate. This meant that the *Luftwaffe* was unhindered operating at such low levels that it could hand-pick targets and destroy them at will. This also meant that dangerous night bombing was totally unnecessary. The result of German air operations, which eventually became indiscriminate, was devastating for the Polish forces. Mechanised armour was also able to push on relentlessly attacking everything and everyone in sight. Gubbins noted that no army so ill-equipped with anti-tank weapons could possibly stand up to the German onslaught without air support. He was a little more positive about Polish infantry, which according to him, had fought gallantly on equal terms with German infantry, but the tank attacks, supported by heavy air bombardment of forward lines, weighed the scales too heavily against it. According to Gubbins the weather also played a very significant part in the German success. The drought conditions that had prevailed during September 1939 had provided tracked vehicles with perfect conditions to prosecute the fight quickly. In his summing up Gubbins, rather dubiously and in the 'British way' informed London that the situation could have been saved if only the Poles had had the luxury of a few days respite in order to 'pull themselves together.' He acknowledged that the Mission's objective was to attempt to ensure that an eastern front was maintained and to convince Romania to permit passage of war material for the Poles. Alas, he concluded, this was not possible and much of the war material would never reach the fighting Poles. Eventually, the Polish High Command felt it had no other option but to retreat across the frontier to Romania with as many men as possible. Gubbins reported that he had tried to convince the Poles to await developments, but understandably, according to him, the Polish General Staff was so spooked by the speed of German armour, that it could not contemplate waiting. Further assessments, highlighted the weakness of the High Command, which was organised according to French military theory and practice. The Head Quarters, according to British assessments, was over centralised, with Śmigly-Rydz[1] and his Chiefs-of-Staff commanding seven armies and one independent brigade without any decent communications.[2] In the turmoil of war, it was impossible for the Polish Marshal to keep track of events and troop movements on the ground and in the field. Soon it became clear that the lack of radio infrastructure in the country meant that the High Command lacked any chance of command and control. During the distressing Polish retreat south to the Romanian border, the General Staff moved four times in a fortnight and it was impossible for it to keep in touch with events on the battlefield. It retreated from Warsaw to Brzecz, then to Włodimierz, then Młynow and finally to Kołomyja. Gubbins reported that on reaching Lwów, on the 13 September, and witnessing the German assault on the town, he travelled quickly to see the Polish High Command at Młynow nearby. When he arrived, he soon realised that the High Command had no knowledge of the attack or of the dire situation which was unfolding in the south east of the country. Poland's High Command, it seemed, was not only failing its soldiers, it was also losing whatever tenuous grip it had on reality.[3] Gubbins reported that he was fortunate to have moved the Mission to Tarnopol, which still retained electric power for the wireless. However, there were petrol shortages in the town and all that was left to do 'was to get the Mission out of there before petrol ran out completely.' He selected those who would travel with him in his group and those who would make their own way back to Britain under their own steam. Poland at the time was spy-ridden and the Mission's departure to Romania was announced on Russian radio the next day. The bulletin said that the Mission was travelling south pursued by German aircraft which 'were going to harass it down until it had left Polish territory.' The British embassy got General Adrian

---

1     Marshal Edward Rydz-Śmigły, also known as Edward Śmigły-Rydz, was Commander-in-Chief of Poland's armed forces during the September Campaign.
2     Kochański, *The Eagle Unbowed*, p. 88.
3     Moorhouse, *First to Fight*, p. 112.

Carton de Wiart out of Romania as quickly as possible whilst the rest of the Mission trickled back to Britain over the following months. Following the war Carton de Wiart remarked in his memoir:

> Thr Polish campaign, though bitter with the taste of defeat, had made me aware of several new developments in warfare. The first—perhaps a premonition—was that with the speed and mobility of mechanized war, it would be very easy to be taken prisoner. The second was the newly acquired power of the air, and the terrorizing effectiveness of bombing, though we were still far from being alive to its full capabilities. The third was a grasp of the full meaning of those strange words "The Fifth Column." The Fifth Columnist as an enemy was most dangerous; he can be felt but not seen, and as an individual he was loathsome as he turned against his own, and loved money or power better than his honour …'[4]

\* \* \*

During the retreat south the War Office wrote to Gubbins regarding the destruction of strategically important infrastructure being left behind on Polish territory. MIR wanted to know how successful demolitions had been, what preparations for future demolitions had been made in the areas from which the Poles were retreating, what preparations existed for the destruction of the Kraków-Lemberg railway and what aid within British means would be useful to the Poles for further action. Gubbins compiled a list of the stores the Poles would require and despatched it to London. Finally, Gubbins was asked to describe the preparations being made for the destruction of Galician oilfields,[5] which would certainly be exploited by the Germans if left intact. He began his reply to London with a warning, saying that he was only able to present what he understood at the time of writing and nothing more. Information was sketchy and it was difficult to ascertain its currency. The Colonel, however, assured that railway lines in the Corridor of the Posen Salient and bridges over the Vistula river had been prepared for destruction, but he was not clear as to how much had already been destroyed. Gubbins was clear, however, that the Kraków-Lemberg-Chernowitz railway had been prepared for wholesale destruction, although he expressed doubt about whether the Poles had made much preparation around Warsaw. In conclusion, Gubbins informed MIR, that clandestine sabotage organisations had been provided with caches of arms and explosives and that each group had been furnished with an order of battle with information regarding the number of operations expected per week.

\* \* \*

---

4   Adrian Carton De Wiart, *Happy Odyssey,* pp. 123-124
5   Oil fields in the Galician region of Southern Poland and Romania.

On 11 October, Gerty went shopping in search of bacon. On returning home she reported that there was no bacon to be had. She also noted that the price of meat had risen by 29 percent. The following Saturday, Gerty and Frank, went to the local Empire cinema to see a film called 'Firefly'. On the way home they were drenched in the rain. By October 1939, the Second Polish Republic had been destroyed and bisected by her two powerful neighbours, Nazi Germany and the Soviet Union. The decision to share Polish territory predated the actual invasion of the country and was formally agreed in the Molotov-Ribbentrop Pact signed in August 1939. Joseph Stalin's suspicion of imperialist powers, combined with a marked reluctance of Britain and France to commit themselves to multilateral treaties influenced the Russian leadership to sign a pact with Nazi Germany, thus forming an alliance between the two of the most unlikely of political bed fellows. The boundary between the two occupation zones of the Second Republic of Poland followed the Narew-Wistula-San rivers in central Poland. The Soviet policy to its newly acquired territory was to 'cleanse' it of Polish bourgeoisie and to create a new Soviet Socialist Republic in the territory; a policy which was later adjusted into forming a People's Republic of Poland. As a first step to the Sovietisation of the Second Republic's eastern territory Polish citizens were rounded up and deported to the depths of Soviet territory, such as Siberia and Kazakhstan, where they slaved for the Bolsheviks. German policy towards the Polish people was simple in its ruthlessness. It aimed at complete annihilation, apart from a nucleus of slaves. Those that were spared were destined to unconditional servitude for the greater glory of the Reich. Polish property was either destroyed or taken over by new tenants from Germany. Polish culture was dismantled and the country's nationhood destroyed. Every means of education was abolished with schools being closed and universities shut down. Only technical schools were allowed to stay open to train boys and girls in the basic skills that were deemed useful for the German economy. During the occupation, Poles could only be slaves, educated to the most rudimentary level. In the Russian occupied region, Polish house owners found themselves evicted from their homes to be replaced by Ukrainian inhabitants. Clothing and shoes were in such short supply in the east that the British Mission, now in Bucharest, reported that Russian women wore no underclothes owing to the shortage of cloth. Soon after the Soviet occupation of Eastern Poland in an act of revenge for the Polish -Soviet war of 1921, a period of ethnic cleansing ensued. The NKVD (the forces of the Interior Ministry) had prepared a plan which was followed systematically and involved murder and forced deportations. The first phase involved the extermination of Polish politicians working in Russia, such as the ambassador and members of the diplomatic service, in the major cities of the Soviet Union. These individuals were murdered in unknown circumstances. Following the liquidation of members of the Polish Diplomatic Service, attention shifted to killing Polish military officers in places such as the Katyń forest. Invariably, Polish officers were promised freedom if they ordered their men to lay down arms, but once they had done so, they were separated out and shot. Following this, their men were condemned to death in their thousands. Then followed the murder of Polish intelligentsia and Catholic clergy including priests and nuns. Finally, Polish families were forcibly deported into the depths of Soviet Russia as slaves. The transports were formed of rolling stock from the provinces, coupled together to form long 'ribbons of misery'. There was no sanitation in the wagons which resulted in outbreaks of disease such as typhus, and the death of the old, the young and the frail. The number of people deported is difficult to ascertain but estimates of one million appear in documents. This is how Joseph Pajdowski described his deportation from his home in Karczowka Settlement, Łuck District:

> We lived in the military settlement Karczowka 20 kilometres from Łuck in Volhynia. In the middle of the night we heard rifle butts slamming on our doors and the words 'Get ready with your possessions.' Father, considering that the danger of being arrested would only affect him as a former legionnaire and not expecting that the whole family would be deported, was in hiding. Mother, half bewildered, packed clothing, shoes and bedding. During this time sledges full of other settlers were arriving in our yard. Come the dawn we were taken to the station in Rozyszcze, where cattle wagons awaited us. Inside, along both walls, were two rows of wooded bunks one on top of the other; in the centre was an iron stove for heating; and in one corner there was a hole with a seat – the toilet – which was screened off with a blanket. The long journey in those wagons proved to be a nightmare … after five weeks journey we were ordered to disembark at Kotlas near Archangel where sledges again awaited us. Now for a further two days we were transported along the frozen River Vychegda in the incredible cold, indeed so cold, that some infants froze to death. We ended up in Nyanda settlement.[6]

\* \* \*

Under these circumstanes it was virtually impossible to organise any effective underground resistance in the Soviet occupied territory of the country, as the population in this part of the republic was in constant flux. The Soviet Union had embarked on wave after wave of ethnic cleansing operations in an attempt to 'depolonise' the region. In German occupied territory (Western Poland) the situation was somewhat different. As the Polish population in this area was relatively stable, (not being deported or moved en masse), it was possible to begin organising clandestine resistance groups. However, one early difficulty facing the leaders of the resistance was the uncertainty regarding the duration of the occupation; would it be long and protracted or short and sharp. Just the same as the British people during the early stages of the war regarding the duration of the conflict, the Poles likewise believed that the occupation of Poland would not last long, especially when the British and the French would come to the rescue. This view spawned plans for just enough guerrilla activity to destabilise the occupiers whilst waiting for help to arrive. Such thinking resulted in the establishment of small clandestine fighting groups with limited military objectives; however,

---

6   Jozef Pajdowski, *Karczowka Settlement,* in *Stalin's Ethnic Cleansing in Eastern Poland* (London: Association of the Families of the Borderlands Settlers, 2000), p. 186.

with the Phoney War (or what the British called 'the Twilight War') in full swing, it soon became clear that the occupation would be a long and protracted affair due to Britain and France hesitating and dithering on the side lines and so failing to deliver the promised help. The prevailing paradigm for resistance, therefore, had to be modified to include holding out for as long as possible whilst preparing for a single decisive blow in the form of an overwhelming uprising. It was the SOE planners in 1940 who were first in devising an ambitious plan for a Polish uprising which ironically was then denounced as fool hardy by the British Chiefs of Staff. The London based Polish staff cloned the plans making them a keystone of their planning for future resistance. Meanwhile, it was realised that a decisive uprising would require one centralised authority to oversee the build-up of resistance capability, the organisation of financial resources and to ensure a successful deployment of men for decisive action. The year was early 1941 and Poland had been erased from the European map for almost two years. At this time, Germany was allied with the Soviet Union and Britain was allied with Poland. It is a moot point why Britain did not protest when the Soviet Union attacked Poland soon after the German onslaught; only being concerned with German aggression. It is possible that Churchill, who unofficially coveted Red Army power, did not want to annoy the Russians in the hope that they would eventually join the western alliance against Nazi Germany, which they did after Barbarossa.

\* \* \*

The objective of Polish political and military leaders at the time of the Polish collapse was to reach sanctuary in France via Romania and Hungary, Poland's nearest ally. There the plan was to regroup, reconstitute the Polish Forces and to continue the fight under French operational command. This also included securing provisions for the Home Army in the occupied homeland. On 30September 1939, a new Polish Government was formed in France with General Wladislaw Sikorski as the Prime Minister. He had also accepted the position of Commander-in-Chief of the Polish Armed Forces. This made Sikorski both politically and militarily very powerful and influential in Polish circles. His government became the exiled government of the Second Republic and was recognised recognised by the Western allies as the true representative of the Polish people. An agreement between the Polish and the French Government, signed 4January, 1940 in Paris, gave the Poles the authority to fight from French soil. By 15 June, this army had grown to 84,500 soldiers. They were distributed amongst the following formations:

    1st Grenadier Division under the command of General Bronislaw Duch
    2nd Rifle Division under the command of General Bronislaw Prugar-Ketling
    10th Motorised Armoured Cavalry Brigade under the command of General Stanisław Maczek
    Independent Podhale Rifle Brigade commanded by General Zygmunt Bohusz-Szyszko
    Carpathian Rifle Brigade commanded by General Stanisław Kopański

3rd Infantry Division (not to full strength) commanded by Colonel Tadeusz Zieleniewski

4th Infantry Division under the command of General Rudolf Dreszer

In addition to these, units were special formations such as officer schools, military hospitals and intelligence organisations. Polish Air Force squadrons were also established and seconded to the French Air Force. Sikorski also authorised the Polish Navy to serve alongside the British Royal Navy.

\* \* \*

Following his escape via the Balkans and subsequent return to London, Gubbins was posted to France and put in charge of 4th Military Mission, with the remit of encouraging the underground activities of the Polish Forces in exile. He met Sikorski there in October 1940 and both men agreed that the first priority was to deliver war material to the Polish underground army, which was at the time called the Union for Armed Struggle. This, it was agreed, would kick-start clandestine operations in the occupied country. In February 1942 Sikorski renamed the Union of Armed Struggle (UAS), the Home Army or Armia Krajowa or AK for short.[7] This was an attempt by Sikorski to unite all the various resistance groups in Poland that had surfaced spontaneously and place them under his command. All recruits to the Home Army, whether they were originally recruited into the UAS or whether they were new recruits, were required to swear allegiance to his government operating in France. The oath, which Sikorski had had a hand in writing, read as follows:

> Before God the almighty, before Holy Mary, Queen of Poland, I put my hand on this Cross, the symbol of martyrdom and salvation, and I swear that I will defend the honour of Poland with all my might, that I will fight with arms in hand to liberate her from slavery, notwithstanding, the sacrifice of my life, that I shall be absolutely obedient to my superiors and I will keep the secret whatever the cost may be.

Any individual who refused was considered 'renegade' and subsequently disowned. One significant resistance group refused to take the oath was the communist People's Army (Armia Ludowa) which took its orders from Moscow. According to communist chronologists about 40 percent of the officers of the independents movement were Soviet specialists in guerrilla warfare. The remaining were: officers of partisan units, men given training in the USSR and parachuted into Poland, Polish officers drafted in from the 'liberated areas' and partisans trained in front line cadet schools. The People's Army had powerful artillery at its disposal and hundreds of tanks many of which had been supplied by Russia and was fighting for a People's Republic.

---

7   TNA:HS4/147: Polish Secret Army, Polish planning for the reoccupation of Poland.

The indefatigable Polish Prime Minister wrote to Allied commanders during January 1940, expressing his thinking regarding the Home Army. He informed them that a general uprising would begin when the Western Allies, including the Polish Forces under British operational command, entered Poland from the west. He envisaged, wrongly as it happened, that the Polish Forces operating in the West under British command, would return to liberate Poland and reinstate the Second Republic. He believed that there was a possibility that this might occur in January 1941 once preparations were complete. Sikorski also explained to General Ironside that German policies of extermination in Poland may provoke a popular revolt sooner than planned and therefore it may be prudent to increase the rate at which British weapons were being delivered to the Home Army. With this in mind Sikorski also approached the French for help, however, this planning was soon overtaken by events on the ground when France surrendered in June 1940. From this point in time Britain became Poland's sole ally and relations between the two countries grew very warm. It was obvious that from now on that the Polish fight for the Second Republic would proceed from British soil and so, with the approval of Churchill, remnants of the Polish Forces in France together with the Polish political authorities were transferred to Britain. With the arrival of the Polish forces in the United Kingdom in June 1940, Churchill reassured Sikorski that Britain would stand by the Poles until the country was free. Meanwhile, Gubbins returned to Britain and continued to work on preparing special forces for operations in occupied Europe including Poland. His mission was later taken over by Peter Wilkinson.

# 5

# Republican Forces in Britain

*By what sweet charm I know not the native land draws all men nor allows them to forget her.*

Ovid, *Epistulae Ex Ponto*, I,3

Southern Britain 1 January 1940 began with a chilly fog which seemed to get thicker as the day progressed. On the 7th, Frank, the Post Master in Staines, went for a short stroll towards the local railway station. Whilst passing the station he happened to notice the posters hanging on the platform walls. The posters on one side of the platform read, 'Come to sunny Broadstairs' and 'All folks go to Folkestone.' On the opposite wall the posters read, 'Coals, shells and food must come first – remember this if your train is late or crowded.' Beneath one of the posters there was a picture of a steam engine with the caption, 'This engine used to pull holiday trains to Weymouth.' Frank pondered these juxtaposed messages and later wrote in his diary,' How typical of things as they are – one foot out of the war and one foot in it. It is still somewhat difficult to grasp that we really are at war.'[1] Across the English Channel, France had just fallen to the German onslaught and Churchill had 'stepped up to the plate' and invited the Poles fighting alongside the French to regroup in Britain. Peter Wilkinson[2] rescued most of the Polish general staff, whilst other ranks joined the Dunkirk evacuation or escaped the continent via Switzerland and Gibraltar. Eventually, 24,000 servicemen had reached Britain, often in extremely dangerous circumstances.[3] Once in Britain and working under the authority of the Anglo-Polish Agreement of June 1940, Sikorski began to ingratiate himself to the British Prime Minister, whose support he required if meaningful Polish resistance was to resume. Churchill too was keen to reciprocate Sikorski's advances in order to

---

1    Peter Minett (ed.), *Frank's Wartime Diary*, p. 1.
2    Later of the SOE.
3    Jozef Gula, *The Roman Catholic Church in the History of the Polish Exiled Community in Great Britain* (London: University of London Press, 1963), p. 75.

demonstrate his support for the Polish ally and to exploit her determination to fight on. Both leaders understood what each could contribute to the war effort, although Sikorski insisted that he be allowed to keep using secret Polish ciphers whilst in Britain. This was agreed. For the second time since evacuating Poland, Sikorski began to rebuild Polish political and military authority in exile. He was convinced that he should send a strong message to the world that, despite the occupation of the Second Republic, the country continued to exist and was determined to fight on. Sikorski proceeded to re-establish a General Head Quarters, a military intelligence bureau, training schools and cadet units, as well as regular military formations. For example, he arranged for the remnants of the Polish Airforce to be seconded to the RAF and supported the training of Polish pilots on British machines. These pilots were later to play a significant role in the Battle of Britain, with the Polish 303 Squadron recording the highest kill rate of any other RAF squadron. He also oversaw the reception of a few updated British battleships, which were then sent to augment the Polish Navy, which had sailed to Scotland in 1939. Some 4,475 officers had made it to Britain via France along with 12,730 other ranks. The men were billeted in camps in and around Glasgow: Coatbridge, Braughton and Ballahaugton. Sikorski's plan was to form two infantry brigades, one tank brigade, a special forces unit and one Polish flight. These were to be kitted out with British equipment. In July the Poles transferred to Biggar, Douglas and Crawford. One difficulty facing Sikorski was the fact that there were more officers in the cohort in Scotland, compared to other ranks. He concluded that retreat routes on the continent for other ranks must have been cut off. As the threat of a German invasion of Britain grew, Sikorski ordered two brigades to be formed from the men stationed at Biggar and Douglas, envisaging that they could contribute to the defence of Scotland. Thus on 13 July, the 1st Rifle Brigade was formed under the command of General Paszkiewicz, followed a few days later by the 2nd Rifle Brigade under General Rudolf Dreszer's command. A mechanised brigade was organised alongside these formations whilst all units in Scotland were put under the command of General Stanisław Burhardt-Bukacki. The make-up of these forces was in constant flux and over the next three years changed as events in the war unfolded. On 22 August 1940 authority was given to the Poles to operate from British territory. The Polish Forces in Scotland at that time numbered approximately 20,000 men and comprised two rifle brigades, three reserve brigades and a tank brigade. In September Polish General Head Quarters started to establish a Corps out of these units, which eventually was named the 1st Polish Corps. This was a significant political move designed to raise the profile of the Poles in Britain. By 8 October, the nature of the 1st Corps was clear, it comprised: a General Headquarters, one reconnaissance division, one artillery division, a tank regiment, a communication company, a battalion of sappers, two columns of ambulances, three quartermasters, two military hospitals and a reserve. The First Corps was designated to defend the line from Firth of Forth to Montrose. The first phase of establishing a Polish military force in Scotland ended when Polish units took up their positions on this defence line.

\* \* \*

Meanwhile in Staines, on Saturday 29 June, Frank went shopping for a new suit. He bought a ready-made garment and as noted in his diary it was a 'wonderful fit', the only thing that needed doing was the lengthening of the trouser legs by an inch. He paid three pounds seven shillings and six pence for it, which he thought was good value. If he had chosen to have a suit made to measure the price would have jumped to four pounds and 15 shillings, because cloth was continually becoming more and more expensive.[4]

In London the Polish Government's intelligence section, under the command of General Sosnkowski, was established on 21 June 1940, and was known as the 6th Bureau of the General Staff. Its predominant responsibility was to establish and maintain radio and courier links with the occupied Republic and to be the contact point between SOE Polish Section and the Polish High Command.[5] After Sosnkowski's resignation the bureau fell under the command of General Klimecki. Following the air accident in Gibraltar, which claimed the life of Klimecki and the Polish Prime Minister Władysław Sikorski, the command was taken over by General S. Tartar. The role of the bureau was to be a conduit between the Polish General Staff, the SOE Polish Section and the High Command of the Home Army in Poland. This function required the maintenance of radio encrypted communication between London and Warsaw. The Bureau was also responsible for the base in Brindisi which operated flights to Poland, 640 reception committees, training schools and radio stations. As well as a military role, the Bureau had a political function in maintaining relations between the exiled Polish Government in London and the government's delegate in Warsaw. To this end it had to take a lead in training political emissaries and organise their transfer to Poland. The Bureau also liaised with the BBC (code name 'Jodoform') which broadcasted secret messages on behalf of the exiled Polish Government to the Home Army regarding clandestine flights. The messages were broadcast in the form of short, coded melodies carrying information in a secret format. Between June 1940 to December 1941 the day to day running of the bureau was managed by Colonel J. Smoleński, then from 15 December 1941 to March 1942 by Lieutenant Colonel T.Rudnicki, Director of Polish Military Inteligence, followed by Lieutenant Colonel M. Protasiewicz until July 1944 and finally by Lieutenant Colonel M. Utnik until the closure of the Bureau in 1945.

---

4 Peter Minett (ed.), *Frank's Wartime Diary*, p. 117
5 Zygmunt Banulski, (ed.), *Wojsko Polskie* (Warszawa: Bellona, 1994), p. 145.

# 6

# The Polish Resistance

*There is an honour…which may be ranked amongst the greatest, which happeneth rarely; that is, of such as sacrifice themselves to death or danger for the good of their country.*

Bacon, *Of Honour and Reputation*

Between 1772 and 1918, Poland was absent from maps. The country had been occupied and shared out between her three great neighbours; Tsarist Russia, Prussia (Germany) and the Habsburg Empire (Austro-Hungary). They had partitioned the country into three segments and incorporated them into their own jurisdictions. This condemned the Poles to years of protest, acts of resistance and desperate uprisings in an attempt to prevent complete national annihilation. Perhaps the first notable uprising was the armed rebellion against the Russian Empire, sometimes called the Russo-Polish War of 1830-1831. The Poles called this rising the November Uprising since it began in that month. After a year of bitter fighting, the conflict ended with a Russian victory and the liquidation of Polish autonomy. No sooner than the November Uprising had failed, Polish émigré's in France began to plot the next bid for independence. This subsequent insurrection was scheduled to begin on 20 February, 1846; unfortunately, the Austrians had learnt of the plans, which resulted in a massacre of the insurgents. The so-called 'January Uprising' of 1863-1864, lasted for one and half years and consisted of 1,200 individual skirmishes and minor battles. All in all, Polish history during the 18th, 19th and early 20th centuries was peppered with battles and uprisings of varying size and ferocity. Things only improved for the Poles in 1918 when the partitioning powers floundered during the Great War and when the Versailles Treaty was passed. the Second Republic of Poland was born. However, the existence of the Second Republic was short lived as the Germans and Russians returned in 1939 precipitating the subsequent partitioning of the country. Yet again the Poles were required to fight for their cultural and national existence

* * *

On Saturday 13 January, Frank finished work at the post office early, at 13.25 to be precise. He met Girty and they both walked to the Regal cinema in Clarence Street adjacent to Staines Bridge. The whole week had been very cold and the pavement was frost bound. They pondered the new rationing scheme, which had just come into force and lamented the shortage of some foods. Lard, for example, was unobtainable but Lardex, a poor substitute at six pence per pound was still in the shops (lard was 5 pence per pound). Trex, an excellent vegetable fat manufactured by Bibby's of Liverpool, was also unavailable. Frank turned to Girty and said, 'We have nothing to grumble about for we will have an excellent Sunday dinner: New Zealand lamb, roast potatoes, sprouts and onion sauce. For afters, we will have rice pudding'. On returning home Frank decided to look up a map of Finland in order to learn something of the Soviet invasion of the country. He had discovered that two out of three atlases seemed to have dismissed Finland as of no consequence and information was rather sketchy. The third atlas was acceptable except the place names differed from those in current use. He noticed that in fact Swedish names and explained this away by the fact that until the nineteenth century the country formed had part of the Swedish Kingdom. The Kings of Sweden were also the Kings of Finland.[1]

\* \* \*

The troubled history of Poland had made the Poles hyper-sensitive to anything which appeared to threatened their independence and they were quick to respond to any national emergency. It is not surprising, therefore, that soon after the 'September debacle' in 1939, when the Second Republic fell to the binary invasion of Germany and the Soviet Union and so beginning the Second World War, numerous resistance groups formed spontaneously in the occupied country. Various elements of the population were involved in these grass root events for example, such as politicians, teachers, scouts groups, priests, students, company owners, the intelligentsia and so on, Approximately, 300 groups were formed, all believing that the preservation of the Republic could only be realised through active struggle. Soon, local resistance groups coalesced into larger and larger organisations until the 'Legion of Liberation' and the 'Fatherland' (Ojczyzna) were formed. Some were non-combatant formations and were solely concerned with nurturing and protecting the spirit of national freedom. They either operated on a local level or a national level, both in rural as well as urban areas. They were led by community elders such as university lecturers, ex-members of parliament and the clergy. Combatant groups, such as the 'Union for Armed Struggle' (later renamed the Home Army) were usually led by ex-army officers who had managed to escape the German and Soviet round-ups and had gone underground to continue the fight from within. For example, on 17 September the hawkish General Wacław Stachiewicz passed an order to Colonel Jan Mazurkiewcz to open a secret resistance group operating behind the front line. On the same day General Józef Olszyna-Wilczyński in Grodno, passed an order to Colonel Franczek

---

1   Peter Minett (ed.), *Frank's Wartime Diary*, pp. 28-29.

Sledczce to commence conspiracy work in the Białystok region. These were individuals were those who refused to lay down their arms when the Second Republic capitulated. However, it would be wrong to assume that everyone who had joined the resistance had been born in Poland and were of Polish nationality. As with many European nations, pre-war Poland had people of other nationalities living within its borders. One interesting example, was a Nigerian man called August Browne who was 44 years of age when he settled in Poland. Born in Lagos, Nigeria, he made a living as an accomplished jazz musician appearing in Kraków and Warsaw night clubs. He married a Polish girl called Zofia Pyków, with whom he had two children. Unfortunately, the marriage failed, but when war broke out, he arranged for all of them to take refuge in England. Browne himself remained in Poland, where he joined the resistance. During his service he had a number of different roles, such as distributing clandestine newspapers, sheltering Jewish refugees who had escaped the Warsaw Ghetto and trading in electronic equipment. August also fought in the Warsaw Uprising in 1944. He is noted as the only African person to have done so. Being a citizen of the British Empire, he had had the opportunity to leave Poland after the war in 1945 but decided to remain in Warsaw where he lived with his second wife. They eventually moved to England in 1956 and settled in London. He died in London in 1976 at the age of 81.[2] In 2019 a small stone monument to commemorate Browne's life was unveiled in Warsaw.

\* \* \*

The guiding principle of the Polish resistance movement was the doctrine of 'two enemies', Germany and the Soviet Union – the two countries which had collaborated in the invasion of Poland in 1939. Consequently, it had two objectives, military and political; the first being to rid the Second Republic of occupiers and the second to oppose the rise of communism in the country. The fear was that in the turmoil of war Polish communists, with Russian assistance, would make a grab for power. However, following 'Barbarossa', Polish resistance activity had to be realigned as Russia was now Poland's new ally. This realignment did not mean that Russia had had a change of heart regarding her aim of sovietising Poland and thus removing the Second Republic. More to the contrary, Russia joining the western alliance presented both the SOE Polish Section and the Foreign Office with a conundrum – how to support the Polish resistance of the Second Republic without antagonising Moscow? This puzzle also taxed the Republic's authorities exiled in Britain, who split into a number of factions. For example those, such as the Sikorskiites (supporters of General Sikorski), who believed that striking a deal with Stalin would protect the Second Republic, and those anti-Russian elements, such as the Sanationists (members of the pre-war *Sanacja* regime), many of whom were in the Polish High Command in the West and were opposed to making any negotiations with Stalin on Polish matters. The SOE found itself between a rock and a hard place, because from now on, it

2   BBC News Website. Accessed 5.10.20.

would have to support both the allied Poles, as well as the allied Russians, both latent enemies. However, the underlying question was, at what cost would Britain be prepared to pay for Russian fire power? The answer was clear at the end of the Warsaw Uprising, when Churchill decided to keep anti-Soviet Poles at arms-length.

\* \* \*

In 1942 General Sikorski, the Prime Minister of the Second Republic exiled in Britain, came to the conclusion that the it would be better if the numerous Polish resistance groups were to unite under one command structure should they have to spearhead the fight for the return of a free Second Republic. With this in mind he renamed the 'Union for Armed Struggle' the 'Home Army' and insisted that all independent resistance groups, large or small, align themselves with this new organisation. The Home Army was, therefore, considered to be the premier underground army of the Second Republic. Secrecy was of the upmost importance when recruitment for the Home Army was taking place and the identity of recruits was never shared as this threatened the penetration of units by German and Soviet 'fifth columnists.' Members of the Home Army were organised into groups of men/women called Cells. Each cell was made up of five fighters. Each member knew the other four in the group but no more. Individual members were allowed to recruit another four people to form a new cell if he/she wished and, in this way, the 'pyramid of cells' grew. The people who presented themselves for service in these formations were usually young and often inexperienced in guerrilla warfare. Those with experience and training were either lost during the failed September Campaign or were in German or Soviet captivity. Since the Home Army was mainly dealing with untrained people secret military training schools were established throughout the Second Republic in order to improve fighting skills. The use of real names in the secret army was forbidden and hence pseudonyms were used. As with names, private addresses were codified to make it difficult, or indeed impossible, to identify the homes of Home Army members, as well as the meeting places they frequented. The number of secret meeting places grew forming underground 'liaison networks.' Complete anonymity was also secured through the issue of false identity papers, which were produced on underground printing presses by experienced draughtsmen with high level skills. Other forms of deception saw men shaving off beards or growing moustaches and changing hairstyles frequently to throw off German and Soviet surveillance. The Home Army's High Command divided Polish territory into sectors based on the pre-war administrative postal regions; however, some resistance groups refused to align themselves with the exiled government in London. These were communist formations and participated in the Soviet sponsored partisan movement.[3] These Polish groups had been trained in the Soviet Union and thus worked for the sovietisation of Poland and the formation of a People's Republic after the war. One such group was commanded by General Aleksander Saburov, and

---

3   Mieczyslaw Juchniewicz, *Poles in the European Resistance Movement, 1939-1945* (Warsaw: Interpress Publishers, 1972) pp. 129, 130.

later by General Vasili Begma, in the Równe district. In the unit commanded by Ivan Szytov, the Feliks Dzierzynski fighters, commanded by Grigorij Sitajlo, Kazimierz Turewicz and Siemion Ladyszew. These units carried out guerrilla activity along the enemy's communication lines. According to communist historians, several hundred paratroopers, scouts and guerrilla fighters were trained in the assault battalions attached to the Polish Partisan Headquarters. After training in Russia these men were dropped as reconnaissance and guerrilla units behind the German front on the Bug, Vistula, and Odra rivers. Substantial quantities of arms and war supplies were made available by Moscow for these communist partisan units. Ironically, there were reports that these communist units sometimes fought other partisan units which were not communist. During such skirmishes Home Army sought armaments from German forces which were ready supplied.

\* \* \*

Up to the time of his untimely death off Gibraltar, when in 1943 his plane crashed into the Mediterranean on take-off, General Sikorski was the Commander in Chief of all Polish Forces fighting under British operational command, as well as in command of the Home Army fighting for the Second Republic in the occupied homeland and he was also the Polish Prime Minster. After Sikorski's death, President Raczkiewicz, also exiled in London, pondered who should replace him. He considered General Anders for the post of Commander in Chief, whilst political leadership would be passed to either Raczynski, Kot or Mikołajczyk. Apparently, Raczynski was considered to be least contentious, Kot the most able, but alledgedly the least popular due to having been accused of espionage when he was the ambassador in Russia. This was soon overlooked. Finally, the President decided to separate Sikorski's dual responsibilities between Stanisław Mikołajczyk, who became the new Prime Minister, and General Kazimierz Sosnkowski, who became the new Commander-in-Chief. Allegedly, Mikołajczyk had to have his arm twisted to accept Sosnkowski as the two men did not see eye to eye on a number of issues particularly regarding relations with the Soviet Union. Other members of the new cabinet included, Kwapiński, who became Deputy Prime Minister, Romer, who took over at the Foreign Office, General Kukiel who became the Defence Minister and Banaczyk who was instructed to take over at the Ministry of the Interior. On his appointment Sosnkowski immediately cabled Warsaw to say he wished to keep a close eye on military activity in Poland- presumably to keep the communists in check. Political authority in the occupied country rested with the Underground State, which comprised a coalition of four political parties, the Socialist, the Nationalist, the Peasant Party and the Christian Labour Movement. This coalition was in intimate contact with Sikorski's administration and the quasi parliament in exile through each party's representative in London. The Underground State comprised five departments and was responsible for maintaining order and discipline in the occupied country. The Administrative Department was headed by the Chief Delegate to the Polish Government in Exile (London). Regional Delegates represented various districts throughout the country, whilst specially appointed ministers were responsible for the Treasury, Education and the Interior. The Poles refused to take part in the so called German General Government for Central Poland or to adhere to its edicts. The Administrative Department was charged with maintaining order in the occupied country and to be ready to take complete control when the occupiers were removed from Polish territory, pending the return of the government from British exile. Political representation in the Underground State was realised through the functioning of a quasi-parliament. The parliament was responsible to Sikorski's Chief Delegate in Warsaw and the commander of the Home Army. The delegate also controlled the financing of resistance and the number of representatives each political party was entitled to have in parliamentary sittings. The responsibility of the Directorate of Civilian Resistance was to nurture the spirit of resistance in the general population and to dissuade individuals from working with the enemy. This was sometimes done by sentencing conspirators to death for treason during trials and tribunals. Finally, the Directorate coordinated the activities of resistance organisations, whether they be political, economic, educational or religious. The groupings not under its direct control worked on the periphery of the official underground state and were invariably self-financing. A significant contribution of such organisations was their ability to organise and run clandestine schools and vocational colleges, as well as to providing instruction at university level. Military resistance was the responsibility of the domestic underground army. The commanding officer in the occupied country, as well as his regional officers, had the same authority as that of the regular army operating in any war zone. They were empowered to issue edicts and orders as well as to organise the necessary war work, which coordinated effective resistance. Men in the underground army had the usual rights of combatants in the front line bestowed on them by Allied Command. For example, they were entitled to pay and veteran pensions. The Commander in Chief, based in Warsaw, was responsible to the country's President in exile on whose authority he operated. The President in London was authorised to call for total mobilisation or for a regional uprising against the occupiers, be it the Germans or the Russians or both. Operations by the secret army had two objectives, to monitor the enemy's forces and pass information regarding their action to London and to prepare for a general decisive uprising. This required not only the transmission of encrypted messages to the Polish Government in London but to coordinate planning with local political and administrative departments in Poland.[4] Meanwhile, other units planned and executed low level sabotage, diversion and confusion. The British War Cabinet appreciated that the only other dissident element in Poland was the Polish Communist Party, which took its directives from Moscow and was considered renegade until, that is, the Russians switched sides in the war.

---

4   TNA: HS4/171: Planning and policy: Operations to Warsaw, FINCHAM.

# 7

# Special Operations Executive (SOE)

*Your country has a right to your services in sustaining the glory of her position. These are a common source of pride to you all, and you cannot decline the burdens of empire and still expect to share its honours.*

Thucydides, *The Peloponnesian War*, II, 63

During the First World War, Lord Northcliffe, the British newspaper magnate, had had some success in undermining the morale of German soldiers with propaganda. Following Anschluss[1] in March 1938, the German threat could no longer be ignored, and among other things, London revisited Northcliffe's research papers. In doing so the Foreign Office contacted one of his assistants and set him to work on finding out how propaganda worked as a psychological tool. The assistant's name was Sir Campbell Stuart, a Canadian newspaper magnate. Stuart ran propaganda operations for the British throughout the Second World War. He worked in absolute secrecy in his department which was known as Department CS, after his initials.

The Secret Intelligence Service or SIS, known today as Military Intelligence 6 (MI6) was also a secret organisation—and SOE's bitter rival during the war. MI6, created in 1909, was part of the secret service bureau designated to secure secrets from abroad. It was under the control of the Foreign Office. Homeland security was the responsibility of MI5, which was answerable to the Home Office.

\* \* \*

In March 1938, Lord Halifax, of the Foreign Office, gave MI6 permission to hire Major L. D. Grand to set up a new secret department, which would study how an

---

1 The forced annexation of Austria by Nazi Germany.

enemy could be attacked by means other than by conventional methods. The department was called Section D (D for destruction) and its work overlapped with that of MI5 and MI6. Also, in 1938, a new department known as GS(R), was established under Jo Holland who also began working on the methods of irregular warfare. He began by collating information on the Boar War, Lawrence of Arabia and his partners, the Russian Civil War, the Spanish Civil War the struggle between China and Japan, the Palestine-Jewish problem, and the Irish troubles. All these conflicts exploited unconventional methods of fighting, so having studied these events in detail, Holland became convinced of the value of irregular warfare. As a result, he became a strong advocate of this type of fighting. In spring 1939, he was transferred to Military Intelligence Research MI(R) under Beaumont-Nesbitt, whose main interest was the gathering and exploitation of intelligence. With the atmosphere in Europe deteriorating rapidly, the Chiefs-of-Staff turned their attention to the work of MI(R) and Section D. In order to improve efficiency, the two departments agreed to a division of labour so that Section D concentrated on undercover action whilst MI (R) looked at tasks suited to troops in uniform. The boss of MI(R) was Joe Holland. On 23 March 1939 Grand moved from working on theory to devising protocol. He began working on the strategy of sabotage.[2] As the Germans rampaged through Europe, the Foreign Office and the Defence Staff agreed to Section D, MIR and JH uniting. This policy eventually led to the establishment of SOE in 1940.

During the first 10 months of the Second World War, German military achievements, in many cases driven by the use of amphetamine stimulants, were nothing but spectacular; so much so that the ordinary 'Tommy' was beginning to believe that the Germans were superhuman. With the help of the Soviet Union, Nazi Germany erased Poland from the European map; whilst Holland, Belgium, Norway, Luxemburg and France had been occupied. London observed the German successes with alarm and trepidation, as it expected Britain to be Hitler's next target. The French surrender not only exposed Britain to attack but opened the door to Italian aggression on Egypt and Suez. Churchill had two options at the time, either to capitulate and come to some kind of arrangement with Berlin, and certainly there were those in the British establishment who energetically recommended such a move, or to continue resisting. It did not come as a huge surprise when the bellicose British Prime Minister, chose to stand firm and fight. He is reported as having said, 'Let us bear ourselves that if the British commonwealth and empire lasts a thousand years men will say, this was their finest hour'.[3] In preparing to defend the British Isles to the last, the War Office sought to identify reason for the Nazi successes and to ascertain whether British forces could emulate German tactics. One of these, which was thought to have played a significant role, was Blitzkrieg. It was a tactic used for the first time in the First World War which saw shock troops rapidly breaking through Allied trenches and wreaking havoc behind the lines. Surprise and speed characterised the strategy and contrary to much literature on German operations in the Second World War, utilised horses as

---

2    TNA: HS4/163: Sabotage and Guerrilla Warfare in Poland.
3    Martin Gilbert, *Churchill, The Power of Words* (Philadelphia: Perseus Books Group 2012).

well as mechanised formations. A second factor identified by the British as playing a significant role in German military success was the use of air power to soften up the enemy, a function which during World War One was achieved by artillery bombardment. However, Churchill suspected that there was another good reason for German success, the presence of a 'fifth column'; individuals in a country who were sympathetic to the enemy and were prepared to disrupt a country's defences. He probably succumbed to a pervasive obsession with spies and espionage. The use of Fifth Columnists showed that one needn't have massive military forces in order to make a significant impact in conflict. This was demonstrated, for example, in the Second Anglo-Boer War of 1899-1901 whereby a well-equipped British army was, at first, successfully resisted by a citizen force of Dutch farmers ten times smaller using guerrilla tactics. In a similar way, Lawrence of Arabia, waged successful war against the Turks employing irregular fighting methods.

\* \* \*

Meanwhile, on the evening of 21 May, Frank sat in his parlour contemplating the latest news from the continent. Having heard that the Germans had reached Arras and Amiens he concluded that the Germans were indeed audacious and capable. Posing the question, 'What of ourselves? Words fail me', he traipsed out into the garden to check on his roses. Noting that the earth was as hard as 'bell metal,' he gave them a dose of Tonk's Rose Manure and decided that what was needed was some rain.

On 23 May it was officially announced that Abbeville was in enemy hands.[4] Drawing on secret investigations carried out by the British Defence Staff on prevailing conditions in Europe in order to decide whether guerrilla warfare could bring success against the Nazis, Churchill recommended that a clandestine organisation, the SOE, be set up which could spearhead secret resistance behind enemy lines. This plan required total secrecy and so the organisation was not even under the strict control of the War Office. By 16 July a broad mission statement had been agreed which only needed time to be given practical shape. The use of deception and trickery was nothing new in warfare. For example, the story of the Trojan Horse is frequently used to illustrate the effectiveness of trickery in war. The tale describes how during the Trojan War in the sixth century BC the Greeks deceived the Trojans following a long siege of Troy. Odysseus, the King of Ithaca, ordered the building of an enormous hollow wooded horse. Elite Greek fighters hid inside the horse while those remaining sailed away pretending to be bored with the war. The horse was presented to the Trojans as a peace offering and was taken inside the city walls. When the Trojans slept during the night, the Greek fighters crept out of the wooden horse and destroyed the city from within. However, it is not necessary to go back as far as the sixth century in order to illustrate how effective a 'fifth column' might be in battle. We need to look no further than to the minority groups which lived in Poland during September 1939. The Second Republic was a multicultural

---

4   Peter Minett (ed.), *Frank's Wartime Diary*, pp. 98-99.

country with various minority groups living on its territory. These groups, such as the Germans, Ukrainians, Lithuanians and Jews, proved to be unreliable citizens during the Second World War. For example, the sizeable German population that lived in the Western part of Poland collaborated with the Nazis when they crossed the border. Similarly, the Lithuanian minority, which lived in the north east of Poland, likewise worked with the Germans in order to destroy the Polish Army which they considered an army of occupation. The Ukrainian minority, living in the south east of the Republic, encouraged the progress of the Red Army during September 1939 as it invaded Poland from the east.

\* \* \*

On 22 July, 1940 the British Government established the Special Operations Executive (SOE), which was to support and encourage underground armies in Nazi occupied Europe. Churchill's 'Trojan Horse', was designed to satisfy four important objectives: to fulfil military purposes, to promote the view that the war was being energetically and effectively prosecuted, what Max Hastings called 'military theatre', to oblige Hitler to employ resources on the internal security of his empire and to encourage tension between the Nazis and their subjugated peoples. The minister appointed to take the political responsibility for the new organisation was the socialist Hugh Dalton, the Minister of Economic Warfare and member of the war cabinet. Sir Hugh Dalton (1887–1962) was born in Neath, Glamorgan, was educated at Eaton, King's College Cambridge and the London School of Economics. He saw service during the First World War and later was Labour MP. In 1940 he became Minster of Economic Affairs in Churchill's war-time coalition. After the war he became Labour Chancellor of the Exchequer, nationalised the Bank of England but resigned as a consequence of 'budget leakages' to the press in 1947. Dalton's task was to coordinate all subversive and sabotage operations on the continent and much to the annoyance of other government ministries, was informed by Churchill, to call on all other departments for additional staff. The British Prime Minister recommended that young men with plenty of character and initiative be signed up. Churchill said to Dalton, that he would probably require a large number of staff of officers and senior officials and was told he could recruit and second people from other Whitehall departments however much their superiors objected. Churchill promised to back Dalton on the matter. He also made it known that 'red tape' should be kept to a minimum in case it 'clogged up the system.' Although the work of SOE was highly secretive it was never allowed to be completely independent of what the government and the Chiefs-of-Staff were planning for the war. Dalton had to ensure that SOE operations fitted into the general military picture. When he said to Churchill that there was a danger that if the Germans were attacked from within, it could result in reprisals being taken out on the civilian population of occupied countries, the British Prime Minister was supposed to have replied that there was a war on and 'we cannot win without casualties.' Dalton described the role of SOE as a military force using different methods of combat to the other services including sabotage, labour agitation and terrorist acts even if these were illegal. However, not everyone considered such methods of warfare noble and acceptable. For example, the Foreign Secretary, Anthony Eden, considered the SOE 'a temporary amateur set up.' Similarly, the service chiefs deplored what they called, the 'amateur pirates of SOE' who worked according to their own methods invariably outside the law.[5] But Churchill, if nothing else, appreciated the organisation's moral value and continued supporting it throughout the war.

\* \* \*

On 15 January, Frank reported that there were things preventing him from making entries into his diary. He believed that there was nothing of any great importance to record except the continued British retreat through Malaya which he called a 'disgraceful necessity'. He resumed making entries by recording that the unemployment figures in Britain were at their lowest level for years. He also noted that Monday last saw a reduction in the availability of cooking fat and sugar rations had made a significant impact on meal preparations. However, Gerty managed to make American Hash, a noteworthy innovation in the Balmforth household. Eileen, Frank's daughter, had the weekend off from hospital where she worked as a nurse. She reported that she was very satisfied with her new appointment where she was meeting some 'very interesting people'. That evening Frank cycled home after work at the post office as normal. He cycled down the roads he knew well but with the 'abominable blackouts' and snow and ice on the ground he hit the curve and took a tumble. Trying to save himself, he sprained his left wrist. He limped home where he rested in his armchair. At nine-o-clock he turned on the radio to catch the news. The newsreader read out that the Japanese had claimed to be within 120 miles of Singapore. On 18 January the family enjoyed their first taste of bottled tomatoes. Frank was reading a new book he had purchased the day before called 'Erewhon' by Samuel Butler. He first came across the book when he read some extracts published in a weekly paper. He found it 'very diverting'. On Thursday 22 January, Frank and Gerty travelled to Kingston on a shopping trip. Whilst in the Market Hall they noticed horsemeat on sale for human consumption. No coupons were required to make a purchase and a long queue had formed. It cost one shilling per pound. Frank noted that furniture prices were depressingly high and indeed things generally were dear.[6]

\* \* \*

Initially SOE practical operations were under the control of Sir Frank Nelson who was later replaced by the merchant banker Sir Charles Hambro when Nelson fell ill. Hambro had been the head of the Scandinavian section and Director of the Bank of England. In 1943 Hambro was replaced by Colin Gubbins who became SOE's

---

5   TNA HS8/897/7: Correspondence with Winston Churchill-six-page report on the organisation and activities of SOE.
6   Peter Minett (ed.), *Frank's Wartime Diary*, pp. 318-322.

Director of Operations. Gubbins was born in Tokyo in 1897 (his father worked for the British Legation) and aged thirteen won a scholarship to Cheltenham College, the feeder school for the Woolwich Military Academy. During his early schooling, Gubbins became fascinated with the military and early on in his school career decided that he wanted to become a soldier. Having endured his time at Cheltenham, as he was to put it later, he enrolled at Woolwich. His ultimate objective was to enlist in the Royal Horse Artillery as by then he was a keen and competent horseman. His plans, however, were thwarted by the onset of the First World War. Gubbins' military experience during the Great War, comprised service on the Western Front, in Russia, Ireland and India. Each of these theatres of conflict contributed something different and unique to his understanding of modern warfare. For example, he learned on the western front that the human spirit had the power to withstand almost any assault; whilst in Russia, he came to understand how best to lead a multicultural group of men. It was also the case, that at this time he was introduced to the methods of intelligence and spying by his then Commander in Chief, General Edmund Ironside.[7] Whilst serving in Ireland, during the 'troubles', Gubbins saw that the character of the Republican Volunteers was not too dissimilar to that of the various resistance groups that had emerged in Nazi occupied Europe. It was in Ireland where he came face to face with guerrilla tactics which he would later employ whilst serving with the SOE. During his time in India, Gubbins came to appreciate how to cope with passive resistance and civil disobedience and learnt how difficult it was to run a state without some level of cooperation from the people. Drawing on the conflict with the Bolsheviks in Archangel and dealing with civil unrest and the tactics of Gandhi, gave Gubbins confidence to write three handbooks on irregular warfare: The Art of Guerrilla Warfare, A Partisan's Leaders Handbook and How to use High Explosives. The books were widely translated into various languages including Polish. They were published on pocket sized edible paper and could be consumed in less than two minutes on a mission.[8]

\* \* \*

Gubbins saw the SOE as the '4th Service' charged with hindering the enemy's actions by means of sudden attacks, characterised by surprise and speed. This, he argued, could be done in three stages: penetration of enemy occupied territory, establishment of signals communication and the building of 'cells' of resistance fighters. He described individuals who involved themselves in irregular warfare as, 'rule breakers', 'mavericks' and 'eccentrics', but this was not considered as a criticisms but assets. SOE was based at 64 Baker Street, London and had the cover name 'Inter-Service Research Bureau' and hence the nickname 'The Baker Street irregulars.' At its inception it comprised of three departments known as SO1, SO2 and SO3. SO1 was concerned with propaganda, SO2 with subversion and SO3 was responsible for planning. SO3

---

7   TNA HS8/897/7: Appointed Chief of the Imperial General Staff, 3 September 1939.
8   Giles, *Churchill's Ungentlemanly Warfare*, p. 19.

was soon absorbed by SO2 which became the mainstay of the whole organisation. SOE operations depended on the willingness of ordinary people in occupied countries to risk their lives for the allied cause. It was inevitable that the secret organisation would have to make contact with underground resistance groups throughout occupied Europe, if it was to provide them with the means for fighting. This would include furnishing them with a list of vital targets, a supply of sabotage materials as well as well-trained personnel. In order to keep these arrangements secret, the War Office approved planning of operations without making any reference to the House of Commons. SOE started with twelve telephone lines at its central headquarters which grew to 200 distributed over three exchanges – ABBey, AMBassador, and WELbeck. A postal address was not included with these exchanges. It was clear that SOE's mandate would inevitably require it to work closely with a number of exiled foreign governments including the Polish and by extrapolation, the secret Polish Home Army. However, Britain's interest in using the Poles for subversive activity in case of war with Germany predates the establishment of SOE.[9]

9   See Chapter 1.

# 8

# SOE Polish Section

*Friends and I mean real friends ... reserve nothing: The property of one belongs to the other.*

Euripides, *Andromache*, 376

On 25 July Frank's milkman delivered four eggs each costing two and three quarter pence. Girty cycled to Kingston upon Thames and brought back, among other things, six pounds of red plums at two and a half pence per pound. By bedtime these had been made into nine pounds of plum jam.[1] Meanwhile, Bickham Sweet-Escott (later replaced by Captain ([subsequently Colonel] Harold. B. Perkins[2]) had become the head of SOE's Polish Section and was quite clear about his task; namely, to assist the Poles in their various subversive activities with the conviction that a successful military and civil revolt executed at the appropriate time would have a significant impact on the outcome of the Second Republic's predicament. The Polish Section described its strategic objectives as follows: to equip the secret fighters in Poland with the resources required for the day-to-day sabotage of German communication and installations on the Eastern front, to assist the Poles in making their plans for a general uprising and to assist the Poles in their planning for an intensified sabotage campaign accompanied by maximum increase in guerrilla activity. This was to be planned and timed to take place in support of 'Overlord', the invasion of France by the Western allies in June 1944. In drawing up the details of its task, the SOE Polish Section referred to what had been learnt from operations in Belgium and France. Liaison between the Polish Section of SOE and the Sixth Bureau (Homeland Liaison of the Polish General Staff) ensured that British effort was coordinated with Polish policy regarding resistance, although the Section was not permitted to send any orders directly to the secret Home Army. The British resigned themselves to the fact that the Polish Underground was going to be independent of its direct control

---

1    Peter Minett (ed.), *Frank's Wartime Diary*, p.134.
2    Perkins had an outgoing personality. He served Gubbins loyally throughout the war.

unlike the clandestine movements in most other German occupied countries. In this situation the Polish Section was no more than a transportation agency procuring and delivering military supplies and trained personnel destined for Poland, as specified by the Sixth Bureau on behalf of the Polish General Staff. It also transferred political couriers on behalf of the Polish Ministry of the Interior. Perkins, who took over from Sweet-Escott, spoke good Polish, having spent some time running a textile firm in pre-war Poland, whilst apparently working secretly for MI6. Originally, he made contact with the Sixth Bureau to offer the Poles support. He was put in touch with Colonel Protasiewicz, but his main contact was Major Jazwiński, who was Head of Department Syrena (Mermaid), also known as Department 'S'. This department was responsible for the transfer of material and people to the Second Republic and was run by Captain Klauber, a naturalised Hungarian. In 1943, Klauber was posted to Force 139 at the Mediterranean base. When Perkins was promoted to lead the East European Section in November 1943, he was replaced by Major Pickles. The Polish Section's Intelligence Officers were Major Truszkowski and Captain Massey who were assisted by Ensign P. Harrison of FANY.[3] Truszkowski was of Polish decent and was fluent in Polish. Massey was equally fluent in the language, having spent his early schooling in Warsaw. In 1941 Major Jazwiński recruited Captain Zygmunt Oranowski to work for Department 'S'. His first responsibility was to administer records concerning the procurment of materials such as photographic cameras, wrist watches, radio transmitters and monies for transfer to Poland by couriers on SOE sponsored flights. His activities for the department were somewhat chaotic and not always legal.[4] The young officer became popular with the officers from SOE Polish Section who he worked with even to the extent that he organising riotous parties and get togethers for them. Following enquiries about the officer's approach to his work Colonel Protasiewicz despatched Oranowski to Brindis, where his job was to make final preparations for the transfer of materials to the Home Army in Poland. His work here was reported to be very professional; however, further enquiries of his accounts by Colonel Tysowski allegedly uncovered some irregularities in his record keeping and the young officer was recalled to Britain.[5] On Oranowski's return, General Kopański ordered his arrest and incarceration in a Polish prison in Scotland. However, thanks to his friends in the SOE Polish Section, he was able to escape and was given sanctuary by the British until the war ended. In 1946 the British parachuted Oranowski to the British Sector in Germany, from where he was repatriated back to Poland.

Captain Józef Jankowski worked for Department 'S' from 1942 as a clerk following successful training by the Sixth Bureau in Edinburgh. In the summer of 1944 he was enlisted into the Polish Army in Scotland. He remained in England after the

3   First Aid Nursery Yeomanry.
4   Marian Utnik, Oddzial Lacznikowy Komendanta Glownego AK przy Naczelnym Wodzu na Emigracji (VI Oddzial Sztabu Naczelnego Wodza) in *Wojskowy Przeglad Historyczany* 4 (98) Warszawa, Wojskowowy Instytut Historyczny pp. 151-174
5   Utnik, Oddzial Lacznikowy Komendanta Glownego AK przy Naczelnym Wodzu na Emigracji (VI Oddzial Sztabu Naczelnego Wodza) in *Wojskowy Przeglad Historyczany* 4 (98) Warszawa, Wojskowowy Instytut Historyczny pp 151- 174.

war. Lieutenant Zygmunt Kiernowski volunteered to join the Sixth Bureau in 1943. After retraining by the Sixth Bureau, he was deployed to the section, where he was responsible for the logging of flights to Poland. After the war he emigrated to North America. [6]

\* \* \*

The SOE Polish Section, officially based in Room 38 Whitehall, was actually located at 64 Baker Street. Each department was identified by the initials of its commanding officer, so the Polish Section was known as MPP after Lieutenant Colonel H.P. Perkins. There were four departments in the section: Operations (MPC), Training (MPG) under Captains Gregor, Movement and Supplies (MPN) and Intelligence (MPX1). The third level of the Polish Section was made up of 'Subsections'. This third tier was manned by FANY personnel, who were not part of the regular forces, although they were uniformed. Their role was to support military authorities with special duties, such as taking care of couriers. All officers recruited for the Polish Section had good previous relations with Poland and the Poles. Personnel in 1943 were listed as: Lieutenant Colonel H.P. Perkins, Major R. Truszkowski, Captain L.H. Massey, Captain G.L. Klauber, Captain A. Morgan, Captain C.T. Gregor, Ensign J.R. Aldis, J.A.D. Timms and Captain H.R. Adams. SOE established a network of 10 special training schools (STS) in Britain, which the Poles made use of. Each recruit underwent a three-part training programme, which began with physical training in Scotland, progressing to specialist courses such as forgery, and ending at a 'finishing school'. They then entered a holding camp, usually located in a requisitioned country mansion such as Audley End. 282 Polish individuals had successfully completed the course on marksmanship with 630 having specialised in underground warfare, 325 had learned about sabotage whilst 75 completed a course on liaison. 50 recruits specialised in intelligence and another 64 in propaganda. 161 recruits completed courses on armaments and anti-tank weapons, whilst 529 individuals completed their studies in parachute jumping. The Polish Section occupied seven special training schools: STS 18 Frogmore, Herts, STS 19 Gardener's End, Stevenage, Herts, STS 20a and STS 20b at Pollard's Park, Chalfont St Giles, STS 43, Audley End House, Audley End, Essex, STS 46, Chicheley Hall, Bucks, STS 14, Briggens, Essex and STS 63, Warnham Court, Sussex. The quality of the relationship between the Polish Section and the Sixth Bureau fluctuated throughout the war and was invariably dependent on the personality of the officers in charge at the time. Smoleński was well liked and respected and so the relationship during his tenure was close and warm. Lieutenant Colonel Rudnicki, was allegedly not so popular since being inconsistent in his dealings with the Polish Section, consequently relations between him and the British were problematic. In Spring 1942, Colonel Protasiewicz was put in-charge of

---

6   Utnik, Oddzial Lacznikowy Komendanta Glownego AK przy Naczelnym Wodzu na Emigracji (VI Oddzial Sztabu Naczelnego Wodza) in *Wojskowy Przeglad Historyczany* 4 (98) Warszawa, Wojskowowy Instytut Historyczny pp. 151- 174.

the bureau and was considered to be very professional and relations with the Polish Section improved. In July 1944, Lieutenant Colonel Utnik took over and relations remained cordial but by this time Poland's importance as an ally had waned.

\* \* \*

On 16 June, Frank went to bed deep in thought. He had just finished listening to the first two movements of Beethoven's Symphony No. 4 on the radio. He noted that the Adagio strangely suited his mood and the mood prevalent in the country. He noted in his diary that the coming week would be exceedingly critical and indeed it was. The following day he had learned from the news on the wireless that France had given up the fight. Later that evening he read in the Evening News newspaper, 'In this black hour there must be no illusion, no dreaming of vain dreams. With open eyes and steadfast hearts we must face the fact that the Germans have won the most stupendous military victory in history, and that the battered French Army is out of the battle.'[7] The fall of France and Italy's entry into the war in conjunction with Germany's penetration of Hungary and Romania, resulted in the blocking of overland routes for couriers. But the new situation on the continent, particularly after the fall of France, had rendered such methods extremely dangerous and inefficient and so a new communication system was sought. General Smoleński, argued robustly that the only way of surmounting these difficulties was to establish direct contact with the occupied country via radio transmissions and an air bridge between Britain and Poland. Both the Chief of the British Secret Intelligence Service, Steward Menzies, and Hugh Dalton agreed with his assessment adding that such arrangements would allow Polish resistance to continue. Hugh Dalton, the minister for SOE, suggested that radio equipment be provided for the Sixth Bureau in Britain and the Home Army in Poland.[8] He also suggested that a unit of the Polish Airforce, which was operating under contract with the RAF, be used to create an airbridge.[9] However, he soon realised that such initiatives would require a large allocation of men and machines and this would take time to arrange. Consequently, he recommended that RAF pilots should carryout missions until the Poles were ready to take over. Major General Hasting 'Pug' Ismay, cabled Dalton on 22 January, 1941, informing him that he was sure that there would be no objection from the COS to his suggestion, provided the Air Ministry was able to provide the necessary aircraft. Dalton was particularly pleased that finally something concrete was going to happen, proving to the Polish people that they had not been forgotten. The dependence on Britain for equipment and war materials put a great strain on Polish authorities, as they had to plan missions without the full knowledge of what war material was actually available

---

7   Peter Minett (ed.), *Frank's Wartime Diary*, p. 113.
8   Eventually, in occupied Poland, 57 radio transmitters operated, 25 in Warsaw, 10 Home Army receivers. Up to June 1944, 800 W/T stations dropped into Poland. Out of the 316 agents dropped 50 were radio operators.
9   TNA HS4/148: Liaison with Poland by means of air.

or could be procured. Under the agreement between Britain and Poland, signed 5 August, 1940 [10], all items were charged against a loan. But even now the situation was not so straight forward for the British had limited access to equipment and just presenting a 'shopping list' to SOE Polish Section did not guarantee delivery. The situation eased somewhat when the Lend-Lease Act came into force which saw the United States directing war material to Europe.

\* \* \*

According to General Sikorski, the Polish Prime Minister, the existance of the Home Army was very important for Polish morale and because of its knowledge of local terrain would be indispensable when the time came for the Western Allies to move onto the continent and to free Poland. At this time Sikorski believed, incorrectly as it happened, that the Second Republic of Poland would be liberated by British and American forces entering Polish territory from the west. This belief made him conclude that clandestine flights to Poland should be started immediately in order to facilitate the action and coordinate resistance with 'Overlord'. In the meantime, SOE Polish Section made an assessment of the Home Army and its operational methods. In its report, it had concluded that it would be the Soviet Army that was more likely to liberate Poland from German occupation and noted that the majority of the Forces available to the Allies for the prosecution of the Polish war were inside Poland. It concluded that when the Polish High Command evacuated to Romania in 1939 it left behind a nucleus of a well organised secret Home Army capable of operating on a national scale. The sophistication of the organisation was such that the Army considered itself to be an official sovereign formation of the Second Republic, with rights under the Geneva Convention. In 1944 and the invasion of Normandy, the Western allies were minded to place French underground fighters in such a protected category. However, the British were reluctant to do this in the case of the Home Army, lest it offended the Soviets. They preferred to leave it to Mikołajczyk to negotiate during his visit to Moscow.[11] The official status of the Home Army was later confirmed by the Allies on the 1 August, 1944. SOE also noted that the Poles were past masters at conspiratorial warfare on account of their recent troubled history. The secret army in occupied Poland had already rendered itself invaluable to the Allies by continued sabotage attacks on German communications and by tying down a sizeable number of German divisions in the East. The conclusion reached in the report was that the Home Army was the premier resistance organisation in Poland and that it would be wholly appropriate to continue supporting it with war equipment above all other resistance groups in the country. It was also noted that the Home Army continued to be loyal to the exiled Polish Government of the Second Republic in London. According to SOE assessments, the Home Army was an adaptation of a typical military organisation with a 'normal' command structure modified for conspiratorial conditions. The basic operational unit was the Platoon, which consisted

---

10   Garliński, *Poland, SOE and the Allies*, p. 95.
11   TNA HS4/144.

of groups or 'Cells' of five men and women. There were four categories of platoon; Full Conspiratorial Platoons, Cadre Conspiratorial Platoons, Sabotage Platoons and Diversionary Platoons. Platoons were divided into units; those for use in the event of a general rising and those which would be called upon prior to a general rising. Sabotage platoons were permanently embodied and were, therefore, available for action all year round and at any time of the day. The Diversionary Platoons were expected to take control and show social leadership. All platoons were officered by trained Polish special forces despatched from Britain by SOE Polish Section and the Sixth Bureau. The report estimated that there would be approximately 350 reception committees distributed throughout Poland and ready to receive personnel and equipment flown from Britain. The Home Army did not have any vehicular transport at its disposal and, as a result, was immobile. In an attempt to compensate for any disadvantage, the strength of any local platoon in a particular district was adjusted in such a way as to match the size and importance of its strategic and tactical value. The territory of the country was divided into provinces which consisted of regions and sub-regions, based on their strategic importance. Areas and sub-areas were divided into districts and sub-districts, each with its own Head Quarters. It was estimated that the strength of the Home Army was 250,000 officers, men and women. Out of these only 50,000 were lightly armed. In any area two thirds of the total weapons were under the control of GHQ in Warsaw and could only be used with its authority. Partisan units, existing under guerrilla conditions in rural regions, were equipped with weapons that had been kept in hiding since 1939. It was envisaged that these weapons would be supplemented with equipment dropped by the British. The Home Army, according to SOE's assessment, possessed only such weapons that could be stored conspiratorially, which meant that the heaviest weapons in its possession were machine guns and mortars (only those that could be carried). It did not possess mobile artillery and therefore could not be expected to engage in mobile warfare against a modern army equipped with tanks and aircraft. The main items of armament were listed as being anti-tank rifles, Bren guns, captured German automatic weapons, Thompson sub-machine guns, pistols, grenades and explosives. Such weaponry would only allow the Home Army to carryout sabotage activities and no other wider battles. If these were to be attempted, heavier armaments would have had to be made available. In SOE's assessment it was also noted that the Home Army's intelligence department was responsible for the gathering and collating of such intelligence as was required by the army and was more often than not despatched to Britain.[12] SIS considered this material to be of excellent quality and therefore it was highly valued. External operational communications were carried out using clandestine radio channels between Polish GHQ in London and Warsaw. Messages of an important nature, such as those dealing with operational matters, were initially transmitted to GHQ Warsaw and then disseminated to the leaders of districts, where operations were put into practice. The time lag between despatch from London and receipt in the operation area was noted to be no more than 48 hours. Internal communications of a non-operational character were passed on using couriers. Despite such methods taking much longer

---

12 TNA HS4/147: Polish Secret Army, Polish planning for the reoccupation of Poland.

to reach their destination, sometimes days or even weeks, their use was continued, as they were considered to be relatively secure and reliable. In its report SOE also considered possible German penetration of the Home Army. It concluded that there was no doubt that the German counter-espionage services had made local penetrations but considered them to be of little significance owing to the conspiratorial 'cell system'. Interrogation of German POWs in the Middle East confirmed that there was little or no penetration of the secret Home Army. SOE concluded, therefore, that the Home Army could be relied upon to carryout sabotage missions on behalf of the exiled Polish Government in London.[13] In the closing remarks of the assessment, SOE wrote that the Poles considered the Home Army to be an integral part of their sovereign forces and as such under the command of the Polish Commander in Chief in London. If action by the Home Army was required the line of command ran as follows: Polish Chief of Staff in London, the Sixth Bureau, SOE Polish Section, Officer in Charge (GOC) in Poland, who would pass on the message to those lower down in the command structure of the conspiracy. However, it was noted that the GOC Warsaw enjoyed a certain individual freedom to make operational decisions with little reference being made to the Sixth Bureau. This was allowed in view of Britain appreciating the tactical difficulties and sometimes strategic conditions that existed in Poland. SOE Polish Section would also receive orders from the War Office, although these were never operational.

\* \* \*

On 12 September 1939, the Anglo-French High Command decided to disengage from fighting the German Forces in France and Belgium and retreat to Dunkirk. This decision left the Polish Forces under French command isolated and disorientated. Following Polish appeals to Churchill it was agreed to transfer as many Polish soldiers as possible to Britain and so approximately 20,000 Polish servicemen, who had been serving under French command, joined the Dunkirk evacuation. Others escaped through Spain, Switzerland and Gibraltar finally reaching the British Isles a few months later. This event marked the beginning of Great Britain assuming special responsibility for the fate of the Poles in the war. In June 1940, Churchill reassured General Sikorski, that England would keep faith with Poland, whilst at the same time Sikorski reassured Churchill that the Poles would continue fighting on the condition that his government was given the full rights and privileges of a sovereign government in exile. This was agreed as was Sikorski's request that he retain full control over secret Polish ciphers used in communications with Poland. In order to coordinate the secret activities of Britain and Poland, both sides cultivated an understanding by reorganising and coordinating their intelligence services. The British established a new department called Number 4 Military Mission commanded by Charles Bridges, and the Poles, the Sixth Bureau led by Józef Smoleński, the former Chief of Polish Intelligence. The SOE Polish Section started with fourteen officers and three typists. On 29 June, 1940 senior officers of Polish Intelligence met with Colonel Holland and

---

13   TNA HS4/163: Sabotage and Guerrilla Warfare in Poland.

Major Wilkinson of MIR at the war office. Colonel Gano of the Second Bureau of the Polish Intelligence Service, informed the meeting that Polish intelligence activities fell under two headings: 'Information Services', which he himself was in charge of and 'Subversion', which was under the direction of Colonel Smoleński. The meeting was informed that it was General Sikorski's wish that both of these departments, would be collectively known as the Sixth Bureau, and would work as closely as possible with their British counterparts. It was decided that Colonel Gano would report to MI6, while Captain H.B. Perkins of MIR would maintain close liaison with Polish GHQ. On 22 July, the war cabinet approved the final character of SOE Polish Section.

\* \* \*

Dalton had great affinity for the Poles, even making an effort to speak a little Polish. In December 1940 he spent Christmas with Polish troops in Scotland and later informed Churchill how much he was moved by the experience. He was thought to be sound on the 'Polish Question', often saying what the Poles wanted to hear, namely Polish freedom and the preservation of the Second Republic. Unfortunately for Dalton, the Foreign Office was not so secure on the 'Polish Question', as for most of the war it had worked for rapprochement with the Soviet Union and appeared to be willing to sacrifice the territorial rights of a junior ally to achieve this. For example, Foreign Secretary Lord Halifax, champion of appeasement, pointed out that the Soviet advance into Poland in 1939 merely took back the territory which the British had earmarked for Russia in 1919. His apparent 'Polanophobia' was in clear contrast to SOE's enthusiastic support for the Polish cause. Perkins was chosen by Dalton to take over from Sweet-Escott as head of the SOE Polish Section which he did in November 1940. No time was lost when in December, Sikorski invited Perkins to attend a meeting with both Professor Kot and General Sosnkowski, in order to start a liaison between the men. The first Polish request was for an advance of money to be used by the Home Army in Poland. Kot suggested 20,000,000 RM[14] and 100,000 US Dollars. This was agreed to and was provided in order to maintain morale in Poland and to demonstrate Britain's gratitude to the Polish nation for its continued heroic resistance against the Nazi threat. Perkins, however, missed one crucial point regarding the Home Army, which was that lightly armed fighters were no match for a genocidal enemy equipped with tanks and aircraft. The second difficulty which surfaced during the early meetings were the demands SOE would have to place on the RAF, given that it did not have aircraft of its own. The Air Ministry would later resent such demands, as there was a shortage of aeroplanes with a myriad of military objectives to satisfy.[15]

\* \* \*

14   Reich Marks.
15   Lynne Olson, and Stanley Cloud, *For your Freedom and Ours* (London: William Heineman, 2003), p. 282.

A third significant request made by the Poles was for the provision of training programmes for Polish special forces; who could then parachute into the occupied Republic in support of the Home Army. The request was made on the initiative of Captain J. Górski and Captain M. Kalankiewicz in conjunction with Department Three of the Sixth Bureau, which was responsible for the transfer of materials and men to Poland. SOE was to take a leading role in this training as well as the transfer of men and material but not for recruitment. All potential recruits came from the exiled Polish Forces in the west. They continued to be members of these forces until they landed safely in Poland, when they became members of the Home Army. Technically, therefore, it would be wrong to call them 'SOE agents', for they were 'simply' Polish Special Forces in the service of the Second Republic. Although the word 'SOE agent' appears in many publications, including this one, strictly speaking this is incorrect. Once in Poland the men would join the secret war by taking up various roles in the Home Army's organisational structure such as sub-area organisers, wireless/telephony (w/t) operators, trainers and so on. The cost for the material and transport was met by a British government loan. When the American Lend-Lease Act came into force the supplies were placed under the Act. The type and nature of equipment was dependent on what the Polish Chiefs of Staff in London had identified as being a priority. This was communicated via the Sixth Bureau to the Polish Section at SOE which undertook procurement and delivery. However, there were difficulties with this process, one being the lack of available equipment and another being the shortage of aircraft. During this period Britain had not yet gone over to full scale war production, which was desperately required, so despite Polish requests being sent to the British there was no guarantee that supplies would be forthcoming. The goodwill of the SOE, which it had to be said, was greatly appreciated by the Poles, was not enough to prosecute extensive sabotage by the Home Army. Under these circumstances the Polish authorities seemed to have no other option but to attempt to obtain urgent supplies from unofficial sources such as the open market. Unfortunately, the quality of unofficial supplies could not be guaranteed and this persuaded Sikorski to visit Washington to seek help from the Americans. America's late entry into the war, December 1941, meant that war materials were not available in significant amounts until America herself had gone over to a war footing. This meant that America's help only became significant during the years following 1942. Sikorski asked for various supplies, which also included office stationery such as duplicators and printers. At first the supply was slow in coming on account of transport difficulties which invariably included a long and dangerous sea crossing across the Atlantic. Urgent equipment was sometimes delivered by air. Once in Britain, the material was stored by SOE Polish Section until it was time to despatch it to Poland. When the transfer was earmarked for Poland it was repackaged and placed in special metal containers and then air lifted by the RAF.

* * *

In 1943 the British protested to the Poles for having made a direct approach to the Americans, because Poland, according to London, was the responsibility of Britain.

London, therefore, encouraged Washington to have no truck with the Poles. To resolve the differences, SOE proposed to classify the equipment earmarked for the Poles into three categories: equipment not available in Britain but which could be procured from America, war material available in Britain which could be supplied by SOE and thirdly items which the Poles could purchase on the open market. This procedure appeared to satisfy the War Office and the system was put into practice. The Polish Section of the SOE was also required to work closely with the Poles regarding the training and despatch of their operatives to the occupied country. The Poles were given the more freedom in recruiting and training their 'agents' than any other ally before handing them over to the RAF for transfer to Poland.

# 9

# The 'Silent and Invisible' (Cichociemni) Polish Special Forces

*I do my duty: other things trouble me not; for they are either things without life, or things without reason, or things that have rambled and know not the way.*
                                        Marcus Aurelius, *Meditations*, VI, 22

The sobriquet 'Silent and Invisible' (Cichociemni) was the vernacular for Polish Special Forces, which had completed their training in guerrilla warfare in Britain with the SOE and were ready to be parachuted into occupied Poland by the RAF.[1] The motto 'Silent and Invisible' was more of a nickname which described the organisation's modus operandi; silent to approach a target and invisible between operations. The use of the phrase became so popular amongst the recruits during parachute training sessions in 1941, that it became a semi-official name for them particularly after the war. In occupied Poland the term Silent and Invisible was not used, although terms such as 'Birds in the Sky' or 'Drops' were. The plan to establish special forces and utilise them in Poland was originally laid down in December 1939 in Paris, where Polish authorities of the Second Republic had regrouped after the fall of the Polish homeland. Captain Jan Górski, contacted Sikorski, the Commander in Chief, with the suggestion that there should be some link between the exiled authorities and the occupied country. His suggestion was, that in addition to radio communication an air bridge should be established. Captain Maciej Kalenkiewicz worked with Górski and prepared a plan to demonstrate to the Polish High Command how this could be done. Meanwhile Gorski had gathered 16 Officers who were sympathetic to the idea and who would be prepared to be dropped behind the lines. Both

---

1   Order Number: SNWL.dz 780/tjn/v/41.

Górski and Kalenkiewicz added their own names to the list. Eventually, in February 1941, General Sikorski ordered General J. Zając, Air Marshal of the Polish Airforce in exile, to begin planning air corridors to the main cities in Poland namely; Lwów, Warsaw, Kraków and if possible, Poznań. Communication was established between the General Head Quarters in Paris (later in London) and the underground Union of Armed Struggle[2]. General Michał Karaszewicz-Tokarzewski was the commander of clandestine fighting units in the Soviet occupied region of Poland, while Colonel Stefan Rowecki was commander of units in the German occupied region. When Rowecki heard of the new developments being planned he contacted Polish Headquarters in Paris to ask for cash for the underground movement. GHQ approved the request and also approached the French for aircraft. However, commitments in Norway, Denmark and the Benelux countries, meant the request could not be fulfilled. On 22 June, 1940, France capitulated and the Poles decamped to Britain. They carried on with the air corridor plan, but this time using RAF planes flying from Britain. A new department was set up to oversee the initiative and Colonel Józef Smoleński was put in charge. The new set up continued to operate as the Sixth Bureau and was the link between the SOE Polish Section and the Home Army in Poland. Its responsibility was to identify potential recruits, oversee their training and maintain contact with the British authorities on behalf of the Polish High Command. It also had to work with a new organisation called the Parachute Training Unit.

\* \* \*

On 20 June, 1941 General Sikorski signed an order for an emblem to be designed for the 'Silent and Invisible'. The final design was drawn up by Marian Walentyn, an illustrator from pre-war Poland. His design comprised an eagle (paying homage to the White Eagle on the Polish Coat of Arms) with its talons exposed whilst swooping down to make a kill. The motto of the Silent and Invisible was 'Win Back Freedom or Die' and before deployment recruits had to swear they would maintain complete secrecy on how they had been transferred to Poland and what their mission was. They also promised never to divulge any secrets concerning the Polish Home Army, get drunk, or take part in any political activity. They were also forbidden to make contact with family members whilst serving in the homeland. Finally, all recruits promised to carry out their orders without hesitation. The men (and women) were volunteers from the Polish sovereign army exiled in the West. Although they were trained to operate as individuals but fought embedded in units of the secret Home Army in Poland. If captured they were never treated as prisoners of war by the Germans and therefore were executed immediately. They did not have any protection under the Geneva Convention until much later in the war, when the Allies gave them official recognition as members of the sovereign army of the Second Republic. Their training concentrated on intelligence gathering, communication, subversion and sabotage. All aspects of Cichociemni activity was treated in the strictest of confidence. Their aim

---

2   Precursor to the Home Army.

was to join the ranks of the Home Army and use their specialist knowledge and skills to lead groups of volunteer fighters in covert acts of sabotage, intelligence gathering and demolition.[3]

\* \* \*

The process of recruitment began with order number SNWL.dz.780/tjn/v/41 being issued, which saw Officers of the Sixth Bureau combing Polish units stationed in Scotland and the Middle East for suitable candidates.[4] Potential recruits would receive an oral invitation to come and have a 'chat' with a recruiting officer, where the possibility of returning to occupied Poland to prosecute irregular warfare on special missions was discussed. Following the casual conversation, individuals who had shown an interest were invited to attend a more formal interview, where they were given a short time to consider whether the opportunity of serving in occupied Poland on special missions was something that would appeal. If the decision was positive the individual signed a declaration which amounting to a contract. There then followed a detailed examination of the person's background by counterintelligence officers in order to assess suitability of the candidate on a psychological level and on physical health. Recruits volunteered for a number of unique reasons. For example, some believed that a life in clandestine work was a far more exciting proposition, rather than hanging around as a regular soldier waiting for the order to 'go'. Others thought that fighting in the homeland was a better life than fighting in some unknown alien foreign territory far from home. Few were no more than thrill seekers, but all were committed patriots. According to the British, the best candidates for insurgent work were individuals who were not impulsive but reflective and calm. The Head Quarters of the Polish underground army made it known that they would prefer men with strong leadership qualities. This probably explains why those who were selected for training were predominately from the officer class; well informed individuals educated to university level. However, it must also be remembered that there was a predominance of officers in the cohort of Polish personnel who had made it to the West and therefore it was more likely than not that an officer would be recruited. The Poles preferred individuals who were young, physically fit, enterprising, intelligent with a high sense of independence, brave and even brutal. Those with specialist knowledge of sabotage, intelligence and communications were of particular interest and so were sought out vigorously. Female recruits invariably came from the leisured classes or the old Polish aristocracy. Out of 2,413 candidates that had shown an interest, 579 were chosen for training and had to swear allegiance to the Home Army. The youngest recruit was 17 years of age, whilst the oldest was

---

3   TNA HS4/163: Sabotage and Guerrilla Warfare in Poland.
4   The Polish Second Corps commanded by General Anders, was formed from Polish troops who had fought in Tobruk, El Alamein and the army which had been taken out of the Soviet Union in an armistice. The corps fought up the Italian peninsula as part of the Eighth Army and concluded its operation in north Italy.

54. Of these 316 recruits and 28 couriers were actually airlifted to Poland and their courage in agreeing to fly, merits special respect.

\* \* \*

The individuals who passed the initial assessments and general training progressed on to specialist training programmes, beginning at the Special Training Section (STS) at Briggens, Essex which began operating in January 1941. Both male and female recruits had to attend compulsory classes in marksmanship, exploiting topography followed by learning how to handle explosives such as mines. Training in the use of firearms in various situations, such as shooting from the hip whilst running or firing whilst lying flat on the ground was obligatory. Pistols or light machine guns of German origin were used in this training as these were the types of fire arms most likely to be encounter in occupied Poland. Recruits were expected to know how to dismantle, reassemble, load and fire weapons instinctively and in darkness when necessary. The Poles used the bent knee position and a two-handed grip with straight arms when firing a pistol at shoulder hight. All SOE personnel were trained to fire two shots in quick succession, which had to be decisive. Also included, was training in unarmed combat using martial arts such as karate and jiu-jitsu. Tradecraft was also included, which involved learning how to drop in a pre-arranged password in a bar, how to spot if one was being followed and how to move onto a moving tram in order to shed a follower. During training Polish recruits were accompanied by Polish officer mentors who monitored an individual's progress. Students were encouraged to share their worries and even express doubt about continuing with training, so that no one felt stigmatised about falling out. Every detail was considered, with recruits even learning about what the German police service was like and how it operated in Poland. Scotland Yard and MI5, as well as SOE, gave advice on how to deal with snap police raids and how not to draw attention to oneself by running away from any road blocks or identity checks. An ingenious training session was designed to find if an agent would be tempted to give away secrets in a 'honey trap'. During this training an attractive woman would be introduced to an unbeknown agent and put at ease with a drink and restful atmosphere. The men with 'loose tongues' were either reprimanded or thrown out of training.

\* \* \*

Obviously, parachute training was compulsory as was training in specialist areas such as wireless operation, forgery and micro-photography. Training courses began with the very serious topic of security. This was a core subject and meant that no person was allowed to leave his/her training school during any course unless they were accompanied or had special permission to do so. Relaxation and recreational walks in the grounds of the training schools were at the discretion of the on-duty security officer. Persons undergoing training could not at any time disclose to anyone that that had attended a course and it was also forbidden to acknowledge anyone from a course, except on official business. During training, recruits were required to hand in their own standard issue firearms, cameras and personal notebooks until the training programme had been completed. Any monies above five pounds plus any other valuables had to be handed in for safe keeping until departure from the training school.[5] Any outgoing mail had to be presented initially for censoring in an open envelope. No recruit was to mention that his/her letter had been censored and all letters were posted in London. Incoming mail, including telegrams, was censored before being delivered to the addressee. Finally, as far as telephone calls were concerned only the telephones at the training centre could be used.

* * *

Following an introductory session on security, specialist training began in earnest beginning with the reading of SOE's mission statement, which was summarised as the 'art of subversion'. Described by tutors as one of the most potent weapons at the allies disposal and as the 'fourth arm' of the services, SOE were presented as being threefold: to damage the enemy's resources of man-power, to undermine the morale of the enemy and to raise the morale of the population in the occupied country. The subsequent training sessions concentrated on how this was to be achieved. For example, damage to German materials and their means of production was achieved through sabotage. This action had three levels of action: 'passive resistance', consisting of small acts which posed minimal risk to the agent, 'industrial sabotage' which carried some risk to the agent but not excessively and 'isolated acts of definite destruction', such as blowing up a bridge. Industrial sabotage included preventing workers going to factories and damaging production lines. Recruits were also informed about which type of act of destruction should be used in what context, for example, during a Nazi military tattoo. Subsequent sessions concentrated on how to undermine the morale of the occupying enemy troops. Trainers described that one way of doing this was to work on the grievances which German soldiers harboured. This approach fanned disaffection and any anxiety that they felt about their families back home. The recruits were also taught how to work on a soldier's feeling of loneliness, particularly if in remote postings. This series of training sessions ended with methods which could be used to raise the Polish population's morale through careful use of propaganda. The function of such propaganda was to unify the population in a common hatred of the German forces. However, the warning went out, that all the above actions could easily occur in a haphazard way and therefore be very wasteful. In order to reduce duplication a shared plan of action of action was required. The subsequent training sessions were devoted to the methods used to develop such plans. The first lesson to learn was that there were two distinct phases to action: planning and execution. The planning phase included dividing occupied Poland into regions.[6] This allowed the agents to assess the characteristics of each region, which could then be dealt with one at a time. The

---

5   *Special Operations Executive Manual* (London: William Collins, 2014) p. 1.
6   TNA HS4/171: Planning and policy: Operations to Warsaw.

nature of the execution phase would depend solely on the equipment available to resistance fighters at the time.

\* \* \*

Individual security was introduced as an agent's first priority.[7] Recruits were warned that apart from the danger to an individual, an arrest could jeopardise the safety of the whole Home Army. Certain basic rules had to be learned throughout the training period. Examples of such rules were listed as: cover, information, alertness, inconspicuousness, discretion, discipline, and planning for an emergency. The trainees were instructed that it was essential to prepare a comprehensive cover story or 'legend' before transfer to occupied Poland. The story had to be well learned and delivered almost like a 'reflex' and as if it were true. The management of information was introduced as a fundamental of an agent's work. As with a cover story, basic information was to be prepared before departure but would need to be supplemented on arrival. This would have to take into account local conditions and regulations. The agents were reminded that they could not rely on the local law for protection. On the contrary they could only depend on their own skills of staying alert and paying attention to detail. They would also need to be acquainted with local security arrangements, including police regulations and the operations of German security forces. An obvious message perhaps, was that an agent must not give himself away by attracting attention to him or herself. Therefore, inconspicuousness was vitally important, as even a small infringement could bring an individual into contact with local police. Consequently, an agent must become a model citizen whilst in the field. Under the topic of 'personal behaviour', recruits were instructed to consider their physical appearance. A good agent, according to instructors, merges with the background and behaves in the same way as those around him. Also, an agent must not give himself away through carelessness. He/she should adopt a 'hush hush' approach not mentioning anything he/she was not supposed to know. Also, he/she should not mention isolated facts that could later be placed with other facts to produce a 'big picture'.

Later, courses covered topics such as: 'interrogation management', 'the cell system', 'security of organisations', 'enemy forces', 'German counter espionage', 'intelligence reports', 'sabotage of road signs', 'morale warfare', 'letter opening', 'disposal of parachutes', 'reconnaissance', 'selection of dropping points' and 'counter measures.' The lecture on interrogation concentrated on methodology, types of interrogation and questioning techniques. It was during these sessions that individuals were taught how to be assertive in various situations. An important topic in the lectures on surveillance, was how an agent should protect him/herself from being surveyed or followed. For example, it was recommended that no agent should go straight to their destination but make an innocent visit on the way. Trainees were also taught not to 'hang about' in places where they could easily be watched without their knowledge, nor to

---

7   *Special Operations Executive Manual*, p. 13.

use their place of residence and/or their place of occupation for subversive activity. There was also a course called 'Living off the Land'.[8] During this course the recruits had to sustain themselves with what they could find in the wild. Later this course was discontinued for the Poles. The lectures on external communications, included information on how BBC broadcasts were used to send secret messages to personnel in occupied Poland. For example, a piece of music could be used to signal the start of an operation such as an incoming parachute drop. The BBC's role in the Polish Project was agreed with the Sixth Bureau. Almost every Polish broadcast on the antennae of the BBC included coded messages in the form of melodies and pre-arranged music.[9] The music was always broadcast just before close-down and was introduced by a special phrase at 1.45 a.m. The announcer would say, 'And now in conclusion we will play for you …' Normal transmissions, that is the melodies which carried no hidden massage, would end with the announcer saying, 'And now comes a short programme of Polish music.'[10] These melodies were called 'cover tunes'. Other messages were sent as crack signals embedded in programmes destined for the Home Army. Each drop zone was identified by its own melody. Once this melody was heard the appropriate receiving committee would prepare the site for a parachute drop by clearing the area from debris, setting up landing lights and getting them ready for illumination.[11] The sessions on emergency planning[12] emphasised the importance of preparing a strategy designed to cope with unforeseen events; for example, what to do if a break in the chain of cells of fighters occurred and so leaving some cells in isolation. In this event trainees were instructed that the last cell in the chain had to be linked to the leader of the whole chain, thus making it circular again. Lectures described drop zones as an open space not less than 400 square metres and, if possible, 800 square metres. The chosen terrain was to be smooth and level if people were being dropped, and that uncultivated land should be used to avoid leaving evidence in the form of foot prints. Sites should also be free from high tension cables and tall trees. The Poles were also informed how to lay out landing lights for incoming RAF aircraft. The norm was three white lights in line 100 metres apart, with the downwind light duplicated at a distance of 10 metres by a flashing light. Each light had to be set at 10 degrees of tilt pointing towards the incoming aircraft. Lectures on German espionage comprised 12 sessions including topics such as enemy police and enemy armed forces. Four types of organisations of counter espionage were discussed: German counter espionage authorities, German uniformed police, Polish police working in the service of the Gestapo, and Nazi or pro-Nazi party organisations. A very important series of lectures concerned 'fieldcraft' and 'survival'. The objective of these sessions was to give practice in moving around woods and closed country. Recruits were trained at

8   *Special Operations Executive Manual*, p. 150.
9   Garliński, *Poland, SOE and the Allies*, p. 79.
10  Garliński, p. 79.
11  Testimony of Stanisław Jankowski <http://www.vod.tvp.pl/video/dawno-temu-cichociemny> (accessed 14.09.2020).
12  TNA HS4/171: Planning and policy: operations to Warsaw.

observing the tilt of trees as a way of finding directions. For example, trees in England usually tilt to the East and could be used to identify the other points of a compass. Recruits were also taught how to examine animal tracks of domestic animals as they could lead to a village or water. Agents had to be wary of domestic animals for a village dog could easily give away a person's presence. The skill of making a fire for boiling, frying or grilling on a spit, was also considered. Recruits were taught how to make bread, how to cook poultry, hares, rabbits and chapatis. Training was concluded at a finishing school where the way to behave in Poland was included, although this was often done when an agent had successfully reached the country and had been met by a mentor. Volunteers who were accidently injured during training had to leave the course and were returned to their units without appeal. The first training station, which was identified as Station 38, was set up on the isolated estate of Lord Aldenham at Briggens, Hertfordshire. On welcoming the first cohort, his Lordship passed them over to the care of his wife before leaving for London on business. Lady Aldenham treated the young Poles as members of her own family. Lieutenant Colonel Evans was the commander at the station with a staff of three other officers. Captain F. Koprowski, who was a Physical Trainer at the Grudziądz Cavalry School before the war, looked after physical fitness training whilst Captain J. Szymański and Lieutenant Morawicz ran sabotage and mining courses. Later Evans was replaced by Major Angus Kennedy and Koprowski was replaced by Major Hartman, who also was also in charge of all Polish training matters at the Sixth Bureau. By February 1941 the first tranche of 27 individuals graduated.

\* \* \*

Typically, British SOE recruits came from universities, the 'old boy network' or from the upper echelons of the business community. However, Polish recruits were volunteers from the officer class of the displaced Polish Forces in Britain and the Polish units stationed in the Middle East fighting under British command . All were Polish nationals who had been trained by both the British and the Poles. All men who qualified successfully had to swear allegiance to the Home Army and the Polish Second Republic by reciting:

> As God Almighty is my witness, and in the name of the Virgin Mary, Queen of Poland, I swear to be loyal to the nation the Second Republic and protect her honour. I shall confront all enemies of the Republic until the end of my life. I shall be obedient to the President and the Commander in Chief and to the officers of the Home Army. I shall keep all codes secret irrespective of what threat I shall face, so help me God.[13]

---

13  *Testimony of Stanisław Jankowski* <www.vod.tvp.pl/video/dawno-temu-cichociemny> (accessed 14.09.2020).

On completing this, the individual received the badge of the 'Silent and Invisible' (Cichociemnych). Initially 74 individuals graduated. During the years 1942-1944 a further 208 individuals had graduated at STS 25, Inverness. Training was run by British and Polish officers, namely Captain Antoni Strawiński, Colonel Stefan Kaczmarek and Colonel Aleksander Legin amongst others. Psychological training was concerned either with the mental stability of the recruits or how to use psychological methods to undermine a German soldier's motivation. This training took place at STS 7 in Guildford, southern England. As far as the psychology of the recruits themselves was concerned, the individual had to be prepared for subversive and sabotage action under conspiratorial conditions.[14] This took much personal courage and conviction. The course lasted one week although they could run for two. 194 candidates graduated from Guildford.

Parachute training involved packing parachutes as well as jumping and landing safely. The course was held at STS 51, Ringway near Manchester (now Manchester Airport). Apart from the Poles, individuals from Czechoslovakia, Norway, France, Holland, Yugoslavia and Hungary also attended. Trainees carried out five jumps during their training including one jump at night. The training programme at Ringway was under constant review, which resulted in frequent changes being made to the curriculum. For example, the original four jumps from an aircraft required in early training were changed to 14 jumps: two from an adapted barrage balloon in daylight, five from an aircraft and seven during night time. From January 1944, parachute training also took place at Base 10 in Italy. The Polish training schools were supplied with Irvin QD type parachutes, the canopy measuring eight metres in diameter when opened flat, with a surface area of 50 square metres. It was made from the finest quality silk and could support 18 Kilograms per square centimetre. The canopy was made from 28 triangular segments sown together with the best silk threads each capable of holding 3.5 Kilograms. Attached to the canopy were suspension lines which were eventually woven together to form two carrying lines, left and right, which were attached to the parachutist's harness.

\* \* \*

Training on how to deal with German tanks began with the operation of British and German machines. These courses lasted between two to eight weeks where the candidate learned about the vulnerability of enemy tanks and how to lead a tank platoon. A subsidiary course covered training in driving and servicing German cars and motorbikes. It lasted approximately eight weeks, with almost all recruits taking part. The Polish Intelligence School, trained individuals in techniques and methods of intelligence and counter intelligence, ways of gathering information, ciphers, radiotelegraphy and recruiting and training other agents in Poland. English language courses included training in the use of British military terminology. Three centres for radio communication were eventually set up: Chipperfield Lodge was used for

---

14   TNA HS4/163: Sabotage and Guerrilla Warfare in Poland.

transmissions, Barnes Lodge in Kings Langley was a reception station and Polmot, Stirlingshire was set up as a training station. Eventually 16 transmitter stations were in operation, 39 reception stations and 48 antennae which were either of American manufacture or made in the Polish research laboratory in Stanmore, London.[15] The training centres (called Special Training Schools [STS]) were identified using Arabic numbers. In the final analysis, the aim of training was to prepare men and women for conspiratorial fighting and to lead small units of the Home Army in clandestine operations in Poland. Considered something akin to finishing schools, final training was designed to change regular Polish soldiers into a resistance fighters and prepare them for operation behind German lines. Dispatch training started in July 1942 at Audley End but after 15 July was transferred to STS 46 near Newport owing to the rapid increase in the number of recruits. During this final phase of training the agent prepared his cover story tailored to his new persona. Between summer 1940 and autumn 1943, 2,413 officers had volunteered but 606 completed training successfully. Between February 1941 and December 1944 SOE managed to organise 82 flights to the occupied country transferring 316 commandoes including one female recruit. Out of these, nine perished before they could reach their target, three were lost when their aircraft crashed en route, three were lost when their aircraft came under fire over Denmark, whilst three died when their parachutes failed to open. 91 commandoes fought in the Warsaw Uprising with eighteen losses. The total losses during the war were 112. The Poles had extensive autonomy in recruitment and training which is why the Polish Sixth Bureau managed all Polish specials although it had to liaise with SOE on account that it did not have access to all the war material that was required nor did it have aircraft for transportation.

\* \* \*

The Silent and Invisible special forces were parachuted into Poland by the RAF since SOE Polish Section had no aircraft of its own. Eventually, five types of bombers were employed: Whitleys, Halifaxes, Liberators, Flying Fortresses and Dakotas (see Appendix 2). The last three models were of American manufacture. All of these aircraft were bombers and so were heavy, slow and difficult to manoeuvre in the sky. It was a case of deciding which aircraft had the range and the best carrying capacity for any one mission. The acquisition of aircraft for Polish missions was always a struggle. The Poles and the SOE pushed the RAF for aircraft where and when they needed them, whilst the Air Ministry tried to hold back planes for RAF missions which were invariably considered to be far more urgent than any SOE/Polish operation. Although anyone who was sympathetic to the Polish predicament would have acknowledged SOE pleas, Polish missions never reached the status of purely RAF operations such as the bombing campaign over Germany.[16] A further complication for the RAF was the

---

15 TNA HS4/186: Polish military wireless research unit Stanmore, Anglo-Polish wireless meetings.
16 Lynne Olson and Stanley Cloud, *For your Freedom and Ours*, p. 282.

need to make modifications to the aircraft for SOE use. The distance from southern Britain to central Poland was approximately 800 miles about 1200 kilometres one way which was the operational limit of most of the aircraft available. This problem was solved by inserted fuel tanks into the fuselage to increase the range; however, this could only be done at the expense of carrying capacity. The Cichociemni were Polish Special Forces, who were trained by SOE and parachuted into Poland by the RAF. They were not SOE agents in the strictest sense, because they were selected by the Poles and did not take orders from British officers. Nevertheless, there were a few that were Poles who had been recruited by the British and became true SOE agents. Such an individual was Maria Skarbek, OBE, GM. Her legendary espionage work included intelligence gathering in the Middle East, passing information on Polish resistance groups to British authorities in London and working behind the lines in Nazi Germany. Perhaps her most important work was done when SOE sent her to France. Although SOE agents in France were answerable to SOE Section F, Maria's mission was launched from Algiers by Section AMF. After the war she remained in the West where she was awarded an OBE and the George Medal.[17]

---

17   Madeleine Massoon, *Christine: SOE Agent and Churchill's Favourite Spy* (London: Virago Books, 2005).

# 10

# Trial Flight

*Fortune Befriends the Bold*
            Virgil, *Aeneid*, X

Initial contact made between the Government of the Second Republic exiled in Paris) and the resistance organisations in occupied Poland occurred in November 1939. Communications were based on couriers travelling overland via Italy and the Balkans but as these routes became increasingly dangerous the office of General Sosnkowski proposed the use aircraft to make transfers to the occupied country. Unfortunately, the French had neither any suitable aircraft for such missions nor the experience needed to run such operations. The Poles approached the Americans with the intention of buying aircraft, but this did not provide the answer when France was occupied by German forces. In June the Polish Government evacuated to Britain, which meant that all contact with the occupied country was temporarily lost. The British were already planning to make parachute drops in occupied countries on the continent, although they were fearful that that this could result in information about what was going on in Britain leaking out. Sikorski was convinced that this was the best way to keep contact with resistance fighters for couriers on the ground could only pass on small quantities of material and short messages. Large bits of information were being transferred by couriers learning texts off by heart and then repeating them on arrival. Dalton also believed that Poland could only be helped meaningfully if the 'Silent and Invisible',[1] together with government couriers, were able to get in and out of the occupied country on a regular basis. This would require an air corridor between Britain and the Second Republic. When Dalton looked at the proposal, two issues immediately came to mind, one was the acute shortage of aircraft, which Sir Archibald Sinclair, the Secretary of State for Air, had previously highlighted on numerous occasions and the second was the difficulty of landing aircraft in occupied territory. In the light of these concerns, it was agreed that parachute drops would

---

1   Cichociemni.

solve the problems, and as far as the shortage of aircraft was concerned, it was hoped that further down the line, production increases would solve the shortage problem. SIS agreed to the establishment of a sub-unit of the RAF crewed by Polish personnel. Despite his disapproval, Sinclair promised Dalton that he would look into securing further supplies for Poland as a consolation. General Sosnkowski argued that the courier system was working well and that it required no alteration, but Sikorski did not agree and ordered the Third Bureau (Operation) to prepare plans for an air bridge. Captain Kalenkiewicz worked tirelessly to hatch a plan. In December the Sixth Bureau and the Inspector of the Polish Airforce accepted his work and things were put into practice. Despite the shortage of aircraft and after months of trying, Sikorski obtained British agreement to fly Whitleys and Wellingtons modified with the addition of extra fuel tanks.

* * *

Early flights to Poland took off from British airfields, although the distance between the two countries appeared prohibitive and dangerous. Consequently, airfields in other locations were considered. Greece was seriously mulled over until it became occupied by the Germans in 1941. Airfields in North Africa were also examined but it was eventually decided to establish a base in Brindisi in Italy. This became the primary airfield for later operations.[2] At the same time the best locations of drop zones were being considered. Western Poland, the nearest Polish territory to Britain was not available for SOE missions because this region had been annexed by Germany and was now considered by Berlin to be German territory and therefore, as a result, heavily defended. Eastern Poland, on the other hand, was out of range for most of the aircraft available and in any case, was now under Soviet occupation and considered to be part of the Soviet Union. Consequently, the most suitable pre-war Polish territory, which was within range and comparatively safe was central Poland renamed by Berlin as General Government territory (see appendix 5). This central area of pre-war Poland was considered to be and treated as a German colony headed by Governor General Hans Frank. The direct distance between RAF airports in Cambridgeshire and this area was approximately 1,300 kilometres so such a distance required an aircraft with a range of approximately 2,600 kilometres if it was to complete the round trip without the need for landing and refuelling. However, it was not only the distance between Britain and Poland that was exercising minds but also the hazards caused by German defences in central Europe which were being continuously upgraded. Other obstacles to successful missions were meteorological conditions over the North Sea since the aircraft would be operating close to their operational limits in headwinds and storms, which could easily jeopardise the success of a mission. The type of aircraft chosen would also have to be equipped with instrumentation for night flying, since it was decided to operate under the cover of darkness.

2   See Chapter 14.

\* \* \*

According to the Air Ministry the only aircraft available for the trial run was the Armstrong Whitworth Whitley Z-6473 twin engine bomber. This type, a twin-engine bomber, came into service in 1937 which meant that it was not the most modern of aircraft when it was called upon to serve in operations to Poland. The Z-6473 was crewed by five personnel and had a lift capacity of 7,000 pounds (3175.1 Kilograms). It was equipped with crude instrumentation for night flying and with only a range of 870 miles (1400 Kilometres) had to be modified by fitting three extra fuel tanks into the fuselage to extend its range before being sent to Poland. However, this adaptation was at a cost to carrying capacity. Meanwhile, the Polish General Staff in Britain could not hold back its enthusiasm that a flight was finally being organised and contacted the Head Quarters of the secret Home Army in Warsaw to inform it of the impending mission. This flight was to be the litmus test for all future flights not only to Poland, but to occupied Europe as a whole. In his excitement, General Sikorski, the indefatigable Polish Prime Minister and Commander in Chief, wrote to Sinclair enquiring on the progress of preparations for the mission. Sinclair reassured him that all would be ready by late autumn, 1940. On the strength of Sinclair's confidence and assurance, Sikorski contacted Gubbins requesting that preparations be started for regular flights to Poland commencing in September/October. Gubbins replied that the Air Ministry would endeavour to do everything in its power to make this happen, provided that the trial run was a success. Meanwhile, the underground army was informed that airlifts would be inaugurated in September, but in the end these did not materialise. Preparations for the trial mission took far longer than had been anticipated. The first trial flight was organised by SOE Polish Section in cooperation with the London based Sixth Bureau which was in communication with the Head of Aviation in underground Poland. The flight would take place without the use of radio communication, although maps and astronavigation methods would be used for direction finding. The plan was for the aircraft to leave southern Britain, climb over the North Sea until it reached its approximate cruising height of 3,000 metres over the Baltic Sea. The flying conditions over the North Sea were known to be invariably turbulent and so the flight over this stretch of water could be bumpy and uncomfortable. The flight would then continue at cruising altitude over the Low Countries and Germany and then on to Warsaw, where the aircraft would descend to 200 metres to make its rendezvous with Home Army reception units. It was to take place under the cover of darkness, which was considered to be safer, meaning that subsequent flights would fly during the long nights of autumn and winter. By October, 60trained Polish officers awaited to see if they would be chosen to fly, but there was still no aircraft available for the mission. Even the expected 138 Special Operations Squadron had not yet been formed. Norman Bottomley (Air Vice Marshal) suggested using Whitley's with a refuelling stop in Russia. The advantage of this was clear to him, but the disadvantage for the Poles was that this risked the infiltration and interference of the Polish Home Army by the Russians. Furthermore, SOE would need to establish complex ground facilities in Russia which Stalin would not allow.

Eventually, an aircraft was found with the identification number Z-6473 and the decision was taken to make an attempt at a round trip during the night of 15/16 February, 1941. Planning for the mission started in October 1940, at the Parachute Depot at Ringway near Manchester. The planning lasted two weeks with 12 individuals identified as a possible crew.[3] The flight was given the classification number of 'zero' and the code name 'Adolphus'. A crew of six flew on the mission: Captain Keast, of the RAF Number 419 Flight, Co-Pilot Flight Officer McMurdie, Navigator Pilot officer Baker, along with a rear gunner, a W/T operator, and despatcher.

\* \* \*

Three men of the Polish special forces were sent on this mission after receiving their final orders from Sixth Bureau officers. The information, which was given to them individually for security reasons, included details of the drop zone, the name of the nearest town to the zone, a password for the reception committee and a local map on a scale of 1:1,000,000. Following this the men were driven to the airfield at Stradishall and placed on 'stand-by'. Just before boarding the aircraft, a final body search took place in case they were in possession of any item which could divulge their true identity and so incriminate them. Following the search each man was issued with his parachute. The leader of the group received final orders and was German and Polish currency for the Home Army. Following a farewell hug from their commanding officer, they boarded the aircraft. General Sosnkowski addressed the men before their departure saying, 'you are flying to Poland as an advance guard.' The flight, manned by a British crew of 138 Division, took off at 18.35 hours on 15 February 1941and took five hours and 30 minutes to reach the drop zone. The three members of Polish special forces on board were: Flight Captain Stanisław Krzymowski, code name 'Kostek', Colonel Józef Zabielski, code name 'Zbik' and political courier Czesław Raczkowski. Each man flew in civilian clothes of non-British manufacture and was issued with standard kit. It comprised two automatic pistols with 50 rounds of ammunition, a torch, a small shovel, a knife, a compass, a first aid kit and a cyanide pill. The pill, referred to as Tablet L, was usually hidden on their person and only used as a last resort when conditions became impossible. The capsule had a rubber coating, which prevented it from dissolving in the mouth, but when bitten death followed quickly. 10 men would later have to use their suicide capsule on their missions.[4] Personal items that were issued included a civilian suit, an overcoat, headgear, a scarf, two shirts, a pair of shoes, two pairs of thick underpants, three pairs of thick socks, three handkerchiefs, a pair of warm gloves, razor blades and several packets of cigarettes of German origin. It was the agent's responsibility to obtain a watch, which had to be made in either Poland or Germany and certainly not one with English markings. Each agent had on his person false letters and diaries

---

3   Later Polish instructors worked with individuals of various nationality on parachute training.
4   Stella-Sawicki, Garliński and Mucha (eds.), *First to Fight* (London: The Polish Ex-Combatant's Association of Great Britain, 2009) p. 131.

written in such a way as to suggest that he lived in Poland. These men were pioneers in the sense that all future air missions would depend on their success. During the flight the mood on board was taut, with no one wanting to talk much. The men sat exchanging few words, with the only light penetrating the darkness coming from the cockpit instrument panel with shafts of intermittent moonlight. The men sat in the noisy aircraft on low benches leaning against the fuselage wall with outstretched legs. They wondered about what they would find in their homeland, which they had not seen for some years. They were about to find out in a few hours' time. As the aircraft skimmed along the cloud base at an approximate speed of 104 knots[5], each man rehearsed in his mind what he had practised in parachute training. However, every now and then these technical thoughts were interrupted by emotional feelings of excitement followed by periods of trepidation. The men were returning to their homeland after two or more years absence. They wondered about their homes, their parents and siblings and whether they were still alive and whether they would get a chance to meet with them? This was highly unlikely as they had been forbidden to make any contact with anyone they knew whilst on their mission. Despite the twin-engine Whitley being modified with three extra fuel tanks it was far from certain whether the aircraft would reach the designated drop zone and return safely and so Flight Lieutenant Keast, decided to risk a direct route[6] to the drop zone which would take them over Dusseldorf and Berlin then south to Silesia. This was a precarious route since it would take the aircraft deep into German airspace which was protected by a heavy presence of Luftwaffe fighters. Later operations to Poland used different routes which took aircraft over northern Denmark, the southern tip of Sweden and the Baltic Sea, thus avoiding German airspace. These were coded as Route 1 and 2. Route 1 crossed the North Sea to the north of the Island of Sylt, dashed across Denmark, then around Bornholm, whereupon the aircraft would turn south and head for Jamno and the Bukowo Lakes. From there the route proceded towards Torun and then onto the Płock region. The pilot then headed towards the designated drop zone. Unfortunately, Keast never reached the designated drop zone due to a navigation error. They were 138 kilometres off target near a town called Dembowiec. Nevertheless, the three agents on board decided to jump even though they had overshot the precise target. They sat at the open side door (the aircraft had not yet been modified with a hatch in the floor) and waited for the signal to jump. Eventually, the dispatcher touched them on the shoulder and each man launched himself into the darkness. One by one they toppled out of the aircraft until their parachutes engaged. Suddenly the roar and vibrations of the aircraft, which had accompanied from the time of leaving Britain, was replaced by the whisper of the wind as the men glided in ambient silence towards the ground. The first man to exit was followed by a container of equipment pushed out by the dispatcher. Then the others followed. Unluckily, the containers were lost and Colonel Zabielski had had a heavy landing hurting his leg for he did not realise that the aircraft was considerably lower than

5   120 mph.
6   TNA HS4/148: Liaison with Poland by aerial means.

the 500 feet his training had prepared him for. Raczkowski was captured almost immediately by German security forces. Soon after Zabielski and Krzymowski were picked up by members of the Home Army and transferred to Warsaw reaching the Polish capital on 20 February. Meanwhile, Keast swung the aircraft to the West and headed home. The return journey took approximately six hours and when he finally landed safely at 0605 hours, he had barely 50 litres of fuel left in the tanks. This spurred the Air Ministry to decide not to continue using Whitley's as the aircraft of choice in future missions, adding that its low ceiling, short range and slow cruising speed rendered the aircraft too vulnerable. All flights to Poland were suspended until a suitable replacement was found. Despite the Whitley being slightly damaged over Germany, the British crew was awarded the Polish Virtuti Militari Cross for bravery. Sadly this award was made posthumously as the whole crew was shot down soon on a later mission and perished. The first parachute landing in occupied Poland lifted the populations morale and had a significant effect on recruitment to the Home Army. In response the German authorities hung up posters throughout the region urging people to pass on information if they knew of the whereabouts of three dangerous 'bandits'.

\* \* \*

Following the first mission to Poland, an extensive post-mortem was undertaken in order to assess the value of the operation and to gauge the feasibility of future missions to occupied Europe. The Mission Report was written by the RAF, the SOE Polish Section and the Sixth Bureau and then was sent on to the Chiefs of Staff and the Polish Government in London. Apart from the relief that the aircraft had returned safely and that the men had been successfully dropped over Poland, a detailed evaluation had to be carried out of the protocol used. One of the first conclusions to be made was that the Whitley aircraft was wholly inadequate for future missions.[7] This view saw the two engine aircraft replaced by the four engine Halifax.[8] Although it was acknowledged that it was also noisy and uncomfortable for passengers, after some modifications, made its range, speed and carrying capacity it a better proposition. Range was an issue and a major adaptation involving the addition of extra fuel tanks was carried out, despite this compromising carrying capacity. The lack of radio navigation was also a serious drawback however, some assistance was forthcoming when it was proposed that lights arranged on the ground by reception committees would help in guiding pilots to their target. Another difficulty, particularly during cloudy conditions, had been the use of astronomical navigation methods which had to be employed as Poland was not covered by British radar signalling. Radio communication was tried on subsequent missions. The next concern raised was the fact that the area selected for the drop had been 'crawling with Germans'. Although a note

---

7   TNA HS8/897/7: Correspondence with Winston Churchill – six-page report on the organisation and activities of SOE.
8   Hadley Page Halifax. Produced 1940-1946. Four-engine heavy bomber.

had been recorded about this misfortune, it was explained away by the fact that the aircraft was off course and should not have been in the locality. A recommendation was made to exercise greater vigilance when selecting future drop zones. The Home Army also informed the Polish General Staff that it was taking up to six days to organise reception committees, something which should be taken into account when planning future missions. This would hopefully reduce the time of 'hanging around' when they would be at their most vulnerable. The Polish High Command in London concluded that, in the light of these difficulties, only equipment of the highest quality should be used in future missions along with the most highly-trained staff. Another conclusion was to choose only remote areas for drop zones and to camouflage them in order to minimise the chance of their detection. The Home Army's High Command also recommended that, if missions were not met by a reception group at the planned rendezvous, the agents should separate and disperse quickly, avoiding main roads. Also, it was decided that on landing they should clean their shoes and brush down their clothes carefully removing mud and dirt from garments and equipment in order not to attract unwanted attention when moving about towns. In order to make flights cost effective it was decided to load aircraft 'up to the gunnels.' Although this made the aircraft heavy and cumbersome, and therefore vulnerable to attack, it was felt that this was a risk worth taking especially during the periods of plane shortages. When it came to flightpaths, the British suggested route two which took aircraft over the northern tip of Denmark and southern tip of Sweden, avoiding German radar altogether.[9] Having avoided German airspace at approximately 400 feet, it was recommended that the aircraft should climb over the Baltic Sea until Gdańsk was reached. On reaching the free city the pilots should then bank to the south and pick up the river Vistula which would lead them onto central Poland and the dropping region. (see Appendix 7) It was agreed that the selection of drop zones would be made by the High Command of the Home Army in collaboration with the Sixth Bureau in London and then relayed to SOE Polish Section and onwards to the RAF. It was also agreed that when an aircraft left England, a signal would be sent to Warsaw via BBC coded broadcasts, so that preparations for its reception could be started. The signal would be in the form of a coded melody or piece of music, which both sides would recognise. It was decided that a precise protocol be followed when drops were made. The first point of contact with the incoming aircraft was designated as Point A. As the pilot approached four bursts of light (two long followed by two short) would be flashed at the cockpit. In reply the pilot would repeat the sequence using his landing lights. This confirmed that formal recognition had been established. Following this, men standing on the perimeter of the drop zone would light up torches or paraffin lamps which shone in such a way that they could easily be seen by the incoming aircraft. The configuration of the lights, the pattern of which was pre-arranged with London, not only identified the drop zone, but indicated the direction of the wind across the site. The pilot would then circle the zone in order to approach it from up wind. The pilot would flash his landing lights twice when the drop was about to

---

9   TNA HS4/148: Liaison with Poland by Means of Air.

commence. Containers were released first, followed by personnel, thus reducing the chance of collisions. On completing the drop the pilot would flash his landing lights once before departing for England. On missions from England to Poland the aircraft would have left any formation separate so as to arrive at the drop zone individually. As the parachuting of men was an act of combat, each was promoted by one rank when he touched down on Polish soil.

\* \* \*

Meanwhile, on the home front, Frank Balmforth decided to travel to London to see how the city had faired since his last visit. Bomb damage became increasingly prevalent the nearer he got to the capital. He noticed that the control tower was being repaired at the Feltham marshalling yard after a recent blitz. Further down the line, houses at Richmond and North Sheen had been wrecked by recent bombing. Frank alighted at Clapham Junction, South London, and caught the 77 bus to Southampton Row via Wandsworth Road, Albert Embankment, Lambeth Bridge, Millbank, Whitehall and Strand. As the journey progressed it began to snow and he noted how drab everything looked south of the river with many damaged properties. When he got off the bus at Cosmo Place the snow had settled and was quite thick. He walked towards Great Ormond Street and was glad to see that the new wing of the hospital was still intact. He popped into a bookshop and bought 'The Woodlanders' for two shillings, and 'Teach Yourself German' for two shillings and sixpence. After wandering for a while, he reached St. Paul's Cathedral. He went in and noticed that a large part of it was closed to visitors. From there he made his way to St. Martin's-le-Grand. In that district he came upon serious damage. Shops, banks and cafes were completely bombed out and, where large buildings once stood, there now were heaps of rubble. At Bank Underground Station he received another shock. The Waterloo Line had been closed due to damage in the subways. A temporary bridge had been constructed to carry road traffic over the destroyed booking hall. As a result his return, journey to Waterloo Station via Charing Cross took longer than expected. At Waterloo Station, Frank was struck by how efficient the dispatch women staff were in their neat uniforms.[10]

---

10   Peter Minett (ed.), *Frank's Wartime Diary*, pp. 212-213.

Marshal Józef Piłsudski

General Edward Smigły-Rydz

General Władysław Sikorski

General Władysław Anders

Premier Stanisław Mikołajczyk

President Władysław Raczkiewicz

# 11

# Planning Air Corridors to Occupied Poland

*It is necessary to hope, though hope should always be deluded; for hope itself is happiness, and its frustrations, however frequent, are yet less dreadful than its extinction.*
Johnson, Idler, No. 58

Nineteen forty-one was a period of preparation. Planning was carried out by the Sixth Bureau and the High Command of the Home Army, based on their assessment of needs and requirements. The Poles requested that flights take place at night preferably during full moons. The Air Ministry transferred two fresh Polish crew to 138 Division then after intervention from Churchill, a further six aircraft and 10 crew were added by the end of 1941. Dalton took heart from the success of the trial run, which was but a prologue to operations to occupied Europe. The success of the run also enthused the Poles, who began preparing for regular deliveries of war materials. A special department entitled *Syrena* (Mermaid) also known as Department 'S' was set up by Home Army HQ in Warsaw. The department was divided into subsections each with a specific responsibility, for example, subsection 'Import' was responsible for seeking out and preparing suitable drop zones, whilst subsection 'Ewa' was responsible for organising the collection and the initial dispersal of special forces men into local safe houses. The criteria for selecting drop zones was refined following the trial run. Each zone was to measure approximately 650 yards by 200 yards (594.3 metres by 182.8 metres) and was to be sited in a remote location. It was believed that a concave topography with poor road connections would hinder the Germans discovering and reaching the site easily. The drop zone would also have to be free from tree stumps and large stones in order to reduce the risk of injury and should contain an obvious natural feature that could easily be recognised from the air. The drop zone was to be marked out in one of two ways, either with red lights on the edge of the zone or with white lights arranged in such a way as to delineate the zone and indicate the direction of the wind across the site. The reception group was assigned specific tasks, such as the gathering of parachutists or securing parachute canopies and dropped containers. The individuals who made up a reception group were always drawn from the local community since they would be best familiar with the natural characteristics of the drop zone and the surrounding geography. All members of the reception committees would have sworn allegiance to the Polish Government in London to prove their loyalty to the Second Republic. A representative of the Home Army HQ in Warsaw was present at each rendezvous, although he was under the control of the local commander.

\* \* \*

During early missions the whole dropping operation was under central control, namely GHQ in Warsaw. On landing special forces were under orders to report to General Headquarters along with the supplies that had been brought over. The reception group overseeing the procedures on the ground had three responsibilities: to gather the agents together; to evacuate them to safehouses and to secure the dropped containers. Once in the safe house money and orders from London were passed to the Home Army representative. Receipts were issued. The men were then introduced to 'liaison girls' (sometimes called 'Aunts' or *ciotki* in Polish), who would take responsibility for the men's initial safety. At the appropriate time and when the coast was clear, the agents or couriers were issued with railway tickets to the Polish capital and delivered to the local railway station in time for departure. During 1941-1942 the drop zones were few in number and could be counted in tens. They required a small number of personnel to service them and could deal with loads of up to 480 kgs, about one half of a possible plane load. In these early days the provision of security for the smaller and cruder sites was more symbolic than realistic. It was even the case that the only equipment prepared for use in some sites was no more than a spade and a pair of galoshes for the digging in of emptied containers and parachute canopies. Axes and shears were also available to cut down trees in which a parachute had snarled. During 1943 the whole secret infrastructure to receive RAF planes grew in number, size and complexity. By now each mission comprised a number of aircraft flying as a group which required more sophisticated reception procedures. As the number of drops increased, it soon became clear that central control would be overwhelmed and so each regional authority was given the autonomy to maintain, supervise and defend its own district.[1] These larger sites, sometimes called 'Bastions', were also provided with an armed guard made up of approximately 100 men. The Bastions were capable of handling seven or so drops at any one time. The Sixth Bureau in London was responsible for informing the Home Army of up and coming flights, such as the dates of missions, the codes related to the mission, the types of aircraft to expect, the range and carrying capacity and so on. As missions became more frequent, each piece of information was codified using so called 'Stellas', each carrying one piece of vital information. Reception committees organised themselves according to this

---

1 Garliński, *Poland, SOE and the Allies*, p. 145.

information. Each mission was also allotted a secret 'identifying melody' which was broadcast by the BBC in order to inform the reception group that a mission was going ahead or if a mission had been abandoned. After each successful parachute drop the reception committee was disbanded to avoid throwing suspicion onto the group. It was the responsibility of Department 'S', using radio transmissions or more than likely couriers, to disseminate the message of an impending operation to the appropriate local reception station. Once the message had been received the local unit it would prepare for the rendezvous with the aircraft. This would include organising the signalling equipment, arranging the availability of horse drawn carriages for transporting received materials, allotting responsibilities to personnel and putting together an armed guard to protect the site and so on. Individuals in the reception group were made responsible for particular responsibilities such as gathering operatives and taking them to a safe house or hiding parachutes. All this had to be done under the cover of darkness and in such a way that it did not alert the attention of the occupying forces. Reception groups were expected to wait in position until day light hours if an aircraft failed to show, before standing down. Those waiting to receive a drop had to be able to distinguish between the engine noise of British and German aircraft. There was no specific training for this and this critical skill could only be gained from experience, Each pilot and navigator, would have given details regarding the drop site. This consisted of a specific letter, which identified the zone followed by its map coordinates. This information would have been passed to the crew by the Sixth Bureau and shared with the resistance in Warsaw using morse code. As the aircraft approached the designated zone, the men on the ground would use the code to identify themselves using flash lights, whereupon the pilot would reply by echoing the code using his landing lights. Once recognition had been established, ground lights were lit with further information for the pilot such as the wind direction across the drop zone. The direction was codified by lamps arranged in the configuration of the letter 'T'. The horizontal bar of the letter was lined up in the direction of the prevailing wind. The distance between each of the lights forming the horizontal bar was 20 paces whilst the distance between each light on the vertical was 30 paces. Other signals such as crosses, triangles and circles, were also used. If the pilot failed to recognise the identifiers, parachute drops would be aborted and he would fly on to a back-up site, where a drop would be made. If successful contact was made, the pilot would circle the site until he was down wind, before commencing the drop. He would descend to 400 feet, which was considered to be the most appropriate height for drops to be made safely.

\* \* \*

Gubbins was encouraged by the success of the trial mission and so, in May 1941, he proposed, rather fancifully, 8,000 sorties to be flown to secret armies in occupied Europe. This proved to be unrealistic, since it was estimated that such a programme would require the deployment of most, if not all, of the aircraft available to bomber command for a period of four months which, understandably, the RAF could ill afford. Furthermore, there was no chance of the Air Ministry abandoning its priority of bombing German cities in order to satisfy SOE plans. In fact, Arthur Harris[2] was so obsessed with the bombing campaign of Germany that he became very possessive of the aircraft available to him and would never have shared them, unless pressed to do so by a higher authority. His contention was that the defeat of Germany would only be brought about by the systematic bombing of German cities. In April 1941, Sikorski pressed the British to establish an independent Polish Flight. He also looked around for up to date equipment, such as the latest version of the Halifax aircraft. At the same time Polish COS instructed the Polish Military Attaché in Washington to enquire about the possibility of obtaining American aircraft for the Polish project. They had the B17 Boeing in mind. In order to champion the request, Sikorski travelled to Washington, a move that did not please the British who considered Poland to be outside America's sphere of responsibility. Since the Poles and the British were 'fishing in the same pond' for equipment, London felt that it should not be in competition with Sikorski and protested. However, Sikorski continued to negotiate on both fronts for nearly two years. The negotiation with the British resulted in the dedication of Liberator aircraft for Polish use, whilst the Polish Airforce was promised 12 new bombers under the American 'lend-lease' arrangements. When the Liberators were finally delivered, the Air Ministry established the independent Polish Flight within 138 Squadron, which as well as three Liberators comprised three Halifax aircraft, a maintenance crew and six flying officers with one in reserve. With the deployment of the Liberators, flights could proceed over Denmark (route 2). This possibility buoyed Polish morale, for it would mean that German airspace could be avoided all together hence increasing the possibility of successful deliveries being completed to the homeland. In September 1941, three Polish bomber crews from 301 Squadron were attached to 138 Squadron, which in August took over duties from 1419 Flight. In November the new squadron was moved to Stradishall Airfield, Suffolk and then in March the following year to Tempsford, Bedfordshire. RAF Tempsford was located some four miles south of St. Neots and a mile from Tempsford Village. The airfield was built in 1940 and constructed in such a way as to give overflying aircraft the impression that it was disused. It became fully operational in February 1942. It was built to Class A standards and was originally planned as a satellite airfield to Bassingbourn. Three concrete runways were constructed with the usual 36 pan hard standings. In March 1942, No. 138 Squadron flying Halifaxes and Lysanders arrived there to be joined by 161 Squadron flying Whitley aircraft one month later. In November 1943, 138 Squadron became 1586 Special Duty Flight which in 1944 was reclassified back to 301 Transport Squadron.[3] By this time Tempsford had become the main spring board for SOE missions to Europe. In order to accommodate the Halifax aircraft, the runways were lengthened. Despite a modicum of improvement

2   Air Chief Marshal Sir Arthur Harris, the most outspoken proponent of the RAF policy for area bombing.
3   138 Squadron which became 1586 Flight which later was reclassified as 301 Squadron flew 423 missions to Poland

in aircraft supply, Dalton, Smoleński and Gubbins pushed for further increases. So that it could not be said that there was a lack of personnel to man the extra aircraft, the training of Polish pilots was increased. Early training started at Largo, Fife, in Scotland ending with parachute jumps using British equipment at Ringway Airfield. 5,000,000 pounds sterling was set aside for the Polish war effort which allowed the Poles to send one instalment of 20,000 pounds followed by monthly instalments of 10,000 pounds to Poland.

\* \* \*

Meanwhile, on 11 May Frank Balmforth had written a long entry into his diary. Firstly, he reported that the Sunday papers had not arrived and that domestic gas pressure was low. This resulted in the cessation of trains beyond Feltham in Surrey, but that was the only effect. For dinner Frank reports that he had English rump steak at two shillings and two pence per pound. For 'afters' he had rice pudding, although he notes as a footnote, that rice was in short supply. On 25 May Frank spent several hours in his garden weeding and hoeing. He reports in his diary that the bluebells, lilies-of-the-valley, woodruff, aubretia and forget-me-nots were 'looking good'. He refers to a passage he was reading in *England's Hour* by Vera Brittain, and quotes, 'A small middle-aged woman in black says to her gardener, 'When things went wrong in the last war, looking at flowers was sometimes the only comfort I had. If you can't have safety, you seem to need beauty all the more.'[4]

\* \* \*

In June 1941 Germany attacked her ally, the Soviet Union, in a momentous act of betrayal known as 'Operation Barbarossa'. The invasion of the Soviet Union by Germany was a complete surprise, not least to Józef Stalin, despite his spies informing him of Hitler's action. Rather than taking his spies seriously, he castigated them for incompetence and criticised them for spreading rumours. Meanwhile, three huge German armies smashed into Russia, one pushing eastward directly towards the Soviet capital, Moscow, with two armies, north and south, protecting its flanks. From now on the whole of Poland would be occupied by one enemy, Nazi Germany. Such was the early success of the German Forces in the Soviet campaign,, that an overconfident German High Command believed that the war in Russia had all but been won during the first few weeks of the campaign. Once Stalin was convinced that indeed the Soviet Union had been betrayed by her ally, Adolf Hitler, he sought friends in the West and approved the signing of a pact with Britain. This was done in London on 12 July, 1941. The pact was signed by Vyacheslav Molotov, the People's Commissar of Foreign Affairs and Stafford Cripps, the British Ambassador to Russia. This meant that Russia had switched sides in the war and was now a member of the 'Western Alliance.' Gubbins thought that this was the best news to

---

4    Peter Minett (ed.), *Frank's Wartime Diary*, p. 245.

come out of the war for some time, as it meant that the huge fighting potential of the Red Army was coming over to fight alongside the Allies, something that had been secretly coveted by Churchill from 1939. Britain's glee that Russia was now a member of the Western alliance was palpable. Not only was Churchill buoyed by the fact that the huge Red Army was now fighting the Nazis on the British side, but he was also prepared to go further and support the Russian war effort with the sharing of equipment and tactical knowhow. In June 1941, The Daily Mail reproduced Churchill's rhetoric, 'No one has been a more consistent opponent of Communism than I have been for the last 23 years. I will unsay no word that I have spoken about it. But all this fades away before the spectacle that is now unfolding.' The article continued, 'We have offered to the Government of Soviet Russia any technical or economic assistance which is in our power and which is likely to be of service to them.'[5] Soon Royal Navy and merchant ships were ploughing their way north in the so called 'Arctic Convoys' with war supplies for the Russian Forces delivering them via Archangel and Murmansk. In order to recruit public opinion Britain unleashed a wave of propaganda to convince the British people that Russia was a worthy ally and that 'Uncle Joe' was a good friend of their country. From now on the issue of arming the Home Army to the extent desired by the Polish authorities and of tying it into strategic planning had become one of the major dilemmas of Polish – British relations since Poland and Soviet Russia were latent enemies. Just as Russia had been supplying Nazi Germany with fuel up to the time of Barbarossa, now Britain was doing something similar with Soviet Russia. Stalin immediately asked for dramatic steps to be taken in the West in order to relieve military pressure on the Eastern Front, where the German forces were rampant; but D-Day was some time in coming. Soon British ships carrying Hawker Hurricane fighters and American produced Curtiss Tomahawk aircraft were sent to aid the Soviet Union. Alongside the hardware came RAF instructors, whilst the Americans sent out Hub Zemke a young 'ace pilot' dressed in civilian. Their mission was to train Russian pilots on how to fly the British and American machines which had been made available for the Russian air force. Eventually, the British sent hundreds of Hurricanes to the new ally.

\* \* \*

Meanwhile, on 6 September, 1941, Frank took his family on holiday to Oswestry. He noted that Paddington Station was unusually crowded and, whilst waiting for their train, he reported in his diary that the incoming Cornish express was running 40 minutes late and was made up of 4 parts. The book stall on the platform was well stocked. At a kiosk he was able to buy some 'very good' shortbread biscuits made by Huntley and Palmers, in packets of five for two and a half pence. Their journey north was uneventful but as soon as it got dark and the blackouts were pulled down, everyone in the compartment seemed to relax and became quite sociable, particularly

---

5   *The Daily Mail*, 23.06.1941

two RAF men. It was just after 11 o'clock when they reached Oswestry and Frank was relieved that their taxi was waiting for them at the station.[6]

\* \* \*

Russia joining the Western Alliance had important implications for SOE's Polish Section. One of these was how to deal with the Poles in the west, given that the Soviet Union's political aim was to remove the Polish Second Republic and its forces and to replace it with a left wing People's Republic. However, with Russia's fire power at stake, which was coveted by Britain, SOE Polish Section's programme concerning the Second Republic would have to be betrayed if Russia's support on the eastern front was to be exploited. This required London to reconcile the competing interests of the Soviet ally, with the guarantee given to the continued existence of the Second Republic. As Churchill remarked:

> The fact, however, that at every stage we had to consider the interests of our Russian Allies … makes it all the more necessary—imperative even—that I and my colleagues should be particularly careful about any pronouncement, explanations, or forecasts in which we might otherwise be tempted to indulge.[7]

Eventually, COS warned SOE that Russian reaction to any attempt to equip the Home Army with heavy ordinance would draw a hostile reaction from Moscow and so heavy weapons should not be delivered to the Poles.[8] This clearly put the SOE Polish Section in a difficult position. How do you support two allies each with competing and opposing political objectives? Sooner or later one of them would have to be betrayed. When the Germans seemed invincible, London's preference was to support Russia given the Red Army's fire power, but this had to be done in such a way so as not to appear that the Second Republic of Poland had been betrayed, hence tarnishing Britain's reputation as an ally. Nevertheless, one consequence of the conundrum was that however hard the Poles pushed for British assistance for its Home Army there was no response until the Polish Section had checked with the COS as to what the Soviet Union's attitude to the request was likely to be. As a British officer was to say, 'To spurn communist help when the principal communist power was grinding the Wehrmacht into the mud and dust on the Eastern front was not likely to bring the day of victory any closer'. Whilst the German Forces were unrestrained, these complicating issues were left on the back burner. The Poles concentrated on ridding Polish territory of the German invader, whilst the Soviet leadership was willing, for the time being, to make duplicitous concessions to the government of the Second Republic, which in 1939 it had asserted no longer existed. Meanwhile, Britain, played along with Moscow's pretence that it was

---

6    Peter Minett (ed.), *Frank's Wartime Diary*, pp. 279-280.
7    *The Daily Mail*, 29.09.41.
8    Lynne Olson and Stanley Cloud, *For your Freedom and Ours*, p. 285.

a friend of the Second Republic of Poland and encouraged the Republic's authorities in London to do the same. In other words, the dissonance within the allied camp was covered up. An agreement signed between the Poles and the Soviets on 30 July, implying full Soviet recognition of the Polish Government in London; declared that the Soviet-German treaty of 1939 was invalid and authorised the release of hundreds of thousands Polish prisoners being held in slave labour and political camps (gulags) throughout the Soviet Union. Those of fighting age were formed into a new Polish Army. Recruiting stations were organised at Koltubanka, Tatiszewo, and Tockoje with the main garrison being established at Buzuluk. General Anders, the commander of this army, who himself had been freed from the famous prison in Lubyanka, did not want these forces to fight alongside the Red Army (which had been the initial plan) preferring them to serve alongside the British. The nearest British Forces were stationed in the Middle East, where they were protecting the Suez Canal and Arabian oil fields for the allies, and so with Sikorski's approval and Stalin's grudging authorisation, the Poles were evacuated to the British protectorate of Palestine, where the nearest British Forces were stationed. This Army called the Second Polish Corps eventually became a part of the British Eighth Army and fought in the Italian Campaign. The units were moved to the Middle East via Iran and Iraq. Tens of thousands of Polish refugees, that is children, women and the elderly, who had also been released from slavery in Russia, accompanied the army out of the Soviet Union and were temporarily resettled in British safe havens in the commonwealth, places such as India, Southern Rhodesia and Mozambique, pending a return to a free Republic. According to Russian historians this army was moved out from the eastern theatre by the Polish Government in London to fight for the British war effort. This meant that they could not take part in the decisive battles for Poland or take the shortest route back to its homeland. The official communist line was that the Polish workers and left wing peasants who remained in the Soviet Union thought it would be proper to set up a communist Polish Army and fight for Poland under Soviet command. These leaders formed the new officer corps of Polish communist forces in the east and were given full support by the Soviet Union who supplied them with the necessary materials and modern arms, as well as political commissars. Stalin designated these forces as the First Army commanded by General Zybmunt Berling, who was awarded the Order of the Builders of People's Poland after the war.

\* \* \*

The assistance Britain was providing the Soviet Union with after Barbarossa did not only include the supplying of war material, it also included intellectual know-how.[9] Barely a week after the first British convoy left for Russia, Brigadier George Hill, SOE's representative, travelled to Moscow. In September 1941 his opposite number,

---

9   The People's Commissariat for Internal Affairs. Conducted regular police work and overseeing Soviet labour camps and prisons. Also, the Secret Service of the Soviet Union.

Lieutenant Iwan Cziczajev, arrived in London. Following discussion the NKVD agreed to suspend secret operations in the United Kingdom, Saudi Arabia, Egypt, Iraq, Syria and Yemen in exchange for the dropping of Russian agents into eastern European countries. Meanwhile, Lieutenant Gano received a letter, suggesting that the newly formed Polish Army stationed in Palestine should attack the axis oil pipeline in the Caucuses; but SOE had already signed a secret agreement with the NKVD forbidding allied action in each other's sphere of operation.. Stalin's objective of destroying the Second Republic and its government in exile, in order to establish a PRP in its place, had to be temporarily set aside until Germany had been defeated and British and American support was no longer required. When this was achieved, Stalin returned to the old agenda of destroying the Second Republic of Poland and eradicating the exiled Polish Government in London despite Maisky saying to Churchill, 'We do not intend to set up any kind of parallel government in Moscow.' 'Really?' Churchill replied, 'Yes really', Maisky replied.[10]

\* \* \*

What to do about Russia's attitude towards the Second Republic of Poland fractured the Polish diaspora in the West into two factions; eventually causing a crisis in the exiled cabinet in London. There were those, such as General Sikorski, the Polish Prime Minister, and Stanisław Mikołajczyk, his deputy, who believed that cooperation with Moscow would make the likelihood of the continued existence of the Second Republic more likely. Sikorski had said to Churchill that if the Germans held Poland, the Second Republic would be lost, but under the Russians, the chance of the Republic surviving, albeit in a different form, would be a possibility. He said, 'Let it be a Soviet Poland but still Poland;[11] suggesting that Sikorski was prepared to appease Stalin and his post war plans. However, there were those in the Polish diaspora, mainly in the military as it happened, allegedly individuals such as General Anders and General Sosnkowski among others, who argued that the Poles should not negotiate with Stalin over the future of the Republic. Whilst Sikorski in power, he was able to suppress the anti-Soviet faction. The official line of his administration was to work with Moscow and take advantage of Russia's predicament in the war.[12] By the same token, Russia was minded not to antagonize the Poles over the matter in order not to distress the British whose support in the Allied camp at the time was required. Just as soon as Germany was defeated in 1944 and Britain's cooperation became less important, Stalin returned to his old intention of establishing a People's Democratic Republic. As Maisky, the Russian ambassador to Britain , said, 'Our objective is, as it seems to me, to explode Sikorski's Government and clear the way for the creation of a more democratic and friendly Polish government by the time or at the time when the

---

10  Gabriel Gorodetsky (ed.), *The Maisky Diaries* (London: Yale University Press, 2015), p. 516.
11  Gorodetsky, Gabriel, (ed.) *The Maisky Diaries*, p. 289.
12  Michael Peszke, British Special Operations Executive Archives and Poland, *The Polish Review*, Vol. XLll, No 4, 1997, pp. 431-446.

Red Army enters Polish territory. This course is correct. Over the last two years and a half I have reached the conclusion that the London émigrés, including Sikorski's Government, are quite hopeless'.[13] However, Sikorski's tragic death, in an air accident off the coast of Gibraltar in 1943, allowed those among the Polish diaspora with anti-Russian sentiments to came to the fore, something that concerned the British greatly since such sentiment could easily undermine allied solidarity. London did not want anti-Russian Poles to complicate relations with Moscow, especially while Russia was carrying the heavy burden of the war on the Eastern Front. In order to calm the situation, Churchill argued robustly that the matter of Stalin's policy towards the Second Republic of Poland should be considered after the war. Although Britain, Poland and Russia, were allies, in reality they were fighting for different and opposing political objectives. As far as the Russians were concerned, they wanted to spread communism into central Europe, which of course included Poland. The Polish objective of those exiled in London was to preserve the Second Republic and reinstate the exiled government to Warsaw. The British aim was to maintain the integrity of the British Empire and to preserve Britain's super-power status. As far as the Americans were concerned the war was about establishing the United States as the premier economic and military super-power in the world.

\* \* \*

Once Russia had switched sides in the war and joined the Western allies, Britain decided to alter its attitude to the work of SOE's Polish Section. The British strategy from now on was to leave Eastern Europe to Stalin's design, and to offer the Second Republic little more than symbolic support.[14] From this point in time the mission that SOE Polish Section was not as straightforward as it had been. It was not only a question of supplying material to the Republic's Home Army, but also deciding what kind of equipment to make available without antagonizing Moscow. Nor was it clear who in Poland was the enemy, the Germans or the Germans and the Soviets or Polish communists? Unfortunately, for the British Government, this question was never satisfactorily resolved for in supporting the Polish authorities in the West it was actually working for the continued existence of the Second Republic of Poland, which was contrary to Soviet policy. This was an impossible situation. The SOE Polish Section has originally been established to support the Home Army, which was loyal to the Second Republic; but as far as the SOE Soviet Section was concerned it was Britain's responsibility to aid the Soviets, which would ultimately lead to the betrayal of the government of the Polish Second Republic. Clearly a compromise had to be found, although the preferred option would be to support Soviet Russia instead the Poles on account of her immense fire power. As far as Beaverbrook, member of Churchill's wartime cabinet was concerned, the problem arose out of Chamberlain's 'unfortunate guarantee' given to the Second Republic in 1939. He was reported to

---

13　Gorodetsky, (ed.). *The Maisky Diaries*, p. 512.
14　Jonathan Walker, *Poland Alone*, p.148.

have said to Moscow's ambassador in London, Ivan Maisky, 'Cursed be the day when Chamberlain gave our guarantees to Poland.'[15]

* * *

Meantime, on 7 November, 1941, the next SOE mission to Poland departed. The mission named Ruction, was commanded by Stanisław Król and was carrying Niemir Bidziński (pseudonym, 'Karol Ziege') Jan Piwnoik (pseudonym, 'Ponury') and Courier Napoleon Segiera (pseudonym 'Bronek'), as well as war material. The course was set for Lyszkowice. On the return leg the aircraft developed a fault and had to land in neutral Sweden. On hearing that an aircraft had to put down in Sweden, the Air Ministry wondered whether the Halifax Mk II allotted to the Poles was indeed reliable and robust enough for the arduous missions to Poland after all. It asked for modifications to be made before further flights were permitted. Perkins believed that this would only result in further delays which Poland could ill afford. He contacted the manufacturer, Hadley-Page, to obtain engineering drawings which he passed onto the Air Ministry asking for the decision to be reversed or at least speeded up. General Rudkowski argued that the Halifax was perfectly adequate so long as the aircraft was fitted with the more powerful type '20' Engines. This mission was followed by Operation Jacket on 27 December, commanded by Mariusz Wodzicki. On board were Marian Jurecki, (pseudonym 'Orawa') Maciej Kalenkiewicz (pseudonym 'Kotwicz') Alfred Paczkowski (pseudonym 'Wania') Andrzej Swiatkowski (pseudonym 'Armurat') and couriers Tadeusz Chciuk ('Celt') and Wiktor Strzelecki ('Buka'). Due to bad weather there was no reception committee waiting at the rendezvous point, Brozow Stary, but nevertheless the six men and four containers were dropped. Two of the agents, Marian Jurecki and Andrzej Swiatkowski ran into a German patrol whilst making their way to Warsaw and were shot. The others regained the containers and made contact with officers of the Home Army. They made it to Warsaw arriving on 3 January, 1942.

On 6 January 1942, Operation Shirt took off with the course set for Stefanow. The captain on the mission was Mariusz Wolzicki. Onboard ware Tadeusz Klimowski, (code name 'Klon'), Henryk Krajewski, ('Wicher'), Jan Marek, ('Walka'), Zbigniew Piasecki, ('Orlik'), Jan Smela, ('Wir') and courier Benedykt Moszynski, ('Andrzej'). The Poles were still troubled by the frequency of operations to Poland and called for Polish engineers to take over the servicing of the aircraft of Squadron 138,[16] in order to speed up the turnaround of the aircraft. However, the Poles were reminded that the Halifax fleet was not exclusively for Polish use and that they should not behave

---

15 Gorodetsky, (ed.) *The Maisky Diaries*, p. 239.
16 On 25 August 1941, No. 1419 (Special Duties) Flight was renumbered 138 Squadron. The unit's task was to maintain communications with resistance groups in occupied Europe. Not only did it make supply drops but it also landed in German occupied territory to drop and pick up agents. In October 1942 it discontinued pickup duties to concentrate on the delivery of supplies.

as if it was. Meanwhile, Air Vice Marshal Medhurst, informed SOE Polish Section that there would be no extra four-engine aircraft available for flights to Poland until the middle of 1942. Consequently, the Polish Section continued to rely on Whitleys. This of course then, limited drops to the West of Warsaw on account of the aircraft's range. Gubbins was correct in predicting that the news would spread despondency and a feeling of loss of hope amongst the Poles. The news also precipitated a crisis in the Polish cabinet. In an attempt to improve the mood, Portal wrote to Sikorski to inform him that special operation Flight 1419 was being made up to squadron strength using Polish personnel. At the same time, the Americans also extended lend-lease to the Poles which opened the door to obtaining the coveted Liberator aircraft. The Poles favoured the Liberator over the Halifax as it was easier to jump out of and was not so sensitive to icing and cross winds on take-off. It also had more reliable engines, which only required an overhaul every 700 flying hours compared to 250 hours of the Halifax. Its range was also greater, which was 2,210 miles of the Halifax. However, Portal, who did not want to lose these American machines to the Poles, wrote to Sikorski to tell him that the Liberators were unsuitable for flights to Poland and so would not be automatically deployed for Polish operations. Perkins disagreed and recommended that the Poles go ahead with the purchase of the aircraft, but despite this, Portal held his ground and made it known that the Poles should purchase Halifax aircraft instead. Consequently, three were delivered to 138 Squadron so flights could commence immediately. The Poles, felt aggrieved when they found out that the machines were to be shared with other SOE sections. It also became clear that some of the machines were not even airworthy and required major modifications before they could fly.

\* \* \*

Meantime, Frank dined at what he called the Ritz, commonly known as an ordinary British restaurant. These were part of a chain of Government run eateries. Frank had a stew costing eleven pence, potatoes and carrots and a bread roll followed by sultana pudding and custard and a cup of tea. The whole meal was 'quite tasty'. On the Saturday, Frank and Gerty went to the cinema to see the film 'It Started with Eve', which starred Charles Laughton and Deanna Durbin appeared. Frank noted in his diary that British Forces in Malaya had withdrawn to Singapore Island, putting a gap in the Lahore Causeway.[17] On 3 February Frank returned to the British Restaurant for lunch only to be told at 1.30 pm that there was no pudding left. After a short wait some Huntley & Palmers chocolate biscuits appeared together with 'Peak Freans' wafers. He noted that sugar was no longer served with tea.[18]

---

17  Peter Minett (ed.), *Frank's Wartime Diary*, pp. 328-329.
18  Minett, p.329.

# 12

# In Pursuit of Freedom

*In order for a war to be just ... it is necessary that the belligerents should have a right intention, so that they intend the advancement of good, or the avoidance of evil.*

Aquinas, *Summa Theologica*, II-II,4.1

Early 1942 was a dark time for the Allies. The Japanese advance in the Pacific reached its apogee with the conquest of Singapore whilst the Germans engaged in a titanic struggle with the Soviet Union the outcome of which was still uncertain. Rommel's Afrika Korps waged a ding-dong struggle with Allied forces in the North African desert which included the 3rd Polish Carpathian Brigade. Meantime, U-boats, prowling the Atlantic almost at will, threatened to starve Britain into submission before the United States, following the Pearl Harbor attack, entry into the conflict could make an impact. Before the year was out, the tide would turn at El Alamein, Stalingrad, Midway and Guadalcanal.

\* \* \*

By 30 April three additional SOE missions had successfully reached Poland, which brought the current 'operational season' to a close. According to Garliński[1], 12 flights (ten Polish, two British) had completed missions during this period which resulted in nine successful drops. As a result 48 parachutists, 19 containers and 13 packages had been successfully delivered. Losses amounted to one aircraft, two personnel, five containers and two parcels. The next flying period, called 'Intonation', was scheduled to begin on the 1 August 1942 and was scheduled to end on 30 April 1943. Meanwhile, Smoleński prepared a budget for the new year. He was planning for a decisive uprising to take place either in late 1942 or early 1943. He believed that 1942 would be his last chance to plan for a general uprising in the occupied country. Perkins was warned, that owing to price increases in Poland, more money would

---

1   Garliński, *Poland SOE and the Allies*, p. 235.

be required if the Home Army was to continue operating. News of the cessation of flights at the end of the Trial Period filtered through to the commander of the Home Army, who responded by lamenting the fact that the break in flights had compromised the plans completed. In order to reverse the fall of morale, Smoleński requested the RAF to extend its bombing campaigns to include German targets in occupied Poland. Dalton seemed taken by the suggestion and wrote to Sinclair requesting a special flight. He argued that this would prevent the Polish Government and the British losing face in the tormented country. In response a third Polish crew was attached to Squadron 138 although no extra bombing raids were planned. In the meantime, Medhurst announced that a Halifax had been successfully modified to meet Polish requirements. Unfortunately, the modification increased the weight of the aircraft to 61,000 lbs (27,600 kgs) which meant that it would require a longer runway. This resulted in the runway at Graveley, where Squadron 138 was stationed, being extended to one mile. The runway at Tempsford in Bedfordshire was likewise made longer. Group Captain Brian Boyle, was against the Poles flying the modified Halifax and even questioned the flying abilities of the current cadre of Polish pilots to do so. It appeared that such bigotry could only be put down to British arrogance.

\* \* \*

Following the departure of Smoleński from the Sixth Bureau on the 15 December 1941, Mikołajczyk the deputy Prime Minister, began to purge the Bureau of 'Sosnkowski's men' who were opposed to working with the Soviets. SOE awaited developments and prepared for the arrival of a new commander at the Bureau. General Tadeusz Rudnicki, who could be described as being a 'Sikorski's man' and therefore one of those who was prepared to work with the Soviets, was appointed. This was seen by the War Office as something positive. He was purported to have understood the difficult relations that existed between the Russians and the Poles and vowed never to discuss the work of the Bureau with Moscow, despite Sikorski's previous agreement to keep the Russians informed of all Polish operations on their territory. The Russians agreed to reciprocate. Gubbins reaffirmed his willingness to work with Rudnicki although he could not vouch for other departments. It was believed that the appointment of Rudnicki realigned the policies of the Sixth Bureau with the views of Sikorski and the War Office . SOE reaffirmed its view that the Sikorskiites were working with the sole intention of ousting the Germans from Poland and as a result, in his view, Sikorski remained the right man to back.

\* \* \*

Following the fall of France , Sikorski accepted that the war was going to be a long and prolonged affair and he warned the Home Army that it should prepare itself for the duration. He also made it known that his government, now exiled in London, was not working to maintain the status quo in the post-war Republic but intended to enable political and social change. Believing that the Poles should consider what they were fighting for rather than just what they wer fighting against, he would say repeatedly that he was not in the business of reviving the pre-war Polish regime but was looking for a fresh liberal democratic path for the Polish people. Put simply Sikorski was looking to reform the Second Republic and make it into a liberal democracy and so insisted that the Home Army must not be confined merely to the needs of resistance but must also play its part in formulating a new vision for the Republic. This meant that when SOE was supporting the Home Army it was by definition also supporting Sikorski's revolutionary ideals. This would antagonize Soviet plans to impose a People's Republic in Poland after the war. Britain's help for the Poles was a moral requirement, whilst its support for the Russians was a pragmatic necessity. In the meantime in autumn 1942, Sinclair, Secretary of State for Air, together with the Minister of Aircraft Production, Moore-Brabazon, promised he Polish Prime Minister the delivery of more aircraft for operations to the occupied country. Based on this information Sikorski enthusiastically wrote to Gubbins asking him to make arrangements for flights to be ready by 1 September. Gubbins contacted the Air Ministry seeking confirmation of the promise.

\* \* \*

As the year turned from 1941 to 1942, more delays hit operations to Poland. Operation Jacket and Operation Shirt, scheduled to fly in November 1941, actually flew on 27 December, 1941 and 6 January, 1942 respectively. The delays were blamed on weather conditions and technical difficulties. Rudnicki grew suitably frutrated and considered the latest missions as pathetically feeble. He wrote a note to Gubbins protesting that further disruption could not be tolerated and that all further planning of flights would be suspended by the Poles until the situation was clarified. His argument was protesting about the fact that operations to Poland seemed more of a patchwork of uncoordinated missions, bordering on political spin rather than a coherent programme of support. The Polish Section was taken aback by Rudnicki's outburst and argued that his action was unnecessary and pointless. Rudnicki eventually calmed down and requested that fresh material be delivered to Poland. He asked for 10,000 metres of Bickford Fuses, 10,000 sapper detonators, 2,000 electric switches and 2,000 quick acting cyanide pills. He did not make it clear how this material was to be delivered. Dalton wrote to Sinclair highlighting that the Poles had been promised a minimum of 12 flights minimum but had only received three to date. Sinclair allegedly sarcastically replied that the Poles should be given the sole responsibility of organising their own flights, so that they do not 'continue badgering us'. It was unclear whether this off-coloured and condescending comment was a serious suggestion, nevertheless, it did show how some were duplicitous towards the Poles.

\* \* \*

On 22 February, 1942 Hugh Dalton left SOE to become president of the Board of Trade. He was replaced by the well-connected 3rd Earl Selborne, who was a friend of Churchill and hence had good reach to the Prime Minister. Dalton had achieved much at SOE and it soon became clear that Selborne was equally up to the job. He was quick to improve relations between the SOE and the Foreign Office, which had been soured in the past by the apparent personal animosity between Dalton and Eden.[2] On 6 January, Operation Shirt took off on a course set for Stefanow. Unfortunately, it arrived one hour behind schedule, which exposed the reception committee to unacceptable danger. Against training protocal, the committee dispersed before the rendezvous was realized. The men and containers were dropped anyhow some 6 kilometres short of the planned rendezvous site. All the containers fell into German hands. Colonel Mitkiewicz-Zalter informed Selborne that it was not a problem if agents were not met by a reception committee, but this could not happen with containers which carried vital supplies. On the 3 March 1942, Operation Collar reached its target, Wyszkowa. It delivered 2,849,031 US Dollars in notes, 170,000 US Dollars in gold, 970,000 Reich Marks, and 70,000 Reich Marks in gold. Meanwhile, a separate Polish Flight was established but with no permanent crew. When Rudnicki heard of this development he by-passed the SOE and approached the Air Ministry directly in order to secure five slots for future missions. As soon as Perkins heard of this, he pointed out to him that the Ministry was not in a position to arrange drops without SOE approval and directed the Polish General back to Gubbins. Rudnicki was also under the misunderstanding that the Liberator Aircraft that had just come on stream were exclusively reserved for Polish use. Meanwhile, Rudnicki was reminded by Perkins that it was wrong of him to have ignored SOE in this way and that it should not be repeated. Rudnicki received the note grumpily, since he considered it to be a personal reprimand. His acidic response lost him some respect at SOE Polish Section and his 'star' fell. Operation Collar, flying on 3 March to Wyszkowa, was followed by Operation Boot on 27 March 1942, which flew to Przyrowa, Operation Legging to Barycz and Operation Belt to Podstoliska, which flew on the 30th. The original plan for Operation Boot was to fly on 27 February but this mission was aborted.

\* \* \*

Meanwhile, back in Staines, Frank wrote in his diary that Gerty had gone to the local butcher at 9.15 am in the hope of obtaining some liver and meat. She was informed that the 40 lbs of liver that had been delivered earlier that week had all been sold. Frank noted that the railings outside of the local Police Station had been removed for scrap and only a low white painted wall remained in position. In his diary Frank recorded that Gerty had ordered a bag of King Edward potatoes for 10 shillings and nine pence, as she feared that rationing would be extended. There was also the suspicion that soap would be put on ration as well as honey. Prices in local shops were also climbing. At Woolworth's feint-lined foolscap writing paper was four pence per sheet, split clothes pegs were 12 for seven pennies, whilst the cheapest

2   Walker, *Poland Alone*, p. 148.

greengrocer had a choice of forced rhubarb at four pence per ordinary stick size and six and a half pence for a bundle of immature sticks. Cups and soucers were no longer available at Woolworths but an unpretentious mug could be bought for one shilling. On 8 February Frank read in the Sunday press that soap was to be rationed and panic buying of what was left in shops ensued. At home Gerty, Frank's wife, had opened the last reserve of greengage jam from New South Wales. The news from Singapore continued to be grim. The only thing that lifted Frank's spirit was listening to the Central Band of His Majesty's RAF playing Eric Coate's 'The Man From the Country' and 'The Man from the Sea' from the 'Three Men Suite'. [3]

\* \* \*

Stanisław Jankowski, code name BUREK, recalled his training and parachute drop as part of the Polish Project. He may have embroidered his story with anecdotes but recalled how he received a letter from his commanding officer ordering him to report for training as an administrator. He thought that this must have been a mistake as he had never made a request for such a move and sought clarification. Stanisław was to learn later that the word 'administrator' was code for special forces training. He described his parachute training as straight forward until, that is, he had to jump from an actual aircraft. The first jump he described as 'scary as hell', but the fear eased with subsequent attempts. After completing his parachute training at Ringway he was awarded the badge of the *Cichociemni*, a swooping eagle. After his mission to Poland his badge was upgraded with the addition of a wreath to the eagle's talons and the phrase, 'For You My Country', engraved on the reverse side of the award.[4] As the time of his mission approached, Stanisław and his colleagues had been taken to a holding station where they were given passwords to be used on landing in the occupied country. They were then searched to check that they were not in possession of any object which could divulge their true identity. Stanisław was then kitted out with his flying tunic and parachute. After this stage had been completed, he and his colleagues had had to wait for further orders. Eventually, a British Officer entered the 'ready-room' and announced, 'Yellow warning for the Collars'. According to Stanisław, British Officers could not pronounce the names of Poish units so it was easier for them to use English code words such as, 'collar', the code name of Stanisław's mission which took place 3 March 1942. The word 'yellow' meant that the group had to stand by. If the mission was going ahead, the message would change to 'Red warning for the Collars'. The word 'Red' in this case meant, 'prepare for departure'. Stanisław and his colleagues gathered themselves and received their side arms. His party comprised six men and unsurprisingly they were allotted a number from one to six. When the party boarded the Halifax, agents one, three, and five sat on one side of the fuselage with their legs outstretched in front of them, whilst two, four and

---

3  Peter Minett (ed.), *Frank's Wartime Diary*, pp. 330-332.
4  *Testimony of Stanisław Jankowski* <http://www.vod.tvp.pl/video/dawno-temu-cichociemny> (accessed 14.09.2020).

six sat on the opposite side of the fuselage with their legs interlocking.[5] Their flight would take them over Denmark, then the southern tip of Sweden, the Baltic Sea and into 'Polish airspace'. However, the first attempt had to be aborted over Denmark, as it came up against heavy flak. He reported hearing bullets rattling against the aircraft as they bounced off the skin of the fuselage. On the second attempt, the pilot informed the men that they would be flying at a low altitude, as it was harder to hit aircraft flying just above sea level. Finally, the Halifax reached the drop zone, which was delineated by lamps. On the navigators green signal, the containers were pushed out of the fuselage, followed by the men jumping out one after the other. Stanisław landed safely, unbuckled his harness and stood up. A young man in civilian clothes ran towards him so he took out his side arm and aimed at the man. He called out, 'Halt, what is the password?' The young man froze and put his hands above his head and said, 'I have forgotten it.' Contrary to all training manuals, Stanisław took him into his arms and hugged him. He whispered, 'Forgive me, you are the first member of the Home Army that I have ever met.' Stanisław recalled that he had left London at 8pm and was in Warsaw by 8am the following morning.[6]

\* \* \*

Meanwhile, Colonel Bogdan Kwieciński, the cautious Air Attaché of the Polish Government, wrote to Gubbins urging that only Polish crews should be used in operations to Poland from now on, the advantage being that there would not be any language problems should an aircraft be forced down. Gubbins made representations to the Air Ministry, only to be rebuffed. However, Air Marshal Medhurst informed Gubbins that there would be a temporary shortage of four-engine aircraft for Polish duties lasting until mid-1942. The Ministry further exacerbated the situation by stating that there would be no possibility of operations to Poland on the scale that had been envisaged. When Sikorski heard of this, he protested that this broke a promise made to him. The information from the Air Ministry meant that operations to Poland would have to rely on the two engine Whitley, which given its slow speed would have to fly during the long nights of December to January under the cover of darkness. The limitations of the aircraft also meant that parachute drops could only be made West of the line from Warsaw to Nowy Sącz. The Air Ministry's news of the policy drift not only disappointed Sikorski but Gubbins too, for according to his understanding the Poles were indeed given a firm commitment that their requests would be met in full during late 1941 and early 1942.

\* \* \*

On 5 April the Staines Home Guard went on night manoeuvers. Frank describes their exercise in his diary and noted that the men left fully equipped with a rifle, steel

---

5    *Testimony of Stanisław Jankowski.*
6    *Testimony of Stanisław Jankowski.*

helmet, respirator, knapsack and so on, with the objective of reaching the railbridge at Longcross, a point on the railway line between Virginia Waters and Sunningdale, South of London. He reported that it was raining hard and 'as dark as a bag'. It was so dark that it was difficult to see the man in front. Nevertheless, they progressed in single file along the pavements and footpaths, where they existed. As the rain continued to fall rainwater soon found its way into their boots. As they reached Holloway Sanatorium, instead of taking the shortest route, they made a detour so that, according to their Officer in Charge, they might get a chance to dry off in the stronger wind there. At one thity in the morning they reached their objective and took off their sodden outer garments, spread out ground-sheets and got down to sleep. They decided to do this under the arch of the railway bridge and as was common with arched bridges, it collected all the 'draughts going' and the men could not warm up. Every now and then an engine or train thundered overhead and by three in the morning the mood of the men collapsed. They decided to build a small fire but it turned out that the bonfire did not produce much heat and the men remained cold. Nevertheless, they were able to make some tea in a can which was unpalatable given that the can had contained raw onions in a previous life. At approximately 5.30 am the Officer in Charge said they had better move or they would end up catching pneumonia. They proceeded to a clump of trees across Chobam Common. Frank reported in his diary, rather sarcastically when the Women's Voluntary Service came to the rescue with tea and sausages 'all good things come to an end'.[7]

\* \* \*

On September 9, the Americans extended lend-lease to the exiled Poles. This allowed them to bypass the Allied Purchase Commission for buying aircraft, which had blocked Polish requests at every turn, claiming that all the available bombers were reserved for Bomber Command. General Rudnicki informed Wilkinson that every effort would be made by the Poles to acquire Liberator aircraft from the Americans and that they would be reserved for Polish operations. However, he was informed in no uncertain terms that this could not be done and that his understanding of the protocol for procuring equipment was misplaced. This should have been obvious to Rudnicki since every aircraft based in Britain required RAF facilities to be able to fly. SOE Polish Section was taken aback by Rudnicki's angry response and made Perkins report that the close relationship that used to exist between the Sixth Bureau and the SOE Polish Section had faultered. He lamented the good old times when Smoleński was in charge of the Bureau and the atmosphere with the Poles had been cordial. Perkins believed that he was witnessing a cooling in relations and when Rudnicki established a new training programme for Polish recruits, Perkins complained that he had been unable to find anything out about the training programme. This seemed to confirm his belief that the relationship with the Poles had waned. What vexed Perkins was that the programme, being under the Allied Wing of the Special Training Centre,

---

7   Peter Minett (ed.), *Frank's Wartime Diary*, p. 346.

was not supervised by SOE. How can the programme, Perkins argued, be verified and approved, if it was unclear whether its training was up to standard? Perkins sent a British Officer, who was fluent in Polish, to enrol on the course and report back on the quality of the teaching. His conclusion was that the course provided students with insufficient technical knowledge for SOE requirements and classified it as 'substandard'. As a result, improvements were called for, with training having to be augmented with an SOE input. Perkins insisted that future training should start with a three week induction programme at Arisaig, run by English SOE personnel. This induction course replaced the one run by the Poles at Inverlochy. Only those individuals who completed the new SOE component of the course successfully could expect to continue with further training. In Perkins' system recruits could progress onto training at Ringway and finish their training at Beaulieu. Following this they would proceed to Audley End to finish their course and await dispatch to Poland. Rudnicki was not given any say regarding the changes. Meanwhile, Colonel Rudkowski approached Perkins with a grievance that General Rudnicki was 'not up to the job' at the Sixth Bureau. Apparently, Rudkowski had divulged that Rudnicki had side-lined Smoleński and was appointing his stooges onto the staff of the Bureau. Perkins appeared to agree. Rudnicki's situation deteriorated when it was alleged that he was attempting to purchase gold bullion which was being diverted from the Polish Project. Further complications arose when Rudnicki allegedly insisted that 12,500 pounds sterling, supplied to the Bureau be used to purchase US dollars in Sweden. Rudkowski suspected that Rudnicki's acquaintances were somehow benefitting from these transactions. When operational matters deteriorated and the relationship between the Sixth Bureau and the Polish Section had reached rock bottom, Perkins decided to get rid of Rudnicki by encouraging General Klimecki to remove him from his position. Rudnicki was replaced by Colonel Michael Protasewicz, a young, energetic individual, well-schooled in fluent French.

\* \* \*

Roundell Cecil Palmer, 3rd Earl of Selborne, known to his friends as 'Top', succeeded Dalton as Minister for SOE. His appointment was a step-up from his previous job as director of cement at the Ministry of Works and now with access to the Prime Minister, was keen to raise the profile of SOE. He sent out enthusiastic reports about SOE operations on a quarterly basis to Downing Street. The reports were also copied to the War Office. Selborne's intention triumphantly reported to Churchill that he had successfully made contact with the Polish Secret Military Organisation and a further 21 Polish special forces had been successfully trained for operations in Poland. In a later communique, he reported that SOE had developed a new piece of equipment that could easily cut through railway tracks and was suitable for use in Poland. To support this view, he reported that the Poles had been successfully trained in using the device and that they could readily train others to do so once they were back in Poland. Selborne concluded, that if a sufficient number of these devices was transported to Poland, enormous damage could be done to German lines of communication in the East of the country. He used this belief to argue for an increase of SOE flights to Poland. His early work for SOE was concerned with persuading the reticent War Cabinet to make more aircraft available for Polish operations — no easy task when the hawkish Arthur 'Bomber' Harris was in post. Selborne pointed out that so far SOE Polish Section had only succeeded in sending barely enough material to Poland to keep the underground organisations alive. The reason given for this situation was the shortage of aircraft. He acknowledged that the Air Ministry had placed a further two Halifax aircraft at SOE's disposal but complained that these were not yet air worthy. He also made a request for more railway sabotage equipment to be delivered to Poland, justifying the request by arguing that it would assist the Russians to withstand the 'German juggernaut'. The response of the COS was to invite the Ministry of Economic Warfare to consult the Secretary of State for Air. to devise the best possible plans to give effect to Selborne's request. The cautious Air Ministry responded by pointing out that flights to Poland in the latest season could only be carried out up to May 1942 and only to an area measuring 30 square miles south east of Płock. When this was put to the Poles, they replied that this region was impractical as it would require the resistance to operate on territory very close to the German border. They argued that the zone should be expanded to some 60 square miles. However, the Air Ministry was unconvinced as even here, it argued, an abnormal risk to aircraft would have to be accepted and furthermore a further two or three flights were unlikely to make very much difference to the situation on the ground. SOE was convinced that RAF policy towards flights to Poland needed clarification. Selborne wrote to Sinclair pointing out that the Poles had been promised 12 flights, whereas to date only three had been attempted. Selborne informed Sinclair that priority should be given to operations to Poland. The Ministry also made enquiries of Selborne as to why SOE appeared to be unwilling to risk Polish pilots before the possible resumption of flights in September 1942.

\* \* \*

In May, Hambro, a successful industrialist, had replaced the tired Frank Nelson as Executive Director of SOE, bringing in important changes to SOE. For example, he relegated SOE operations to a secondary level of importance, placing them behind standard military operation. This drastic change in emphasis came in just as planning for the invasion of Europe by the Western allies was coming on stream. Unfortunately for the Poles, as the importance of Overlord increased the urgency of SOE operations to Poland appeared to recede. This was demonstrated by the fact that the Home Army received a tenth of the supplies that were delivered to Greece and barely one twentieth of that dropped in France and Yugoslavia.[8] This, of course, had serious consequences for the planning of a general uprising in occupied Poland.

\* \* \*

---

8   Lynne Olson, and Stanley Cloud, *For Your Freedom and Ours*, p. 283.

At the Defence Committee meeting on 26 March, Selborne proposed the sole use of Liberator aircraft for flights to Poland. A day later this proposal was approved, leading to a meeting between Selborne and Gubbins, and Sinclair at the Air Ministry. Having pondered Selborne's proposition, Sinclair rejected the idea but offered five extra Halifax aircraft instead. He also promised to make systemic improvements to ensure that Squadron 138 was at the peak of its readiness during the next moon period. In order to gain complete control it was suggested that the squadron it transferred from RAF command to SOE command; however, this was not endorsed. Later that year, 30 September 1942, SOE signed an agreement with the Soviet NKVD.[9] It covered mutual assistance in clandestine work, excluding operations being undertaken in each other's sphere of influence. After scrutinising the agreement, the Poles expressed concern that it suggested that the Western allies would only be able help the Poles if the Soviets agreed. To alleviate this concern the Polish Section agreed to consider the Poles as a special case and therefore outside the terms of agreement, allowing SOE flights to Poland to continue. There were no protests from Moscow about the adjustment. Operation Cravat heading for Drzewicz took off on 8 April 1942, using a Halifax aircraft,. However, SOE repeated to the Poles that significant help could only be assured with Soviet support.

\* \* \*

On 20 April, a Polish crew was lost on a non-Polish mission. As a consequence, Lieutenant Colonel Barry, the Director of Plans, asked the Air Ministry if the remaining Polish crews could be reserved solely for Polish operations. The Ministry did not give any assurance but did provide a list of Polish pilots to replace the losses. In late 1942 efforts were made to improve communications between RAF aircraft and the drop zones reception committees. The introduction of radio/telephones was intended to help pilots make contact with reception groups at greater distances, however, this was not very successful, as signal reception proved unreliable during trials,. One improvement tested was the use of high frequency transmitters at the drop zone, which transmitted a radio beam towards the aircraft in order to assist the pilot to find the glide path to the target.[10] It was envisaged that a wireless beacon would enable accurate drops to be made in the absence moonlight.[11] Despite some improvements in reception being made, the radio equipment was in such short supply that it made little difference and so pilots continued to depend on their own flying skills and the map reading abilities of their navigators. During autumn 1942 the improvements were such that drop zones were able to receive larger loads (960 Kg). Aircraft approached target zones at an altitude of between 300 to 500 metres. Invariably, the first items to be dispatched were metallic containers stuffed with equipment.

---

9   The People's Commissariat for Internal Affairs.
10  TNA HS8/897/7: Correspondence with Winston Churchill – six-page report on the organisation and activities of SOE.
11  TNA HS8/897/7.

Two designs of containers were used so that despatch and delivery methods could be standardised. Type 'C' cylindrical containers were made of galvanised steel with a diameter of approximately one metre, and two and a half metres in length. Known as drop containers they had four carrying handles riveted to the body and opened into two halves. Once dropped they were emptied by the reception group and then hidden or destroyed. The second type of container, designated 'H', was a Polish design. It had similar dimensions to the 'C' type, but the cylindrical body was made up of a set of drums or short cylinders joined together by strong chains. The flexibility of this design was supposed to reduce impact forces when they hit the ground. The containers could be loaded into the bomb bay, but those heavier than 100 weight were stored in the fuselage during the flight and pushed out over the drop zone by the dispatcher. Every container was filled with equipment at Packing Stations working under licence for the SOE. Each shift of packers prided themselves on the speed and efficiency of their skills and were invariably staffed by female personnel. This was particularly the case when it came to the precise folding and packing of parachutes. Typically, the second items to be released from the aeroplane were packages which could withstand impact with the ground and usually contained items issued by the Polish Government. The whole operation was designed to last no longer than approximately 10 minutes.

\* \* \*

In the meantime, on the Home Front, Gerty and her son Michael travelled to Tadworth Court Hospital in Surrey, where Eileen worked as a nurse. Spring had arrived early and the sunshine made the trip 'very pleasant'. With Eileen's probationary period coming to an end Gerty knew that this would be the last opportunity to see Tadworth Court. The journey took them over Epsom Downs Race Course, past the grandstand where she pondered how peaceful and calm the Downs appeared. She looked at the grandstand whilst they drove past and found it odd that the lift shaft had the phrase 'To Boxes Only' painted on them. She was also interested in the heaps of chalk that could be seen all over the racecourse. She thought that the Downs looked so different now than they had done 12 year ago on her first visit. Finally seeing Eileen in her uniform and sharing tea with her during her break made the visit most impressive and memorable.[12]

\* \* \*

Despite Gubbins' enthusiasm following the apparent success of the first operation period, it soon became clear that any future successes would depend on more aircraft being made available for missions. However, at the time this seemed a remote possibility. David Stafford, pondered whether, under such circumstances, using the Polish Home Army as a keystone detonator for individual acts of sabotage was the best way forward. Despite the prevailing problems, preparation for a national uprising

---

12   Peter Minett (ed.), *Frank's Wartime Diary*, p. 343.

remained the ultimate guiding principle for the Polish resistance. After all, the Poles had never been content with isolated acts of sabotage and subversion, preferring a decisive national uprising which, if successful, would finally free the nation from occupation; it was just a question of how and when. In January 1942 the Situation Report for Poland was published. It covered the last quarter of 1941 and stated that 7,446 individual acts of sabotage had been completed resulting in a fall in industrial output (equivalent to 30% of gross national production). The BBC triumphantly announced this success, although unfortunately this precipitated German reprisals on the civilian population. Following this cruel German action, the Home Army insisted that, in future, news of Polish successes should not be broadcast. On 1 September, 1942 two flights, code-named Operation Chickenpox heading for Stanisławow and Operation Smallpox flying to Bogatki, took off successfully using Halifax aircraft. These were followed by Operation Rheumatism to Lyszkowice and Operation Measles heading for Stachlew on 3 September. Despite these successes, the dearth of flights compared to other theatres once again threatened to become a flashpoint between the Poles and the British. To avoid further angst Sikorski suggested setting up a joint Polish and British committee in order to coordinate plans for Poland. On 29 September, the Joint Planning Staff informed Sikorski that SOE had already received specific instructions regarding the coordination of the activities and therefore such a committee was not needed. They also included in the communique that all planning would proceed, as before, with SOE liaising with the Polish Sixth Bureau using staff specifically trained for the purpose. Sikorski was not satisfied and instructed the Polish Military Attaché in Washington to approach the Americans with a request for six B24 Bombers. In a correspondence from Roosevelt to Churchill, the former observed:

> Our good friend, General Sikorski, has been urging us to assign at least six B-24 aircraft for the maintenance of his liaison with Poland. I have just written him that the United States cannot take action on his request without jeopardising basic agreements in which the United States and Great Britain have accepted responsibilities for the provision of aircraft within the various theatres of operations. Poland is within the British theatre of operations and responsibility.[13]

This reply was dated 9 December and pointed out that in accordance with Allied arrangements, Poland was a British responsibility and in any case the US had no spare aircraft available for additional commitments. On 21 December, Gubbins told Hollis that the Poles had already been informed to continue working through the SOE Polish Section as it was charged with planning and procuring all requirements for secret missions to Poland. In frustration Sikorski proposed a scheme to transfer the British based Polish airborne division to concentrate exclusively on missions to Poland. This proposal was rejected by Sir Alan Brooke, Chief of Staff, but to diffuse any tension an assurance was given that assistance for the Poles would not be interrupted, although it

---

13 TNA HS8/897/53: Correspondence with Winston Churchill regarding requests from General Sikorski for B-24s.

was emphasised that SOE could not directly support any military invasion of Poland. Sikorski was reminded again that the SOE was the correct organisation and not the Americans for the procurement of materials for the Home Army. Clearly, the British did not approve of Sikorski freelancing with the Americans; nevertheless, to reduce tension Sikorski reassured Brooke that Poles would continue cooperating and working with SOE. Meanwhile, Brook expressed that equipment was disappearing after it had been landed in Poland. The problem, according to him, was that the equipment was packed in such a way that it could not be hidden easily nor moved from the drop zone without difficulty even if horse-drawn carriages were available. The Poles also requested that the drop zones be no larger than 500 square metres, for anything larger required agents to scour the countryside looking for containers released from aircraft. This, the Poles argued, would also mean a drop height of 400 metres could be employed. It was recommended that about 20 containers should be delivered in any one drop which would mean that the weight of any delivery would not exceed 500 kilograms. SOE Polish Section was shocked to learn of the thefts of equipment taking place on the ground after drops. Following enquiries, it was informed that collection and evacuation was in some cases so slow that it left containers exposed and vulnerable to theft by unauthorised underground units. SOE called for further training to take place designed to speed up the work of reception parties in drop zones.

\* \* \*

On 1 October, 1942 four missions were despatched, Hammer, (heading for Gloskow), Gimlet (flying to Zyczyn), Chisel (flying Lupiny) and Lathe (flying to Zyczyn), all using Halifax aircraft. The last mission of the year took off on 29 October code named Pliers, was captained by Mariusz Wodzicki. It was unfortunately shot down enroute. The change to these missions was that a Polish liaison officer was present at Tempsford to oversee their despatch. His role was to inform the crew on the type and quantity of materials loaded on board their aircraft. Meanwhile training of personnel continued. During 28 October 1942 a meeting between the Polish Section and the Sixth Bureau, announced that further training on railway sabotage would take place at Brickendonbury Manor in Hertfordshire. Also, it was divulged that coaching in the use of anti-tank weapons would soon be available at Audley End. The Poles were further informed that white camouflage clothing would soon be available for winter operations in the Tatra Mountains in Southern Poland. On 30 October, during a debrief of Operation Pliers, agents were warned that no unauthorised material was to be taken on aircraft prior to departure. It had been noted that one agent had taken food on board, which he planned to consume in Poland.

\* \* \*

On the night of 29 October, Flight Lieutenant Stanisław Król flew a twin-engine Whitley on a Polish Government mission to bomb the HQ of the Gestapo in

Warsaw. Uncertain of the precise position of this target he made for his back-up target, Okencie airfield. On dropping his bombs, he turned for home, but on his return journey Król was attacked by two German night fighters which forced him to ditch in the English Channel near Sheringham where the crew was rescued by the coast guard. Król's mission was successful, whereas Operation Wrench, piloted by M. Wodnicki, had crash in Southern Norway killing all on board including Jerzy Bichniewicz, Stanisław Hencel and Wiesław Szapkowski. Their cargo of 156,000 US dollars and 70,000 Reich marks was also lost. In the last two months of 1942 all flights to Poland were suspended even though the weather was good.[14] Bomber crews were reassigned to missions over Norway and France and providing cover for allied landings in North Africa. Such last-minute changes angered the Poles and were also a source of irritation to SOE officials. Lord Selborne wrote to the Air Ministry that those who had delayed or postponed drops to Poland had failed to appreciate the enormous planning that gone into preparing missions.[15]

14  Lynne Olson and Stanley Cloud, *For Your Freedom and Ours*, p. 283.
15  Olson and Stanley, p. 283.

## 13

# Why Can't Life be Simple?

By mid-1943, the Polish Section of SOE was growing into a competent and professional operation. Training of Polish Special Forces was progressing well and recruitment was sound. The SOE Section continued working closely with the Sixth Bureau although significant differences in policy sometimes emerged. One such difference, which cannot be ignored, centred on how the Home Army should react once Overlord was in progress. Should it coordinate its action with the Western Allies (Britain and America) or with Soviet Russian Allies approaching Poland from the east? The Poles wanted to do the former, whilst the British and Americans argued that it would be far more logical if they did the latter. In the meantime the Poles decided that most benefit would be gained if the uprising concentrated Warsaw, the most potent symbol of Polish nationhood. The other concern was timing; when should the rising be launched to ensure maximum effect? The Poles received mixed advice here. On the one hand, the Chiefs of Sstaff were counselling caution and restraint, a message which was endorsed by Churchill and was passed onto the Home Army via Radio Świt (the mouthpiece of the Second Republic's Government broadcasting from Britain). Churchill informed the Poles that they should wait to be told when to rise as they would be given fair warning before anything significant happened on the 'second front'. He also told them to ignore the 'stuff' that the British were putting out for German consumption in London's war of nerves with Berlin. On the other hand after discrediting Radio Świt as a mouthpiece of Nazi sympathising Poles, Moscow, broadcasting from Radio Kościuszko (the mouthpiece of Polish communists exiled in Russia) called upon the Home Army to rise up immediately as the Red Army was not far from Warsaw and was ready to help the insurgency. This contradiction unsettled the Brtish Chiefs-of-Staff in London and so priority was given to harmonising directives. According to the COS it would be wrong to encourage large scale guerrilla activity before the Western allies were ready to invade Europe, as this would result in false hopes. It was now clear to the Poles that it would be the Red Army that would liberate Poland from German occupation and not the western allies as was hoped; however, it was still necessary to counter Russia's advice and to arrive at an agreement on timing. Britain concluded that broadcasts to the Home Army should run along the lines of: organise in secret, but do not be rash, ignore German propaganda about the second front and wait for a message from COS in London. Regarding the harmonisation of British and Soviet policy on timing, two possible strategies were identified: to either take up the matter with the Soviet government as a general question of policy throughout Europe, or to address the specific case of Poland during bilateral meetings. The latter approach would also allow for wider discussion regarding the Polish question, such as Russo-Polish friction, incitement to premature revolt and attempts by the Soviet sponsored press to discredit the more cautious policy of the Polish Government. London decided to make a limited approach at first. In the meantime, the Polish Government in London decided to leave the final decision concerning the start of the uprising to the Home Army command in Warsaw, arguing that it would be best placed to make such a decision. General Bor-Komorowski, the commander of the Home Army, decided that the Warsaw uprising would begin on 1 August 1944 at 17.00 hours[1].

\* \* \*

The Polish authorities of the Second Republic in the West fell into two camps regarding Soviet intentions towards the Second Republic. Camp one, which allegedly included Sikorski and Mikołajczyk, was prepared to believe that Stalin would not destroy the Second Republic, especially in full view of the British. The second camp, which included many in the Polish High Command fighting under British operational command, did not trust a word the Russian leadership was espousing believing that Moscow's intention is to replace the Second Republic in favour of a People's Republic just as soon as the Red Army had reached Berlin. General Anders, commander of the Second Corps, not surprisingly warned against making deals with the Russian regime that had kept him in captivity between 1939 and 1941. Truszkowski, seemingly also in camp two, even went as far as to criticise General Sikorski for not being firm enough with Stalin early on in negotiations regarding the nation's regime change and Poland's territorial integrity, even if this threatened to disrupt allied unity. In Truszkowski's eyes the choice was clear, either resist the Red Army as it swept westward across Polish territory towards Berlin, which would be quite irrational, or risk Poland becoming a Soviet socialist republic. Unfortunately, these fratricidal differences placed SOE Polish Section in a quandary. Should it continue supplying the Home Army at the risk of some of its fighting units 'facing off' the Red Army, or stop supplies altogether and risk the wrath of the allied Poles in London? The British Government was quite clear; if the Poles did not want to critically jeopardise SOE support they should renew diplomatic relations with Moscow. As Robert Bower was to say in the House of Commons, 'I am not prepared to regard Soviet Russia as a freedom loving nation, but we cannot do without her now…I know they have shot a lot of people but there are about 170,000,000 of them still

1   Kochański, *The Eagle Unbowed*, p. 402.

left'.² Sikorski's approach was to adhere to the British preference however, this did not silence his political opponents. Rumours spread that if he refused to change his position an attempt would be made to remove him from office. When Sikorski heard of these unconfirmed rumours, he cancelled all leave, increased manoeuvres, put in closer monitoring of Polish units in Britain and increased security at his headquarters in the Rubens Hotel in London.

\* \* \*

On 25 January 1943, Operations 'Brace', 'Screwdriver' and a day later, 'Gauge' departed for the Second Republic. As far as 'Brace' was concerned everything did not go to plansince it had supposed to fly on 29 October 1942, but it had had to return to base without reaching its planned target. The men on board, Ignacy Bator ('Opór'), Tadeusz Gaworski ('Lawa'), Roman Rudkowski, ('Rudy'), and courier Wiktor Czyzewski ('Cap'), were dropped 'blind' some distance from the target zone on account of German Forces being present at the official drop zone. The speculation was that Wing Commander Rudkowski had ordered the drops to proceed despite the official drop zone being missed. There were also missions in February 1943: Rasp, Vice, Saw, Floor, Wall, Spokeshave, Rivet and File. Operations Vice and Rivet were unsuccessful. This is how Francis Griffiths of the RAF described his mission to Poland. He started by saying that a mission to Poland meant leaving Tempsford in daylight so as to arrive at Skargerrak just after dark. Then, 'nipping across the tip of Sweden' and getting a fix on Bornholm.³ He wrote, 'when we reached Poland it was a question of navigating by moonlight and water (the river Vistula).' Because of fuel shortages the route back had to be shortened so a dash across Denmark between Kiel and Fleensburg was used.⁴ The month of March saw nine missions to Poland taking place followed by a break in operations until the September. Missions were part of the next phase of operations. These referred to as 'Riposte' which lasted from August 1943 to July 1944. Lessons had been learnt from the previous periods and the scene was set for the instigation of more flights. By this time the British war economy had reached full capacity. Experience had shown the advantages of labelling the contents of packages and containers using coded labels. For example, packages were labelled as either containing mining equipment or bombing making materials or medicines and so on. Therefore, a full coding system was inaugurated which improved the efficiency of loading, delivery and distribution of materials. During the Intonation Period of operation (August 1942 to April 1943) 65 missions were completed with 42 successful drops.⁵ Twenty-nine Polish crews and 13 British crews were responsible for the successes during this period. 119 parachutists landed successfully, including 109 military personnel, political couriers and one Hungarian national.

2  Robert Bower MP, House of Commons, *Hansard*, HC Deb 15 March 1939
3  Small inhabited island off Denmark.
4  Adam Zamoyski, *The Forgotten Few* (London: John Murray, 1995), p.146-147.
5  Garliński, *Poland, SOE and the Allies*, p. 235.

241 containers, 86 packages, 58 kit-bags and 13,022,000 worth of US dollars and gold bullion were delivered. 5,000,000 German marks were also landed during the period. Besides arms and explosives, there was a need for signals equipment and so there was a surge during 'Intonation' in the delivery of radio receiver sets and transmitters. It was also the period which saw container design improve. The losses during Intonation amounted to six aircraft, four parachutists, 42 containers, 14 packages and seven kit bags. This amounted to 8.1 tons or about 16.4% of the total dispatched. Out of the losses three crews were saved three were lost – two Polish one British. By late spring 1943, nine agents had lost their lives on active service. The General Staff of the Home Army called for reprisal bombing of German targets. The Air Ministry disagreed, arguing that bombing was already being carried out on industrial complexes and German cities.[6] In early autumn, the Germans erected a strong anti-aircraft battery in Denmark, which became a formidable barrier to RAF planes flying to Poland from Britain. Consequently, a new route was planned taking planes over Gothenburg, Sweden, across the Baltic Sea and then south to the Polish coast. This route was 200 to 300 km longer one way and was beyond the range of the Halifax. In order to help the situation three four engine B24 Liberator aircraft were assigned to 138 Squadron.

\* \* \*

On the death of General Sikorski in July 1943, Stanisław Mikołajczyk became the Prime Minister and General Sosnkowski was appointed the new Commander in Chief of Polish Forces in the West. Sosnkowski met with the British in support of the Home Army. He was able to point to impressive statistics, which demonstrated Poland's ardent underground operations: 20 derailed trains, 180 damaged locomotives and the death of 1,000 German soldiers and so on. His intention was to show that SOE support for Poland yielded positive results and that the work of the Polish Section and the Sixth Bureau should continue. However, he was shocked when he learnt how meagre the actual supplies to Poland were when compared to other countries and so protested to SOE Polish Section regarding the situation. The reason he was given for this state of affairs was that supplying the Home Army continued to be agonizingly difficult because the Germans had established a defensive line of anti-aircraft guns stretching from Denmark to Bavaria. Sosnkowski, who became uncharacteristically agitated, could not accept the explanation and considered the low number of drops as 'foot dragging' by the British and lambasted the SOE for not working in lock step with the Poles. From this point in time the relationship between Sosnkowski and the British became strained. SOE communicated the Polish General's frustration to the War Office in October writing that Polish authorities in London had expressed extreme dissatisfaction with the arrangements being made for the Home Army and had threatened to approach the COS and Secretary of State for Air directly and inform them that they would be forced to give

---

6   Garliński, *Poland SOE and the Allies*, p. 235.

orders for the cessation both of resistance in Poland and the transmission of intelligence to London if the situation did not improve. Selborne informed Churchill of the threat whilst expressing sympathy for the Polish standpoint. Meanwhile, Sosnkowski lobbied General Alan Brooks, Chief of the Imperial General Staff. He confirmed that Gubbins, Executive Director of SOE, promised 12 flights per night which meant 250 flights for the quarter, ending 31 December, with a further 350 the following quarter. According to Sosnkowski the actual number of flights that had taken place was nowhere near the number quoted. Selborne, Minister for SOE, met Sosnkowski to discuss the Polish dissatisfaction. Sosnkowski reiterated the disparity between the number of flights promised and the number which had actually taken place. He warned that the shortage of materials for the secret army was compromising its effectiveness. At the time of this unfortunate flareup, all that SOE had at its disposal was one flight of six aircraft manned by Polish crews. The Poles had been informed that these aircraft were primarily at their disposal but could be used in other theatres at short notice. Prior to the opening of fresh Polish operations in September, SOE Polish Section talked of 300 possible flights during the eight months remaining (36 flights per month) in the season. However, during September, the first month of operations, only 16 flights were completed successfully. This did not take into account that on the first night a special effort had been made and a total of 11 aircraft was dispatched, almost double the usual number that would normally fly. The decision to discontinue these operations occurred because four of the 11 aircraft failed to return. Experience from September demonstrated that enemy defences en route had been strengthened considerably and therefore it was necessary to find a new way of getting to Poland. An alternative would be to fly over the Balkans, which would require the acquisition of a different airfield to Tempsford. Although a number of possible sites was considered, the airfield chosen was at Brindisi in Italy. This land-based airfield was built at Camp Casalle and had opened on 30 July, 1933 by Duce Benito Mussolini. In the meantime, the War Office had compiled a report in answer to Polish protests regarding the suspension of flights. It began by pointing out that all cessations were temporary and were caused solely by the strength of enemy defences encountered during September, which had caused an unacceptable level of losses. It was explained to the Poles that the latest thinking was to find a new route so as to avoid flying over central and northern Europe. Bases in Italy were mentioned as possible alternatives. The War Office then addressed the complaint regarding the diversion of aircraft to operations other than to Poland. The British believed that this complaint showed a fundamental misunderstanding by the Poles, who had already been informed that although primarily intended for work in Poland, the six aircraft manned by Polish crews must be regarded as an integral part of the squadron available for employment in other theatres, as directed by the Station Commander. Regarding the target of 300 flights given to the Poles, this was a theoretical maximum which six aircraft might attain but should not be regarded as a firm commitment.

\* \* \*

At the root of the Polish complaints lay deeper causes of discontent. For example, the Poles did not appreciate why they had to work on matters related to resistance in Poland solely through the SOE Polish Section, which by now they considered to be 'unfit for purpose'. They also failed to realise that, whereas in their own organisation the support of resistance in Poland was of paramount importance, this form of warfare could not occupy a comparable position in relation to the war effort as a whole. Also, because adverse decisions were always communicated to them by the SOE, whatever channel of communication they used, it gave them the impression that it was the SOE that was obstructing Polish plans. Hollis wrote to A. E. Nye 18 October 1943, explaining that the Poles were being 'thoroughly tiresome.' The Sixth Bureau, whilst acknowledging the success of SOE as the supplier of materials for Poland, enquired whether it was possible to recast its relationship with the COS by creating a special Inter–Allied General Staff for planning strategy, which they would expect to participate in. Of course, Hollis knew that the COS 'have not the slightest intention of setting up such a group,' although he was sensitive to the fact that the Poles were, owing to strained Polish–Soviet relations, extremely suspicious and 'capable of seeing the influence of Moscow in even the most trifling incidents which did not accord with their wishes.' Polish HQ, very naturally, desired that it should be the sole authority responsible for the support of resistance in Poland. Sosnkowski wrote to the War Office in late October stating that it was probably the last chance to equip fighters in Warsaw who would contribute to the war effort and consequently all possible measures should be taken immediately to meet Polish demands. The War Office seemed to accept the Polish argument and pressed the Air Ministry to increase flights from the Mediterranean theatre. Selborne urged for an increase in allocated aircraft for Poland from the two which were airworthy. On 30 October, Air-Command in the Mediterranean informed the Air Ministry that Brindisi was ready to receive three Liberators and three Halifaxes of the Polish Flight. It was to be placed under operational control of 334 Wing headquarters. Churchill stipulated, over the head of Air Marshal Porter, a three–fold increase in the allocation of aircraft for missions to Poland arguing that the diversion of 12 aircraft from bomber command was a small price to pay to keep the Poles happy. But there was one serious fact that was being kept from the Poles which rendered their planning for an uprising obsolete and inappropriate. Unbeknown to them the COS had already rejected giving any assistance to an uprising on the grounds that it would be too difficult, if not impossible, to deliver adequate quantities of supplies that such military action would require. It was unfortunate that this decision was not shared with the Polish HQ and so the Poles continued to plan as if the delivery of equipment would not be a problem. At first glance it seemed the decision was a practical problem but in reality it was also a political decision designed so as not to antagonize the Soviet Union. In the meantime, a series of operations, collectively called 'Neon', were flown during the month of September using Halifaxes. The drop sites were Osowiec, Lucznica, Tluszcza, Nieporet, Wyszkowa and Milenia. Operation Neon 9 was shot down. On 18 October, Operation Oxygen 8 was dispatched which was the last fight of 1943. The overall tonnage delivered during this period was barely sufficient for sabotage work, never mind a military uprising. It might also have been the case that Britain did not want a powerful Home Army to exist as it could have snarled up the Red Army's front line in the east.[7]

* * *

SOE operations in 1944 increased significantly as the endgame of the war approached. Many resistance organisations in Europe had become more active in order to assist the allies in their progress to victory, to secure political power in their country, or to prevent an opposition faction becoming all too strong. In Poland the aim of the Home Army was to assist the government of the Second Republic, exiled in London, to return to power in Warsaw, something Stalin had taken note of. This political objective necessitated an increase in SOE flights to Poland and, according to the Home Army, a need to coordinate operations with Overlord. An unfortunate consequence was that this put the British into an awkward position as they did not want to be associated with anti-Russian factions in the Polish diaspora, which had been emboldened by Sikorski's death. It was clear that the British Chief of Staff had to find a compromise between supporting the Poles without antagonising the Russians and visa-versa. The compromise, as the British saw it, was to increase SOE supplies to Poland, which demonstrated commitment to the Poles, but on the proviso that the delivered materials were not used against the Red Army or on territory East of the Curzon Line which the Red Army had liberated and claimed for itself. Cosequently, the British ensured that the nature of the equipment sent to Poland only allowed for sabotage activity and not for full scale military operations, such as a full blown rising. This should have shown the Poles that under such restrictions a successful uprising was well nigh impossible. Unfortunately, this was missed by the Polish High Command and the British failed to make the point forcibly enough. There were some, such as Generals Sosnkowski and Anders, who understood the dangers of a rising under such conditions and argued robustly against it. Others, such as General Bor-Komorowski, the normally cautious Commander in Chief of the Home Army, believed that once a rising had started it would force the hand of the British to step up the supply of military equipment. As things turned out a rising was authorised but the delivery of material remained sporadic despite Selborne promising Sosnkowski that the number of SOE flights would be increased significantly. Similarly, the COS confirmed that the Polish flight based in Brindisi would be increased to 12 aircraft, with the authority to use a further six belonging to 334 Wing when available. Consequently, six Halifaxes were brought from 300 Squadron to the base in Italy. The availability of aircraft from other theatres, due to the arrival of American machines, resulted in the Polish flight growing to 18. For the first time in the conflict the increases were of such magnitude that there was a significant chance that they would be transformative. The increase in the size of the flight also provided SOE Polish Section with

---

7   Michael Peszke, British Special Operations Executive Archives and Poland, *The Polish Review*, Vol. XLII, No. 4, 1997:431-446

much needed flexibility in the planning of operations. Air Ministry misssions saw a temporary increase in tonnage delivered to the Second Republic from three and a half tons in February, March and April 1944, to 240 tons in the period from April to June. However, this proved to be difficult to sustain and so the tonnage fell back to 150 tons during the period from July to September. In comparison the equivalent of 3,400 tons was dropped on Yugoslavia during the same time. Calculations suggested that the possibility of delivering materials to Poland could be increased six-fold although Perkins suggested to Gubbins that no figures should be used when talking to the Poles, as they had a 'tendency to view numbers as promises.' Reassuring communications were also arriving from MAAF in Algiers, which were informing the Air Ministry in London that the Poles could feel assured that, whenever weather permitted, aircraft would be put at their disposal; the only limiting factor being the availability of reception committees. During the night 8/9 April, 1944, three sorties took off with full success. Sosnkowski wrote to Ismay sharing his joy and asked for 'more of the same.' It appeared that a high-water mark had been reached with help for Poland and Perkins (Polish Section) contacted Mikołajczyk to inform him that alas the Polish Parachute Brigade will not be sent to Poland as requested and this despite 130 men being ready to fly. Instead, they were to be redeployed to the Second Corps fighting at the Italian peninsula as part of the British 8th Army's Italian campaign. On the first of June Perkins informed the COS that German industry was being moved eastward, deeper into occupied Poland. This was to avoid it being destroyed by the RAF carpet bombing campaigns. Bomber Command would undoubtedly be interested in these targets; so Perkins offered the services of SOE to set up 'Rebecca', a secret system for guiding bombers to new sites in Poland with the assistance of the Home Army. He informed the air ministry that Home Army units could be used for sabotage instead if bombing was not possible. SOE reassured the RAF of the dependability of the Poles in this task.

\* \* \*

On 18 July, Truszkowski sent a memo to Perkins stating that the Poles intended to carry out an armed uprising as a show of strength to the Soviets and therefore SOE Polish Section should begin planning for this event. It was also suggested that an SOE reconnaissance party be sent to Poland, followed by a military mission to make contact with the High Command of the Home Army. This should help, according to Truszkowski, in providing information about preparedness for the event and indicate the amount and type of equipment that should be delivered to the Warsaw fighters. On 30 July, General Tabor saw Gubbins and informed him that, on the 24th, the Polish Government had given the Deputy Prime Minister and General Headquarters Home Army complete autonomy in deciding on operations in the Warsaw region. He also said the Home Army was ready to launch the uprising just as soon as the order was given. On 25 July, Home Army command had telegraphed General Sosnkowski informing him that the Home Army was ready to fight for Warsaw and that the deployment of the Parachute Brigade to Poland be prepared. Tabor requested the bombing of German positions in the Polish capital in order to soften up the occupiers; four flights to land in Warsaw to render assistance to the Home Army and to be a symbol of Poland's desire to free itself from the chains of occupation. He also requested SOE deliveries of heavy machine guns and anti-tank rockets. These communiques demonstrated that the Poles expected significant British support for their rising. At the time the only Flight capable of helping Warsaw was Flight 1586. Perkins wrote to Tabor explaining that there will be no further support from the Combined COS for operations to Poland until relations between Poland and the Soviet Union had been restored. Gubbins wrote on his copy of the letter that he had spoken to Selborne who had agreed that the Poles were well aware of this view but were only pretending that they were not. On 27 July the Polish request for a British Military Mission was rejected so as to avoid friction with the Soviet Union.

# 14

# Allies at War

*In war the most deeply considered plans have no significance...All depends on the way unexpected movements of the enemy—that cannot be foreseen—are met, and on how and by whom the whole matter is handed.*

Tolstoy, *War and Peace*, IX, 9

On the outbreak of the Second World War, Poland had two enemies: Nazi Germany and her ally the Soviet Union. Following Operation Barbarossa, Poland continued to have the same two enemies, except the Soviet Union was now also an ally. Clearly, this was a strange paradox, for how can a country be both an ally and an enemy at the same time? During Barbarossa, Stalin realised that the Red Army could not defeat the Germans without help and so signed an alliance with Britain and the 'Western allies', which resulted in Russia switching sides in the war. Since the Second Republic of Poland was an existing member of that alliance, it too became Russia's ally; however, this did not remove the fact that Poland and the Soviet Union were latent enemies.

\* \* \*

From the time Russia changed sides, Britain had worked tirelessly to bring the old foes together in order to bolster allied solidarity and to ease the difficult relationship which had developed between London and the exiled Poles. The problem was that, after the war Russian policy was to install a People's Republic in Poland. For the Poles in London the objective was to ensure the continued existence of the Second Republic. These political objectives were so completely at odds with each other that it would prove impossible to reconcile the differing and opposing aims. As far as Britain was concerned her obligations required her to support both allies at the same time. One tactic was to support those in the Polish diaspora in the west, who were prepared to negotiate with the Russians on the future of the Second Republic and to undermine those in the diaspora who were anti-Russian. However, as most of anti-Russian sentiment was found in the High Command of the Polish Army in the west, to do this was no easy task In fact Sikorski had travelled to Polish formations under the command of General Anders fighting in the Middle East to warn them not to 'play politics' regarding Soviet Russia but only to concentrate on military matters. The same sentiment was transmitted to the Home Army. Sikorski's approach suited Britain, as it kept the Russians on side. Consequently, Sikorski and his government were strongly supported in London whilst General Sosnkowski and General Anders, being strongly anti-Russian, were allegedly kept at arms-length. On the premature death of Sikorski in an aircraft accident off the coast of Gibraltar in July 1943, conspiracy theorists suggested that a secret clique of anti-Russian Polish officers was somehow behind the incident in order to remove Sikorski's pro-Russian stance. If this was indeed the case they certainly succeeded. Nevertheless, one thing is clear, the death of Sikorski allowed anti-Russian factions in the Polish exiled diaspora, to came to the fore. The difficulty for the SOE Polish Section was now how to respond to the contradictory political pressure coming from the opposing factions? A diabolically ingenious compromise saw the SOE Polish Section being directed to provide only enough war material for individual acts of sabotage but not enough to make the Home Army believe it could stand up to the Red Army in Poland. In the meantime, the Russians informed London that they could not work with the 'Western Poles' because they were untrustworthy. For a start, they argued, the Poles had their own secret ciphers and it was impossible to know in what spirit messages were being sent to the Home Army in Poland. Moscow insinuated that they were anti-Soviet and, therefore, by definition pro German. The Russians also complained that secret packages flown to Poland on SOE sponsored flights by the RAF were not checked and therefore no one knew what was being transported. The COS, alarmed by Russia's complaints, made enquiries to the SOE and the Foreign Office about the situation regarding communications between the Poles in Britain and underground Poland. The Polish Section responded by pointing out that packages for Poland were being transferred in one of two ways, either on SOE sponsored flights on RAF aircraft, in which case the content was known, or on RAF flights sponsored by the Polish Government in London, in which case the content was not known. The packages dispatched by SOE on behalf of the Sixth Bureau contained small arms, explosives and ammunition at the risk of their falling into enemy hands. No documents or sensitive papers were sent out on these flights. As far as containers transported on behalf of the Polish Government were concerned, these were carried under diplomatic immunity and so their contents remained a secret. The issue of ciphers was a complex one since the Polish exiled Government had been given special permission to operate its secret ciphers from British territory when Sikorski had arrived in Britain after the fall of France. Nevertheless, this did not stop the COS enquiring whether the Poles could be persuaded to surrender their ciphers, although, they warned that these should be kept from the Russians in case they asserted their right to them as Britain's ally. SIS was clear on the matter, as according to its assessment, all Polish broadcasts to occupied Poland should be censored. If the Poles refused to cooperate, a tight grip should be imposed on Polish transmitter stations on British soil. The

War Office, wishing not to appear heavy handed, ordered an unspecified crackdown on Polish communications. SOE pulled back from detailed supervision of the Poles because from its assessments if it was necessary to raise the question of control of secret transmissions, it should be done by His Majesty's Government. A large proportion of radio traffic to Poland was of an SOE nature and therefore of little concern to anyone else. Also, SOE did not want to overstep the mark by appearing to be spying into Polish affairs. The COS did not have such scruples. Their major concern was to win the war at the least possible cost to Britain and to ensure that Polish traffic did not jeopardise Overlord or Britain's relationship with Russia. They warned that if the Poles refused to cooperate, their privileges should be withdrawn. Since such action would disrupt transmissions to Poland, the Poles allowed far more detailed checks being made on the contents of the containers intended for the Home Army but refused to share their diplomatic ciphers. These arrangements, however, did not apply to diplomatic bags which remained classified.[1] Gubbins set up a unit of Polish speaking FANY staff to oversee the checking procedures. This allowed the British to show the Russians that materials being sent to Poland were being monitored and were not a threat to Moscow. The monitoring also gave SOE Polish Section some understanding of what was going on inside occupied Poland. These arrangements were not designed to censor Polish action, but to ascertain whether it would embarrass the Foreign Office in the eyes of the Russians. This was another example of how hard Britain was working so as not to antagonize Stalin.

\* \* \*

On 26 June, Frank took his son to a concert at the Royal Albert Hall where the BBC Promenade Orchestra was performing. Frank noted the remarkable setting for wartime with plenty of colour and 'pleasant artificial lights'. The programme included, among other items, 'Overture Oberon', 'Debussy's Prelude' 'A l'Apres-midi d'un Faune', 'Handel's Largo' and the 'Trumpet Voluntary' by Jeremiah Clarke, the organist of Winchester College and subsequently of St Paul's. The concert was a 'real treat', wrote Frank in his diary, 'I so rarely hear a full orchestra direct'.[2]

---

1   TNA HS/4/166: 1942-1944 The use of Diplomatic Bags.
2   Peter Minett (ed.), *Frank's Wartime Diary*, p. 449.

## 15

# Transfer to Italy

*A general must also be capable of furnishing military equipment and providing supplies for the men; he must be resourceful, active, careful, hardy and quick-witted; he must be both gentle and brutal at once, straightforward and designing, capable of both caution and surprise, lavish and rapacious, generous and mean, skilful in defence and attack; and there are many other qualifications, some natural, some acquired, that are necessary to one who would succeed as a general.*

Xenophon, *Memorabilia*, III, 1

During September 1943 Flight 301 received three new Liberator aircraft that had been modified for night flying by the addition of silencers to the exhaust systems. In October two of the aircraft flew missions to Poland using route two. Although at first this route was relatively safe when compared to route one, it grew increasingly dangerous, necessitating the Polish Section to transfer the Polish base to Brindisi in Italy and so opening up the potential for further routes. This resulted in route one and two becoming redundant. The distance from the heel of Italy to Poland was approximately 1,200 km, not too dissimilar in distance from Tempsford, but was considered safer because it avoided the airspace of occupied northern Europe. Routes would pass over the Caucuses and Hungary allowing Poland to be reached from the south. As if to endorse the decision, in September six aircraft using route one were lost over northern Europe, falling foul of the defensive anti-aircraft belt which stretched from the north of Denmark to the centre of Germany. It had originally been put there to protect German cities from the carpet-bombing operations started by Bomber Command. The result of the September losses convinced Bomber Command, (at that time in control of special operation flights), that the decision to approach Poland from the south was the correct one. The resolution to transfer to a base in Italy involved a great deal of extra work for the Polish Section in that personnel, stores and a signals station had had to be relocated to the Mediterranean theatre. The initial proposal was to fly from Sidi Amor airfield near Tunis where a Polish Flight of three Liberators and three Halifax aircraft was stationed after leaving

137

Britain where thet had been part of 138 Squadron. This flight was later known as 1586 Special Duties Flight. The first attempt to fly three aircraft from Tunis on 15 December failed to reach Poland, as they had to turn back owing to bad weather. However, a further attempt on 18 December brought some success. In January 1944, one flight took place with another taking off in February and a third in March. All three missions only carried supplies. It was also thought that the base at Brindisi in Italy, where the distance to Poland was somewhat shorter, would be a better proposition for missions to the eastern ally.

\* \* \*

The transfer of the Polish base to Italy took some time to complete and resulted in a break in operations to Poland. The new base was designated Base 11 and was commanded by Lieutenant Colonel Threlfall, who was assisted by Majors Klauber, Morgan and Truszkowski. The British codename for the base was Force 139 with a Head Quarters at Monopoli. As with all Polish missions, sorties were under the control of the Polish Section and the Polish Sixth Bureau and answerable to the exiled Polish Government in London. The supreme commander at the base was General Maitland–Wilson, unkindly nicknamed 'Jumbo' by others. Six heavy bombers were transferred to the base opening up the possibility of flying 24 sorties per month. Three routes were approved from the base designated as Routes 3, 4 and 5. Route 3 crossed the Adriatic, Dalmatia and Croatia, then Lake Balaton in Hungary which led the aircraft over the Tatra Mountains into southern Poland. Route 4 differed slightly with aircraft crossing the Dalmatian coast flying over Montenegro towards Budapest and entering Polish airspace east of the Tatra Mountains. Route 5 took aircraft over Albania, then over Serbia onto the Romanian/Yugoslav border and finally to the Lwów region of Poland. Base 11 had much autonomy regarding operations to Poland, including procuring equipment and materials for the resistance, and had a say regarding the airmen that flew. It even had radio contact with the underground in Warsaw, holding currency reserves for the Home Army and the Government's delegate, although its despatch to Warsaw was under the control of the Sixth Bureau in London. The base's strategic function also included the support of allied forces fighting up the Italian peninsula. The Base of the Sixth Bureau was just one element of the British Special Force number 1 operating from Algiers and southern Italy for missions to Italy and Czechoslovakia as well Poland.

\* \* \*

Meanwhile, whilst waiting for the completion of the transfer to Brindisi, air crew bided their time at SOE stations across Britain. At Brickendonbury Manor in Hartford, for example, there were some twelve young fighters awaiting orders. The men were under the care of permanent staff made up of a matron and a score of young female personnel belonging to the First Aid Nursing Yeomanry, FANY. The women drove ambulances, served in canteens and carried out domestic duties with a positive attitude and a 'spring in their step.' They were a credit to the SOE. By the beginning of January 1944, 1586 Polish Flight had been established at Brindisi, together with 148 Squadron RAF, forming the 334 Wing. All subsequent special operations to Poland, with the exception of one large American sortie were flown from Italy. The transfer of flights from Britain meant that a signals station was required with direct communication to Poland and had to be set up in Italy together with the necessary Polish operational staff before flights could commence. By the end of 1943 this was completed at Latiano.[1] The base was given the code name 'Torment'. It was not worth transporting Polish recruits based in the Middle East to Britain for training only to send them back to Italy again for despatch to Poland, so it was decided to establish an SOE training school in Italy alongside Torment where Polish volunteers stationed in the Middle East could be trained. The first school, named 'Impudent' (STS 10), was established at Latiano under the command of Captain Oranowski. A second school commanded by Major Leopold Krizar was established at Ostuni . Both training schools had British liaison officers on their staff to deal with the British military authorities on matters of airlifts and to ensure that Polish special operations fitted into the general framework of SOE activity in the Mediterranean.

Lieutenant Colonel Roper-Caldbeck, was in charge of the advance party in Italy, with Major A.M. Morgan as senior British Officer at Latiano and Major Ferrers-Guy succeeded by Captain A.E. Andrews at Ostuni. The advance party worked as a special section of Number One Special Force and was the first SOE unit to be established in Italy.

\* \* \*

The Anglo-Polish base in Italy was concerned with training and with the operational side of special missions to Poland. All questions of policy or intelligence were dealt with by the Sixth Bureau in London in consultation with SOE Polish Section. When policy had been established it was transmitted to the Latiano base, where the planning and training for operations was completed. On completion, the Latiano base communicated with the Home Army on matters concerning the mounting of operations and the provisions of supplies. Although these stations were Italian but manned by Poles, they were dependent on SOE on all questions regarding airlifts, supplies and general liaison with Head Quarters Special Operations Mediterranean, H.Q.S.O.(M). This arrangement was finalised by April 1944 when Lieutenant Colonel H.M Threlfall and Major G.I. Klauber arrived in Italy. Threlfall was henceforth responsible to H.Q.S.O.M for the administrative side of Polish operations while remaining dependent on SOE in London for policy. The headquarters was set up at Monopoli and, following its amalgamation with various Polish establishments in the heel of Italy, was given the designation 'Force 139.' Threlfall was appointed as commander with Klauber as his deputy. Force 139 differed from other sub-groups in that the

---

1   TNA HS4/184: Colonel Threlfall's report on air operations from Mediterranean theatre; training school at Latiano.

Polish military authorities were in sole control of special operations to Poland, unlike other allied powers exiled in London. This was by virtue of having left behind a well organised underground movement in the Polish Republic and having established a rather more independent modus operandi with the British authorities from the moment of their arrival in Britain. For example, the provisions of false documents for agents going to the field and their briefings, was done by the Poles. Furthermore, the signals station at Latiano, which carried all operational communications with Poland was similarly under Polish control. Force 139 also ran its own packing station for materials to be transferred to Poland, instead of using the central station at Paradise Camp. The Poles also carried out the loading of aircraft themselves. On the basis of the airlift which the British provided, the Poles made their own estimates of requirements and it was then one of the responsibilities of the British element of Force 139 to screen these demands, before putting them forward to H.Q.S.O.M. On the whole these arrangements worked well. On the English side, the division into policy and intelligence in London and operations in Italy was satisfactory, except that the Italian end was sometimes out of touch regarding background intelligence on what was happening in Poland. On the Polish side, there were difficulties which at the end of August 1944 eventually led to the resignation of Major Jazwiński, who felt that the Polish Sixth Bureau in London was giving the Home Army underground movement in Poland reasons to hope for more help than it could operationally send. As a result, Jazwiński came into conflict with the Sixth Bureau on a matter of policy. There was also a later occasion, after he had been succeeded by Lieutenant Colonel Hancza, when the latter's opinion of the inadequacy of air support for the Warsaw rising was transmitted to higher British authorities without the knowledge of the Commander of Force 139, which caused some lively discussion at NAAFI, but such occurrences were fortunately few and far between. In fact, an outstanding feature of the period was the exceptionally happy cooperation which had developed between the British and Polish elements. When the Polish Flight was transferred to the Mediterranean theatre it consisted of six aircraft and there was much debate about the number of sorties they should undertake and whether they should be used exclusively for Poland as well as other theatres. Shortly after Polish representations about the strategic role of the Home Army, a Prime Ministerial ruling laid down that the air effort to Poland be trebled.[2] The Polish flight was doubled by the addition of six more Halifax aircraft, but a further six never materialised. The failure to implement this ruling to the full was the seed of much trouble in later months, for it meant that Polish operations were a constant claim on the British aircraft of 148 Squadron and thus came into conflict with other missions, in particular the Italian and Yugoslavian campaigns. This was simply part of the usual position whereby the supply of four-engine aircraft lagged behind the planning for the expansion of special operations requirements. A pooling arrangement was organised, whereby the British aircraft of 148 Squadron flew to Poland as a first priority, when weather was suitable in return for the help given by 1586 Polish Flight to other countries when operations to Poland were not

---

2  TNA HS4/156: Warsaw Rising; War effort to Poland.

possible. This arrangement continued until August, when the Warsaw rising brought other considerations into play. The first attempt at flying from the new base, on 18 December, comprised two Halifax aircraft from 148 Squadron. Unfortunately, they were unsuccessful, although an attempt from North Africa on the same night succeeded.

\* \* \*

It was envisaged that the southern routes would avoid the frequent difficult weather conditions of the routes over the North Sea, as well as enemy defences which had been put in place in northern Europe. However, operations out of Brindisi during the first three months of 1944 were a disappointment. Out of a total of 23 operations during this period only one mission was successful in January and another in March, whilst two aircraft were lost. The doubt about the wisdom of the decision to switch to the southern route was dispelled, however, by the successes that followed in April, when the weather improved and 132 operations were attempted of which 50 percent were successful. For example, Operation Weller 5 on 3 April 1944, and Weller 4,6 and 7 on the 8 April departed successfully using Halifax aircraft. Weller 1 and 2 flew out on the 9th, while Weller 3, 14 and 11 departed on 14 August. Weller 10, 12 and 15 flew on the 16th whilst Operation Weller 26 flew on the 4 May, Weller 27 flew on the 10th whilst Weller 18 departed on 19 May. The results for May were equally as good as for April, although five aircraft were lost during this period. It was clear that the southern route was proving to be eminently more practical than the northern one, despite its slow start. In these two months 104 operatives were successfully dropped into Poland together with 172 tons of stores, more than twice the weight than that sent in the previous year from Britain.

\* \* \*

The Weller Operations were completed by 30 May with Weller 29 flying to Wierzbno on the 21st, Weller 23 flying to Bochenski on the 24the and finally Weller 30 on 30th, flying to Babrowka. The secret army in Poland was delighted with the increase in supplies and its Commander in Chief, General Bor-Komorowski, sent a warm 'thank you' for the help he had received. In June there were no sorties at all, the reason being partly the short nights and partly bad weather, but in July flying resumed and 63 operations were carried out with a fraction of over 50 percent success rate. This is how Pilot Officer Wlodzimierz Bernhadt recalled his mission:

> 'The flights to Warsaw were of the most nerve-racking kind, and the reasons behind this were technological and emotional. It was so difficult to look down at the burning city and think of what the people were going through … Flight conditions were difficult and we lacked all the electronic radar devices that we had had in Europe since everything ended over the Adriatic … As soon as we reached the Yugoslavian shore after half-an-hour of flying we encountered the

Germans.... We kept low all the way until we approached the Polish border near the Carpathian Mountains. Then we flew higher so as to get over the Tatra Mountains ... On reaching Warsaw all we could see was all-embracing smoke, here and there we could see 'pillars of fire', and we had difficulty in finding the drop zone.'[3]

\* \* \*

On 1 July, 1944, Clark-Kerr informed the Foreign Office that the Russians considered the clandestine People's Army[4] in Poland to be the main resistance organisation and not the Home Army, which it denounced as a lacky of the Polish Government in London. The People's Army, supported and financed by Moscow, was a communist resistance faction fighting to secure the formation of a People's Republic in Poland. Britain was also informed that the NKVD and the People's Army were prepared to confront the Home Army if it stood in the way of the communist takeover, precipitating a civil war if necessary. In order to besmirch the name of the Home Army, Moscow falsely reported that the Home Army had claimed credit for acts of sabotage. The Russians also claimed that ammunition procured by SOE was not being used against the Germans but was being cached, to be used against the Red Army at a later date.

\* \* \*

On 7 July, Threlfall enquired about Polish requirements for 1944. He also asked whether there was a need to change the type of war materials being delivered in case the Home Army was ordered to expand guerrilla activity. He was told to continue without any change to deliveries since action by the Home Army was to remain as sabotage, intelligence gathering and subversion on the current scale. No open guerrilla fighting was planned. Missions continued with Jacek 1 on 30 July, Przemek 1 on 21 September, Wacek 1 and Poldek 1 on 16 October, Kazik 2 on 18 November, Kazik 1 on the 22 November and Staszek 2 on 26 December. Freston (British Military Mission) also flew on 26 December.

---

3   *Polish Air Force* <http://www.polishairforce.pl> (accessed 10.10.2021).
4   Armia Ludowa.

# 16

# Wildhorn Operations

*The result of a battle is decided not by the orders of a commander in chief, nor the place where the troops are stationed, nor by the number of cannon or of slaughtered men, but by that intangible force called the spirit of the army.*

Tolstoy, *War and Peace*, X, 35

Throughout operations to Poland, the Poles thought it would be advantageous if aircraft not only made parachute drops of personnel and equipment but would also be able to land in the occupied country. They believed this strategy would improve the accuracy of missions to designated sites and, more importantly, allow for a repeated exchange of officers and couriers between Britain and Poland. Unfortunately, during the early years of the war, landings were not possible as the aircraft available required long runways which could not be guaranteed by the Home Army. It was not until much later in the war that landings became a possibility due to the delivery of a new type of aircraft built by the Americans called the Douglas C-47 Skytrain better known as the Dakota. This aircraft did not require a long runway to operate, although by this time in the war the relationship between Soviet Russia and Britain was so important that the Chiefs-of-Staff were prompted not to share the aircraft with SOE Polish Section. This policy soon changed when the British learned that the Poles had obtained plans and components of Germany's V-2 rocket, which had wreaked havoc over London in the Blitz. Suddenly, the mood changed and the Chiefs-of-Staff approved the use of a Dakota aircraft to pick up the drawings and rocket parts and bring them back to London. SOE operations where planes landed on Polish soil and then returned were given the code name 'Wildhorn'.[1]

\* \* \*

---

1   TNA HS4/180: Wildhorn and Wildhorn VIV: air landing operations to Poland from N. Africa and Italy.

Once the possibility of making landings was understood, effort was put into finding suitable sites. Secret Home Army units scoured several locations for possible airstrips which were rarely used by the Germans. If a stand-in airstrip had to be used it had to be well away from tall buildings and trees; the ground had to be firm, flat, smooth and free from stones, tree stumps and ditches. If more than three centimetres depth of snow was on the ground, the landing was aborted and either diverted to a substitute runway or called off. Three possible sites were found quickly, one near the city of Lublin and two near Kraków. Planning for the first operation, named Wildhorn I, took place in March, although initially the bad weather prevented the aircraft from flying. The landing took place on an airstrip near Lublin on 10 April, once the Home Army officers decided that the airstrip was thoroughly prepared and ready to receive aircraft. A message was sent to London, 'We are ready to receive'. Wildhorn I was due to fly at night on 15/16 April, 1944. On the 15th a coded melody was broadcast to the Home Army by the BBC; a melody called Koło Mego Ogródeczka[2], which signalled that the operation was on. The melody was repeated in the evening of the 15th signalling that the aircraft should be expected at 01.00 hours the following day. The Dakota departed from Campo Cassale, at 19.32 hours commanded by Flight Lieutenant E. J. Harrod. His crew comprised, Flight Lieutenant Bolesław Korpowski, (Second Pilot) Pilot Officer J. A. Wells (navigator) and radio controller, Pilot Officer N. Wilcock. On board were two Polish couriers and two suitcases stuffed with mail, US dollars and blank counterfeit documents. Also aboard were film cameras with reels of films. Harrod decided to fly over Albania then over Yugoslavia at a height of 9,300 feet. After overflying Yugoslavia, Harrod followed the river Danube to the north. When the aircraft flew into German FLAK, Harrod increased the altitude to 10,500 feet. A second wave of German anti-aircraft guns was met in the Budapest region, but fortunately the Dakota was not hit and was able to continue north. Eventually, Harrod located the river Vistula in Poland, which led him to the landing site near Lublin. He reduced the altitude to 1,000 feet and after signalling to the reception committee using his landing lights, put the aircraft down safely. As Flight Lieutenant Bolesław Korpowski, exited the aircraft he knelt down and kissed the ground, an act reminiscent to the Polish Pope John Paul II when he returned to Poland on a pilgrimage from Rome in 1979. Looking up at those who ran to meet them, Korpowski called out, 'do not stare boys we have missed our Polish homeland for so long.'[3] He continued that he wished to gather up some of the soil to put on General Sikorski's grave on his return to England. He did this and put the soil into the pockets of his flying tunic. Those in the reception committee who had quickly gathered around fetched an empty haversack and filled it with more soil and handed it to Korpowski. The return journey to the Italian base was delayed, because those that were scheduled to fly; General S.Tartar, code name 'Tabor', Colonel Marian Dorotycz-Malewicz, code name 'Hancza', Colonel Andrzej Pomian, code name 'Dowmunt', Stanisław

---

2   Near My Little Garden.
3   TNA HS4/180: Wildhorn and Wildhorn IV: air landing operations to Poland from N. Africa and Italy.

Oltarzewski and Zygmunt Berezwski, were gathered on the other side of the airfield and had to make their way across to the aircraft. Apart from the passengers and packages, a new banner with the Colours of the First Independent Parachute Brigade, freshly sewn in Warsaw, was also loaded on board. The organisation on the ground was excellent and the turnaround lasted only a few minutes, with the aircraft taking off without incident. The Secret Army Forces, which had been detailed to protect the landing site, attracted German attention and there was some gun fire in progress whilst the operation took place. Unfortunately, forty men defending the site were killed. The crew reported that they could see numerous burning villages below them as they departed.

\* \* \*

Wildhorn II, the second flight to land in Poland, was planned and prepared in May 1944.[4] The chosen landing site was near Tarnów on the river Kisielina. The aircraft came from 267 Squadron and was ready to fly on the 17 May. Four extra fuel tanks had been installed in the Dakota which meant that its range was extended by a further 14 flying hours. It was to fly during daylight hours and be accompanied by two fighter aircraft for protection. However, the operation was postponed twice, once on the 24 May and once on the 27th. This was because fighter aircraft for protection could not be found for the mission. Eventually, at 19.35 hours, on the 29th, the mission commenced. The crew was made up of: First Officer O'Donovan, Second Officer Jacek Blocki from 1586 Flight, and Navigator D. R. Thomas. On board were two Polish agents, Colonel Romuald Bielski and General Tadeusz Kossakowski. The mission also carried 440 tons of war material. The escort for the mission was provided by two Liberator aircraft from 1586 Flight, but they turned back as the sun set. Two minutes past mid-night the crew rendezvoused with the landing party. O'Donovan put the aircraft down on the landing strip which had been prepared with one green light at the beginning of the strip and two red lights at the end. He did not switch the engines off whilst on the ground but swung the aircraft through 180 degree in case he had to make a quick get away. Romuald Bielski, Tadeusz Kossakowski were infiltrated whilst Zbigniew Sujkowski, Roman Rudkowski and Jan Domanski were exfiltrated. Just six minutes later the aircraft took off for Italy. The return flight took eight and half hours with the aircraft landing safely at 04.08 hours.

\* \* \*

Wildhorn III[5] was associated with the transport of captured V2 rocket components to London. The Home Army had secretly snatched and spirited away parts of the

---

4   TNA HS4/180: Wildhorn and Wildhorn IV: air landing operations to Poland from North Africa and Italy.
5   TNA HS4/183: Wildhorn III pick up operations for special passengers to come to the Britain from Poland.

weapons of mass destruction which had devastated London during the Blitz. On 11 July, London was informed that the components would be ready for pick up on the 20th. The commander of 267 Squadron was instructed on the 12th to plan and prepare the mission. On the 25th at 19.28 hours, the Dakota left Campo Cassale for Poland heading for a landing site codenamed 'Butterfly'. This site should have been ruled out as the landing strip had been compromised by the Germans on mission Wildhorn II but events had been moving so fast on the Eastern fronts that an alternative could not be found. It was argued that Butterfly had a few things going for it namely an existing reception team, nearby safe houses and signals. The flight commander of Wildhorn III was Flight Lieutenant S. G. Calliford, the Second Pilot was Flight Officer Kazimierz Szrajet of 1586 Flight, navigator was Flight Officer J. P. Williams and the Radio Operator Flight Sargent J. Appelby. On board were four couriers, Captain K. Bilski, Second Lieutenant L. Straszyński, Major B. Wolniak and Lieutenant J. Nowak. Nowak was a courier for the High Command of the Home Army whilst the other three were scheduled to join the secret army as officers.14 packing cases and five packages were also on board. During daylight flying the Dakota was escorted by only one Liberator, as the second aircraft did not fly because of a technical failure. Calliford had had difficulty landing at the chosen site since there was a detachment of German troops stationed nearby. When the plane put down the Germans did not suspect anything untoward and so the alarm was not raised. The second misfortune faced by the crew was a slippery and damp runway, which resulted in the aircraft skidding off the landing strip. The landing wheels bogged themselves into the grassy mud, rooting the aircraft into the ground. This episode lengthened the operation considerably and complicated the take off. Calliford loathed using full throttle to get the aircraft airborne and this made take off very difficult, especially when it was realised that the brakes had seized. After the second attempt to take off, Calliford switched off the engines and prepared to destroy the Dakota, but before he did this, he attempted a last try. Timber planks were placed under the aircrafts wheels and this seemed to do the trick. The Dakota lifted off the ground landing safely in Camp Cassale at 10.15 the following morning. One intriguing mission taking advantage of Wildhorn flights was Mission Salamander. This mission involved Józef Retinger, who had landed in occupied Poland in April 1944. Retinger, one time adviser to Prime Minister General Sikorski, was on a British mission to liaise with the Polish Government's Delegate in Warsaw. The plan was for Retinger to rendezvous with Stanisław Jankowski, aide-de-camp to General Komorowski-Bor, commander of the Home Army, to persuade him to accept Stalin's plans for post-war Poland; namely the annexation of eastern Poland by Russia and the formation of a People's Republic. Churchill had already unilaterally accepted Stalin's plans at the Yalta Conference and was keen to get the Poles in the West to acquiesce. This would require Polish delegates in Warsaw to first weaken then break their ties with the Government of the Second Republic in London. Initially this was done by allowing the formation of the People's Republic to acquire patriotic overtones. Retinger was by now 56 years of age and not in the best of health. Nevertheless, he was pressured by the British to take up the dangerous mission to fly on Woldhorn I with another political courier, Tadeusz Chcuik. The Halifax aircraft was taken over the Adriatic, then the Hungarian plain and finally over the Tatra Mountain range into Polish airspace. When Jankowski received Retinger and heard Churchill's message, he was dumbfounded. Allegedly Jankowski considered the proposal a betrayal of the Second Republic and put Retinger under surveillance as a potential traitor. The best outcome under the circumstances for Retinger would have been a return to Britain on Wildhorn II, but his departure was blocked by the Home Army. Soon Retinger fell ill to a mysterious illness and he lay in his sick bed for some three weeks. Eventually he recovered sufficiently enough to take his place on Wildhorn III. On 26 July, 1944 he returned to Brindisi, where he was met by British officials. He finally returned to London via Morocco. In the final analysis the whole episode was irrelevant as Stalin occupied the Second Republic without making any reference to the representatives of the Second Republic in London.

\* \* \*

The rare and coveted places on Wildhorn flights were not only reserved for supporters of Prime Minister Mikołajczyk's government, for among those brought out was Mr. Arciszewski, who later became Prime Minister after Mikołajczyk's resignation (29 November, 1944). His policies were anything but in agreement with those of Mikołajczyk and could be described as 'anti-Russian'. Among the military representatives that flew were General Tabor, Deputy Commander in the COS of the Polish Secret Army[6] who took over the command of all underground work in Poland soon after his arrival in London, and Lieutenant Colonel Hancza, who after being brought out of Poland on Wildhorn I, took over the command of Polish operations and training bases at Latiano and Ostuni. A fourth Wildhorn operation was standing by waiting for suitable weather in December 1944, with the intention of bringing out some political personalities who, it was hoped, would contribute to the settlement of the Polish question, but bad weather and local German ground activity delayed the operation for so long that the Russian advance overran the landing site before this could be done.

\* \* \*

On 14 March the Polish Finance Ministry contacted John Venner, the SOE's finance chief, in search of a loan. Money became an issue when Polish accounts had uncovered a discrepancy between expenditure and income. Expenditure was calculated to amount to 30 million US dollars for military equipment and 18 million US dollars for civil expenditure, which amounted to a total of 48 million dollars. The Poles had amassed a reserve of 3 million dollars in Zlotys, 1 million dollars in Reichsmarks, 1 million dollars in Pounds Sterling. On-going credit amounted to 9 million US dollars and 2 million US dollars for the Intelligence Services. The grand total amounted to 16 million US dollars which meant a shortfall of 32 million dollars, hence the request

---

6   TNA HS4/147: Polish Secret Army, Polish planning for the reoccupation of Poland.

for a loan. Venner authorised the loan explaining to Harry Sporborg, that despite an agreement between Sikorski and Roosevelt for 12 million dollars per year this money had not materialised because it was drawn on the president's secret account. The Poles were caught short. It was rare for the British to refuse loans to the Poles, as the Foreign Office did not want to appear as if London was refusing to support its ally. The first monetary approval for special operations to Poland was made on March 25 1942. The Defence Committee decided that two thirds of the funds would be provided through the British treasury and one third by the Polish treasury. Apart from these short-term problems, the War Cabinet worked on two long term issues which concerned the administration of liberated Poland and the further equipping of the Polish underground army after the war. With the communist People's Army poised to confront the Home Army after the war, SOE's role was problematical. Should the Home Army be equipped with war material when there was a danger of a civil war breaking out between the two conspiratorial groups or should it drop supplies to the People's Army as well as the Home Army, which could be construed as a betrayal of the Polish Government of the Second Republic? When the Russians were consulted on the first issue, they suggested that the Political-Military Commission at Algiers should deal inter alia with the whole problem of liberated allied territory. The British agreed, believing that such an approach would give the Western Allies some chance of seeing that the Poles were 'treated properly'. Regarding the further arming of the Home Army, the Americans decided that they were against sending more supplies than that required for sabotage and intelligence work. Their reason was both military and political; the shortage of aircraft and the Russian reaction. The general view was that Moscow would be violently hostile to the Polish underground army being equipped to such an extent that it felt embolden to try to oppose Soviet intentions regarding post-war Poland. As a result, the equipping of the underground army for full blown military action was resisted. It was clear to the War Cabinet that the question of whether to supply full military equipment could not be answered until there was some satisfactory solution to the Russo-Polish question. Meanwhile, the British decided to wait until things became clearer.

\* \* \*

On the 20 May the COS re-considered their support for the Polish uprising. They concluded that the short summer months would restrict the number of SOE flights and so hinder any support that could be offered to the Poles. They recommended that the Home Army should concentrate on diversionary action rather than on an insurrection. This recommendation was passed on to Henry Threlfall. The Poles regretted the recommendation for, according to their estimation, 350 reception committees were on standby to receive materials and ordinance. Meanwhile, George Hill, SOE's representative in Moscow, was enquiring about the possibility of cooperation between the Polish underground and the NKVD, but the enquiry was unproductive. The May report on conditions in Poland sited that the Home Army was 350,000 strong although only 70,000 men were armed with small arms. The main equipment in the army's possession comprised anti-tank guns, 3-inch mortars, Bren guns, Sten guns, Thompson submachine guns, explosives, sabotage equipment and captured enemy weapons.[7] SOE also understood that clandestine production of weapons was ongoing. Communication between Warsaw and London was reported to be good and the chances of German penetration of Home Army 'cells' minimal; however, the penetration of political parties in Poland was suspected. The army had no accompanying artillery or transport. On 7 October, CIGS informed the Sixth Bureau that regrettably it was not possible to increase the number of aircraft for Poland. Three Wildhorn landings were made in Poland compared to 103 in France. The latter nation was, of course, of great strategic importance to the Western allies and in a privileged position from the political point of view.

7   TNA HS4/177: Results and Reports, equipment dropped.

# 17

# A Shortage of Trust

*Theirs not to make a reply, theirs not to reason why, theirs but to do and die, into the valley of death rode the six hundred.*

                                        Tennyson, *The Charge of the Light Brigade*

The planning for the invasion of Western Europe by Britain and America was carried out in the strictest secrecy. Under no circumstance were the Germans to learn about where and when the invasion was to take place and much diversionary activity was employed by the Allies in order to keep the Nazis guessing. One such deception was called Operation Fortitude, which saw full scale inflatable dummy tanks and lorries arranged in combat formations on Britain's southern coastal areas. This made it appear that huge armour was poised for an assault on the Pas de Calais.[1] Overlord was so important to the allies that all SOE missions to the continent had to be coordinated so that secret armies could play their part or take advantage of the battle. For some time Stalin had been calling on Churchill to open a second front in the West in order to relieve pressure being exerted on Soviet armies on the eastern front. Discussion on the location of the second front saw a difference of opinion emerge between Churchill and Eisenhower, the American Supreme Commander. The British Prime Minister, being acutely aware of the debacle of the amphibious assault at Gallipoli during the First World War and for which he was partly held responsible, argued against an amphibian attack on the French coast, preferring a full-frontal land attack up the Italian peninsula followed by an assault on southern Germany and beyond. In Churchill's mind such a move would not only take pressure off Soviet Forces but would also have the distinct advantage of giving the Western Allies a chance of reaching Berlin before the Russian Army. Eisenhower, on the other hand, appreciating the low morale of the 8 Army in Italy and fearing a Soviet advance deep into Western Europe, believed that the allies should take the shortest route to Berlin. This meant an amphibious landing on the French coast and

---

1   Straits of Calais.

then fighting through France and the Low countries towards Germany. Eventually, the American view prevailed and planning started for an amphibious invasion of German occupied France.

* * *

Soon after the breakdown of relations between the Poles and the Russians it was shown that General Sosnkowski was correct to be concerned about Russian intentions regarding the Second Republic, for Moscow had started besmirching the name of the Republic's authorities in London, accusing them of working with the Nazis and opposing the advance of the Russian Army across the Polish plain towards Berlin. This was the beginning of the sovietisation of Poland and the establishment of a People's Democratic Republic. However, Britain refused to accept this conclusion and instructed the Poles in the West not to overreact nor support any military action against the Red Army by the Home Army as this would upset the understanding between the British and the Soviets. This decision had a profound re percussion for SOE Polish Section, because from now on it would be more than just a procurer of equipment, but also an arbiter on the type of equipment to be delivered. Despite this the Polish Commander in Chief wrote to Selborne requesting an increase in the number of SOE flights to Poland to be accompanied by a rapid expansion in the delivery of war material. General Sosnkowski justified the request by stating that the Home Army was involved in constant conspiratorial fighting, large scale intelligence work, mass sabotage and general insurrection, all of which required an escalation of deliveries of war equipment. Despite the fact that the Joint Planning Staff had already rejected plans to increase missions to Poland, Selborne opinionated that the only way to deliver meaningful support to the Poles was to increase the number of aircraft allotted to SOE and to fly the 'southern route' to Poland. He wrote to the Air Ministry:

> I confess to great sympathy with the Polish standpoint. They braved Hitler in 1939 on Britain's guaranteed support. They have been crucified. They have not winced. Alone amongst our occupied allies they have no Quislings. They have incurred considerable casualties in very successfully attacking German communications to Russia at our request. They have an organised army of 250,000 in Poland which only needs equipment. To be told that Britain cannot afford them more than 6 aircraft is a bit hard.[2]

Although the SOE base serving Poland was now in Italy it was still felt that the best policy regarding the Home Army was to mend the rift between the Governments of Poland and the Soviet Union. This is how Dalton put it in August 1944:

---

2   TNA AIR 19/815: Document 80530.

> I tell them (the Poles) that unless they make friends with the Russians, who are great favourites in this country, there will be nobody left to back the Poles over here except a few Roman Catholic priests.[3]

One suggestion was to convince the Russians that the Poles in the West posed no threat to the Soviet Union whilst persuading the Poles that they had nothing to fear from Moscow and thus to encourage both sides to work together on a plan for a Polish uprising. The exercise could involve the Home Army, the Soviet Army and partisans in an act of reconciliation. However, Moscow returned to the question of Polish ciphers. How could the exiled Poles be trusted if they had their own secret ciphers to which no one had access? The Soviet fear was that the Poles were secretly fostering anti-Soviet and pro-German activities using secret messaging. London was well aware that an anti-Russian faction existed in the Polish diaspora but tried to play down its importance. On the other hand it was far from clear whether the Russians were using the question of Polish ciphers as an excuse not to cooperate with the Poles and the Home Army, in order to facilitate the establishment of a People's Republic. Nevertheless, the Chief of Staff enquired of the SOE whether the Poles could be persuaded to share their ciphers with the British in order to satisfy Soviet concerns. Also, enquiries were made as to whether the contents of the diplomatic packages being sent on behalf of the Polish Government to Poland on RAF aircraft could be monitored. Although no one held out much hope for this, as this would contravene convention regarding diplomatic traffic, SIS was clear on the matter of ciphers; all Polish broadcasts should be censored along with keeping a tighter grip on Polish radio transmitters in Britain. The War Cabinet, wishing to reassure Moscow, ordered a closer control on Polish communications. There were a number of reasons why SOE refrained from interfering with Polish radio transmissions, the main one being that the issue of Polish cipher censorship was a matter for His Majesty's Government. A large proportion of radio traffic was of an SOE nature and therefore of little concern to anyone else. SOE Polish Section did not want to overstep its authority, as its work was exclusively dependent on the Polish Ministry of the Interior and Polish wireless channels. It did not want to spoil its good relations with the Poles by appearing to be prying into Polish affairs. Although the Polish Section did not want to upset its working relations with the Poles, the COS, on the other hand, did not appear to have any such scruples. Their major concern was that Polish traffic would not compromise planning for Overlord nor jeopardise Britain's relationship with Moscow. When the Poles refused to cooperate on censorship and rebuffed any conditions being placed on them, the COS decided to withdraw privileges and refused to approve any future messages being sent to the Home Army until ciphers were submitted for scrutiny. The Poles compromised and, despite not sharing their government's ciphers, permitted the British to check the contents of their Sixth Bureau bags and containers before despatch by SOE. This compromise did not cover diplomatic bags,[4] which remained a

---

3   TNA HS4/301: Dalton.
4   TNA HS4/166: 1942-1944 Use of Diplomatic Bags.

secret. London signalled to bases across the world that extra security measures would have to be taken prior to D-Day meaning that no telegrams were to be transmitted unless prior approval had been received from SOE. Gubbins had set up a unit using Polish speaking FANYs to read non-governmental ciphers. This allowed the British to know what was going on in Polish circles in the West, both politically and militarily. The only exception were operational messages sent in the Polish language to the occupied country. The monitoring of Polish traffic had allowed SOE to obtain information on maps and battle orders both inside and outside of Poland. The exchange of information improved cooperation between the Poles and the British. However, it was never the intention to censor messages but to ascertain whether they contained anything that the Foreign Office and the Russians would object to.

\* \* \*

In February 1944 the Defence Committee questioned whether it would be prudent to transfer the control of operations to Poland from SOE to General Eisenhower. According to the Committee this would streamline the command structure and facilitate an improvement in Russo-Polish relations. After some consideration the COS disapproved, pointing out that air operations into Poland were now entirely based on the Mediterranean base. The route to Poland from Italy was considered to be safer than across central Europe where German fighters patrolled the airspace in large numbers. It had been understood for some time that the heavier bombers were prospective victims rather than effective protagonists against fighter aircraft . The Allied Commander in Chief, Mediterranean region, would additionally be the officer in command of Polish flights. There was also the complication that special operations to Poland were bound up with political considerations. This meant that it was unworkable to place SOE operations to Poland under Supreme Allied Command in the Mediterranean theatre.

\* \* \*

The death of Sikorski in July 1943 caused a crisis in the Polish cabinet. Mikołajczyk was appointed as the new Prime Minister, and General Sosnkowski as the new Commander in Chief of Polish Forces. These appointments brought out into the open the fissure that Sikorski was able to suppress whilst in office. Mikołajczyk reported that he would adhere to Sikorski's pro-Russian stance whilst General Sosnkowski and General Anders, both allegedly staunch anti-Russians, called for a change in policy. Since Sosnkowski's stance was opposed by Churchill, he did not stay in post for long and was demoted on 30 September 1944. Meanwhile, Mikołajczyk reassured Selborne that his intention was to continue working with the Russians as closely as possible, which also adhered to British policy at the time. However, he did express a need to take control of the Home Army in case certain anti-Russian factions within it decided to confront the Red Army in Poland. The British, counselled caution. Perkins highlighted how well things were going in Poland and how effective SOE involvement there had been until now, stating that no change in arrangements was necessary. However, things became awkward for London when it became clear that Moscow wanted to occupy Poland after the war and to set up a People's Republic in direct opposition to the Polish Government exiled in London. Moscow's plan was to remove the Second Republic, and to use the country as a springboard to spread communism into central Europe. Naturally, the Government of the Second Republic made it known that it opposed any such move vehemently and expected to take control of the Polish state after the war. The Poles in London looked to the British government for support on this matter. This support was not forthcoming whilst the Germans were rampant and Russian military power was needed. Once the Germans were defeated, Britain was far too weak to resist Soviet intentions and in any case Churchill by then had well understood that the nation states of the 1930s were succumbing to a new world order. Furthermore, Churchill also knew that he could not follow through without US support.

# 18

# The Soviet Push to the West

*The wolf ... shall dwell with the lamb, and the leopard shall lie down with the kid; and the calf and the young lion and the fatling together; and a little child shall lead them.*

Isaiah 11:6

On 5 October 1943 the SOE Polish Section published its assessment of the internal situation in Poland. It noted the very close relationship that continued to exist between the Home Army and the exiled Polish Government of the Second Republic exiled in London. This convinced the SOE Polish Section that it was justified in continuing to prioritise the Home Army with the war material above all other clandestine forces in the country. An alternative would have been to supply the People's Army, which was a communist formation sponsored by Moscow. According to the British War Cabinet the Polish Communist Party was working closely with Soviet agents and fifth columnists who had been parachuted into Eastern Poland by the Soviet Airforce in order to prepare the country for sovietisation. It was this fact that prevented the British, who were the champions of the Government of the Second Republic, from supporting openly communist insurgents in Poland although doing so would have pleased Moscow considerably. The report also speculated that the Soviet policy of inciting the Poles to rise up immediately in Warsaw was a ploy to destroy the Home Army and prepare for the installation of a People's Republic. His Majesty's Government was of the opinion that a premature revolt on the ground would only lead to useless bloodshed.

\* \* \*

The Russian advance westward was bringing the Red Army closer and closer to the pre-1939 Polish frontier. The reversal of fortune on the eastern front was spectacular as only a few months ago the Russians had been on their knees. Now it was the Germans who were teetering on the brink; yet the great reversal on the eastern front was causing the exiled Polish Government in London some concern. This was because it was still not clear whether Soviet Russia would indeed proceed to establish a People's Republic in Poland or if they would liberate the Second Republic and allow its continued existance. The immediate question for Bor-Komorowski, was whether to recommend that the Home Army making itself known to Russian officers or whether it should remain underground to see what the true intention of the Russians was going to be. The Polish Government's in London serious concern was the fear that if the underground army revealed itself to Russian officers, it would be destroyed which would lead to the collapse of the whole clandestine organisation. On the other hand, if the Poles remained silent and hidden it would appear that they were indifferent to the sovietisation of Poland handing propaganda victory to the communists. Meanwhile, Britain was certain on one thing, under no circumstances should the Home Army be in the position to jeopardise the Soviet army's progress towards Berlin. This is why on 17 September 1943 no steps were taken by the Combined COS to approve the arming of the Home Army with large military equipment in case it was used against the Red Army. In deciding not to arm the Home Army to such an extent, the COS had relegated Polish resistance to the second tier of importance. This is why it wavered when it came to making transport aircraft available for operations to Poland, and on any decisions regarding the kinds of materials these aircraft should carry. It was envisaged that Soviet intentions should be considered at a future Foreign Ministers Conference. Meanwhile, the general line of the War Office was that the underground movement should confine itself to single acts of sabotage and subversive activity against German targets and withdraw altogether from areas in eastern Poland, beyond the Curzon Line, where the Soviets were making steady progress westward. Improving the relationship between the Poles and the Russians remained a priority. Privately, the War Cabinet felt that the Home Army should declare itself to the Russian forces as they fought their way towards Berlin and in order to encourage this, it reassured the Poles that HMG was in close contact with the Soviet Government and would not allow victimisation of its leaders. Consequently, the British Foreign Office informed the Polish Government in London that, in its view, a first step towards the restoration of normal Polish-Soviet relations was likely to lie in some collaboration between the Home Army and the Soviets. One possibility considered was to get the Home Army to cut German communication lines to the East Front in an act of solidarity with the Russians. The Poles agreed to this in the hope of freeing-up more military equipment from Britain. Perkins approved the idea and contacted the Air Ministry proposing an appropriate aircraft be provided.. He suggested that a Lockheed Hudson would probably do the trick. The Air Ministry did not reject the idea out of hand but requested photographs of suitable drop sites. Perkins passed the request to the Sixth Bureau which acknowledged it could provide such information, but not in the form of photographic evidence. Two airfields were even considered as possible bases for the mission, Norfolk Colttshall and Horsham St. Faith. It was acknowledged that the Lockheed could be used only if its range was extended by the addition of extra fuel tanks. The Air Ministry offered 11 October, as a possible date for the mission; however, this plan was overtaken by events in Eastern

Poland, where it was discovered that the Red Army was arresting Home Army officers and putting them on trial for working for the Government of the Second Republic in London. This was considered by the Russians as treason. Other ranks of the Home Army were being forced to enrol in the Russian Forces.

\* \* \*

On 16 October 1943 the Joint Planning Staff sent fresh directives to SOE Polish Section informing that the Polish Government had proposed an increase in deliveries to Poland. The object of the proposal was to equip it for an uprising at the most suitable moment and seize an area in Poland once the main German forces had retreated in the face of the advancing Red Army. In this way the Poles would secure their capital before the Red Army's arrival. Despite the continued planning for such action, the Polish strategy was rejected by the COS on two grounds: the vast scale of air transport that would be required to equip such action and the hostile reaction which would most likely come from the Russians. Despite this, SOE was informed that it was the intention to increase supplies of equipment for 'petty sabotage' purposes and not for any major military action. The justification for this decision was strategic. Poland lay across the main German lines to the East. The intention here was to ensure that the Home Army was strong enough to harass the Germans but too weak to hinder the progress of the Red Army towards Berlin. The communications to SOE pointed to one thing, Britain will not equip the Home Army with heavy weapons, something that was missed or ignored by the Poles for they continued planning action which would indeed require such equipment. During February and March 1944, aircrews were mainly allocated to operations over the Balkans, however, when Poland was back on the agenda, mechanical faults and bad weather conspired to preventing many from flying.[1]

\* \* \*

The start of the rising occurred in SOE's 'Retaliation' operational phase, which had started on 1 August, 1944. Without special preparation flights from Campo Cassale started to be organised it was not until 21 September, that the first flight, Przemek 1, departed for Warsaw. The next operational flight to Poland, known as Wacek 1, took off on 16 October, some three weeks after the end of the rising. Significant help for Warsaw came from the Americans. (see Chapter 20) The Joint Planning Staff believed that a general rising would not be ordered by the Polish Government as this would lead to the 'butchery' of the Polish population. It therefore argued that Britain should not encourage the Poles to rise, but to intensify sabotage operations accompanied by maximum guerrilla action as far as supplies would allow. This, according to the JPS, required plans to be laid for a sabotage campaign on a grand scale a few days after the start of OVERLORD. This thinking led to three strategic objectives being issued

---

1   Jonathan Walker, *Poland Alone*, p.81.

to SOE Polish Section: 1, to arm the day to day sabotage action targeted on German communications and installations through Poland to the Eastern front; 2, to support action that provides maximum interference with a German withdrawal in the event of the Russian advance reaching the Russo-Polish border before OVERLORD; and 3, planning for an intensified sabotage campaign accompanied by a maximum increase in guerrilla activity timed to take place in support of OVERLORD. The actual timing of this was to be coordinated by Supreme Allied Command. One important limiting factor in trying to coordinate Polish action with Overlord was that the strategy would require extensive use of the airbridge to get adequate material to Poland. Perkins estimated the number of fighters in the Home Army to be 300,000 men, of which 50 percent were organised into formal companies and battalions. Up to 40,000 were armed with small arms such as Sten and Thompson submachine guns. However, Perkins believed that these totals were inadequate. But this did not mean that Polish aspirations were aborted, far from it, for Perkins pointed to the many successful sabotage activities of the Poles against German oil stocks, communication facilities and agriculture which demonstrate that the Polish spirit had not been conquered.

* * *

By late 1943, attacks on bridges and German lines of communication using explosives sent by SOE Polish Section were reported as far east as Minsk, but despite the Home Army helping to relieve some pressure on the Red Army, relations between the governments of Russia and the Second Republic remained strained. On 16 April, 1944, Major General Tabor and Lieutenant Colonel Dorotycz-Malewicz, were flown back from Poland to Britain in Operation Wildhorn I.[2] They reported to SOE Polish Section on Home Army plans to launch a general insurrection. They also reported that all political parties, except for the communists, were united behind the exiled government in London. As far as the insurrection was concerned, Tabor said, the Home Army command planned to unleash an insurrection at the point when the German Forces were at their weakest. This point would come, according to Tabor, when the Germans were being pressed hard by the Red Army fighting from the East and were evacuating the Polish capital. The aim of the insurrection was to put the Poles in a commanding position and provide political authority during negotiations on the future of post war Poland. On 20 June, SOE learnt of Mikołajczyk's request for $97,000,000 to finance the uprising. The American President remained non-committal but put Mikołajczyk in touch with Admiral Leahy who in turn introduced him to the Combined COS. Meanwhile, Tabor requested more wireless sets and between 1200 and 1500 extra missions to Poland in support of the rising. The American Combined COS agreed in principle but asked that the request be made through the proper channels, namely the SOE Polish Section. Meanwhile, Selbourne admitted secretly that the British had made errors 'in suggesting 300 sorties to the

---

2  TNA HS4/180: 1943-1945 Wildhorn and Wildhorn VI air landing: planning and policy.

Poles'.³ Despite Gubbins' belief that SOE should assist home-grown resistance in occupied countries by vast airborne drops, this was not encouraged by either the COS or thr Air Ministry.⁴

\*   \*   \*

Meanwhile, Frank's entry in his diary reads, 'Gerty and I went to town.' (20 June 1944) He describes how they saw evidence of Doodle Bug incidents here and there, for example, at Whitton and Twickenham and on entering Putney Station and Waterloo. He describes how they took tea at Buzzards where they also bought some of their 'unbelievable chocolates and nuts.' Having spent some time in Hyde Park they made for the 7pm Promenade Concert at the Royal Albert Hall. Sir Henry Wood himself conducted the Dvorak symphony. He reports that they enjoyed the programme although they had to leave early in order to catch the last train home. According to Frank, inside the Albert Hall a two electric warning lights had been installed at the conductor's platform. In the event of an air raid warning being received a red light would be flashed, and on receiving the 'All Clear' a green light would flash. As it happened, he writes, there was no occasion to use the lights that night.⁵

3   TNA AIR 19/816: Selbourne to Archibald Sinclair, 21 February 1944.
4   Jonathan Walker, *Poland Alone*, p.147.
5   Peter Minett (ed.), *Frank's Wartime Diary*, p. 546.

# 19

# Sixty-Six Days (Warsaw Rises)

*To renounce liberty is to renounce being a man, to surrender the rights of humanity and even its duties. For him who renounces everything no indemnity is possible. Such a renunciation is incompatible with man's nature; to remove all liberty from his will is to remove all morality from his acts.*

Rousseau, *Social Contract*, I,7

On 23 July 1944, Frank and Gerty celebrated their daughter's 21st birthday. The dinner effects included duck and green peas, Victoria plum pie, cold blackcurrant mould, port, cider and lemonade. At tea time a first class salad, jam tarts and an iced cake was on offer with 21 small coloured candles which had to be lit. 'They looked very cheery indeed,' wrote Frank in his diary. It was a wonderful effort on Gerty's part. In his diary, Frank adds, 'I must also mention the unintentional fun which was provoked by a tea time item called 'fluffy pudding' – it was so sweet and rich that only the very smallest quantity of it could be eaten. We were not able to chill the concoction having no refrigerator'.[1]

\* \* \*

Meanwhile, on the other side of Europe, Bor-Komorowski, Commander of the Home Army, telegraphed London to inform that he was ready to fight for Warsaw. All he needed was the order to 'go'. At the time the only Polish Flight capable of helping Warsaw was 1586 stationed in Brindisi. The commander of this Flight was Squadron Leader S. Król, who was respected at SOE Polish Section. He was originally deployed as liaison officer to the newly formed British Air Group 'The Balkans', commanded by Squadron Leader E. Arciszewski. On 1 August 1944 at 17.00 hours (Godzina W) the

---

1   Peter Minett (ed.), *Frank's Wartime Diary*, p. 557.

Polish Secret Army in Warsaw (Home Army), joined by many of the civilian population in the capital, rose up against the German occupiers. Although Zero Hour was 5 p.m, skirmishes between the occupying German army and the insurgents flared up prematurely when over enthusiastic young fighters could not restrain themselves once they saw ragged German troops retreating from the Eastern Front. According to Bor-Komorowski, national dignity and pride required the Poles to liberate their own capital. The spontaneous begining to the rising, despite an official start time being announced, wrong-footed the High Command to the extent that it began making frantic demands on the Sixth Bureau in London. The great Polish fear was what Stalin would say if the Russians were to clear Warsaw of Germans single-handedly. In that event, it was feared, he would have no difficulty in convincing the other allies that the Home Army and the underground movement as a whole, was nothing more than pure fantasy. The military objective of the rising was to liberate Warsaw; prevent the retreating Germans from destroying the Polish capital and to protect the capital from a possible Russian occupation. When the Red Army was fighting towards Berlin, across Polish territory, it had two objectives: to clear the territory of German forces and to destroy the Home Army which stood in the way of Moscow's intention to establish a People's Democratic Republic in Poland. This meant that the Home Army would have to fight the Germans as well as the Soviets in order to free and preserve the Second Republic until the Republic's Polish Government could return from London. The serious repercussion of this for SOE Polish Project, was how to support the Home Army in its fight against the Germans without empowering it to the extent that it felt empowered to confront the Red Army? One thing that could not be seen happening was that supplies delivered by SOE, were being used against the Russians. The compromise to the conundrum saw SOE being instructed to provide just enough equipment for individual acts of sabotage but not enough to make the Poles believe that they could launch coordinated action against the Red Army. This should have pleased the Russians who had told Eden that they would have preferred it if no arms were sent to the Poles.[2] In the meantime, Warsaw called for more and more equipment whilst the British hesitated. When Warsaw rose in August 1944, the Russian Army had reached Praga, an eastern suburb of the Polish capital. Rather than continuing its advance and help the Home Army Stalin, who had all military decisions under his fountain pen, stopped all army action taking place on the approaches to the Polish capital. This left the Home Army to fight the Germans unaided. Stalin's intention to destroy the Home Army, was slowly being realised. SOE received information regarding Soviet policy on Warsaw from a Russian officer who reported that at the last moment military plans were changed to by-pass Warsaw rather than to enter it. Eventually, the Polish Home Army units in the capital perished in the streets and sewers of the city by crushed by overwhelming superior Nazis forces.[3] Concern rose that reprisals would be taken out on the fighters and so efforts were hurriedly taken to obtain combatant status for the fighters. This was the only sure way of preventing

---

2    Lynne Olson and Stanley Cloud, *For Your Freedom and Ours*, p. 285.
3    Robert Dallek, *The Lost Peace* (London, Harper Perennial, 2010), p. 54.

the captured insurgents being treated as rebels with no protection under the Geneva Convention.

\* \* \*

The objective of the rising was for the Home Army to occupy Warsaw after the German retreat but before the arrival of the Soviets forces. The rising was given the name Operation Tempest. What is not clear is why the decision was taken to reverse previous decisions to begin the rising in rural areas, where the bulk of arms had been secretly cached, and then move on to concentrate on urban areas. This decision meant that the Home Army was destined to fight in Warsaw where there was an acute shortage of weapons. When the rising started the insurgents were unable to seize either the whole city or any key locations. The Red Army far from helping was ordered to stop their advance and concentrate on expanding bridgeheads over the river Vistula. According to Surkov, a Soviet officer, who was questioned by the Home Army, reported that as he approached the Polish capital he was ordered to swing around and by pass the city. In his view this was done for political reasons. All this while the Germans annihilated the Home Army in the Polish capital whilst razing Warsaw to the ground. For days the Soviet Union either refused to send aid or to facilitate the sending of aid by SOE Polish Section. However, when the Germans were gaining the upper hand in Warsaw, Stalin finally decided to reduce tensions with the Western Allies and indicated that he did not object to their helping the Poles as long as their planes did not refuel on Soviet territory. He even provided a little help himself. At the time no one in London or Washington could have foreseen that the Russians might have deliberately halted their offensive on the day of the Rising, however, to those who appreciated Russian intentions towards the Second Republic, the action was true to form. The Poles appealed to Britain for supplies. As the function of Force 139 in supplying the Secret Army was principally operational, no one in the Italian base went into the vexed questions of whether the rising was wise or not; whether the Soviet Military Authorities should have been informed of the start of the rising beforehand or not, or any of the other questions aroused by its tragic course. The facts are that the monitoring of Russian radio broadcasts until 31 July in the Polish language show that the citizens of Warsaw were being urged to rise up as the Soviet army was on the outskirts of the city and was ready to provide help. The eventual cost in lives of the rising amounted to 150,000 losses. This forced SOE Polish Section to question whether flights to Warsaw should continue. As soon as Churchill heard that the rising had begun and not wanting to appear as having betrayed the Poles at a crucial moment, immediately called for more flights to Warsaw irrespective of weather conditions. Major Pickles started to search for more stores whilst he prepared for mass drops. At the request of the Polish Government in London, the COS telegraphed Mediterranean Allied Air Force asking for their opinion on the practicalities of mass drops. Air Marshal Slessor, Commander MAAF, consulted with Major General Stawell, who replied unfavourably and so planning for mass drops was halted. The High Command of the Home Army should have appreciated the significance of this decision.

\* \* \*

On 4 August, 1944 aircraft flew to Poland but were diverted away from Warsaw to other parts of Poland. The Balkan Air Force, which at the time controlled all special operations from the heel of Italy, declared that operations to Poland during the current moon period were too dangerous and stopped authorising them. The reason given for doing so was the presence of German night fighters in the skies over Poland and the new radar belt called the *Kammhuber Line,* erected to protect the Silesian industrial region which had to be traversed in order to reach Warsaw. The position, therefore, was such that just at the time of Poland's greatest need not only was help for Warsaw refused but all support for the Secret Army cancelled. The reality was the fact that the Royal Airforce was unable to undertake accurate mass drops on Warsaw with many of the parachutes ending up in German hands.[4] However, when Churchill called for a resumption, missions began a few days later. In the meantime, Prime Minister Mikołajczyk, travelled to Moscow to appeal for Russian help. Aid was promised and the premier sent an urgent upbeat telegram through diplomatic channels to London on August 9, with details of what Marshal Stalin had promised. He instructed the Sixth Bureau to notify the Home Army Commander in Chief in Warsaw to make contact with the Russian commander stationed across the Vistula River. These efforts proved to be ineffective and despite the joint appeal to Mr. Molotov on 18 August, by the British and American Ambassadors in Moscow, the approach was met with denials of the value of Polish resistance in Warsaw and the wholesale condemnation of the Polish Government in exile for approving it. Consequently, no Russian help was forthcoming until the night of 13 September. Kopański asked Selborne to send a British liaison officer to Warsaw who could observe and perhaps prevent German reprisals, when it appeared that the rising was faltering. The rising was started on the mistaken premise that the British ally would increase the amount of supplies being delivered. The Poles also envisaged that a Polish squadron of fighter planes would be flown to Poland just as soon as an airfields had been captured. Their other hope was that the First Polish Parachute Brigade would be deployed to Warsaw to join in the fight. It seems clear that the Home Army's High Command was unaware that the COS had already decided against supporting a rising and as a result never sanctioned help for it. They had decided that a national uprising by the Home Army was no longer a necessary prerequisite to an Allied victory[5] and that the Home Army should have appreciated that help from the West would be limited.[6] This decision condemned the Home Army to prosecute the rising under equipped, using small

---

4   A.J., Prażmowska, *Civil War in Poland 1942-1948* (Basingstoke: Palgrave Macmillan, 2004). pp. 104-105.
5   Lynne Olson and Stanley Cloud, *For Your Freedom and Ours*, p. 282.
6   A. J., Prażmowska, *Civil War in Poland 1942-1948,* pp. 104-105.

arms and limited ammunition. Furthermore, when Stalin decided to halt the Russian advance on the outskirts of Warsaw the prospect for any kind of victory over the Germans by the isolated Home Army evaporated rapidly.[7] The reason why General Bor-Komorowski did not know of the British decision not to provide further help for Warsaw, which perhaps would have influenced his decision regarding the rising, is a moot point. It was never made forcibly enough by SOE Polish Section or COS that support would be limited and that the planning for a rising carried out by the Poles was no more than a waste of time. Despite this state of affairs, the Poles did not give up and continued pressing for British help. General Kopański, Chief of the Polish General Staff, contacted Selborne whilst General Kukiel, Commander of the First Polish Corps, wrote to General Ismay. As SOE's Polish base was now in Italy, the Polish requests were copied to Air Marshal Slessor, RAF Commander in the Mediterranean and the Middle East, and General Maitland—Wilson, Supreme Commander, Mediterranean. Having received a note from Slessor and Wilson stating that nothing will be achieved by increasing flights to Poland and that such an increase was not an operation of war, the Joint Planning Staff recommended that they return negative answers to all Polish requests. Colonel Perkins, Head of SOE Polish Section, was upset by this instruction, as it appeared that the British were being disrespectful to the Poles. although he appreciated the tone of the message. On 2 August reports from Warsaw informed London that certain districts of Warsaw were under Polish control; however, the cost in lives of securing them was very high. The immediate concern on the ground was the dwindling supplies of ammunition. On 3 August, President Raczkiewicz wrote to Churchill asking that priority be given to drops for Poland that night.

*　*　*

The second stage of help for Warsaw came about because of renewed pressure from SOE and desperate appeals by the Polish Government in London. General Bor-Komorowski despaired and telegraphed London pleading assistance for the rising. He requested ammunition and anti-tank rockets and, according to him, if this was not forthcoming the Home Army would not be able to hold out much longer.[8] In a desperate effort Bor-Komorowski hardened his resolve and decided to curtail any further bitter wrangling and cabled President Roosevelt and Prime Minister Churchill directly, he observed:

> In this desperate struggle, strength of spirit without weapons will not suffice. In the name of the principle that right and justice shall overcome might, in the name of the Atlantic Charter and of the Four Freedoms, confident of having fulfilled our duty to defend the independence of our country, confident of the just part we have played in the war effort of the Anglo-Americans, we have to

---

7　Lynne Olson and Stanley Cloud, *For Your Freedom and Ours*, p. 283.
8　Bor-Komorowski, *The Home Army*, (London: Victor Gollancz, 1950), p.239.

full right to address you, Mr. President and Mr. Prime Minister, this ardent appeal for immediate help to be sent to wounded Warsaw.[9]

This was a despairing message from an exasperated officer trying to bypass Britain's pusillanimity. However, the view in London echoed the belief in Moscow that the Polish General's decision to initiate a rising was a grave mistake and should not have been made. Furthermore, according to COS, he would have realised this as an error if he had consulted closely with SOE Polish Section before initiating the insurrection. The message continued to be that meaningful support for the Polish rising could only come from the Russians as Poland was firmly in the Soviet sphere of operation. Air Marshal Slessor was keen for the Russians to know about the dire situation in Warsaw and requested that the British Mission in Moscow inform Stalin.[10] Moscow replied that it was difficult to support the Poles as ultimately the rising had been badly planned by General Sosnkowski.[11] Stalin was warned that the decision not to help would influence future Polish opinion regarding Russia as an ally but alas this did not concern Moscow. Slessor's exasperation began to show when he cabled the War Office stating that the British are continuing to exert full assistance to Russian activities in Yugoslavia with shuttle operations using B25 aircraft which could be better employed supplying Warsaw. His brutish conclusion was that Russian failure to supply Warsaw was no more than a deliberate policy[12] as was the decision by London to sacrifice Warsaw rather than to antagonize Moscow.

\* \* \*

Perkins was in favour of sending a military mission to Warsaw as it could supply London with up-to-date information regarding conditions prevailing in the Polish capital. Selborne suggested to Churchill that sending the Polish Parachute Brigade would also be a welcome gesture of support and a little pressure from him would push the COS to come to the same conclusion. Komorowski also sent a plea for assistance to Stalin asking for the units of the Red Army on the outskirts of Warsaw, to be ordered to enter the Polish capital and help the Home Army.[13] There was no response from Stalin and the Polish Parachute Brigade was deployed to Arnhem in Operation Market Garden instead. The COS were also minded to refuse intensive bombing of the Warsaw region. The reason given for the refusal was the difficulties associated with coordinating operations with the Russians, the blame for which was placed squarely on the Polish inability to come to an understanding with Moscow. McFarland insisted that for geographical reasons the responsibility for helping Polish home forces

---

9 Bor-Komorowski, p. 263.
10 TNA CAB 121/310: SOE Operations in Poland Vol. II.
11 TNA CAB 121/310: SOE Operations in Poland Vol. II, 275B.
12 TNA CAB 121/310: SOE Operations in Poland Vol. II, 321.
13 TNA HS4/147: Polish Secret Army, Polish planning for the reoccupation of Poland.

in Warsaw should rest primarily with the Russians.[14] This view was endorsed by the Joint COS.[15] General Maitland—Wilson, the Supreme Allied Commander in the Mediterranean, and Air Marshal Slessor were also asked to give all the help they could. A telegram dated 11 August, from Lord Selborne to Prime Minister Churchill, who happened to be in Italy at the time, resulted in a re-examination of the position at MAAF, and the allocation on 13 August of two squadrons of Liberators from 334 Wing. They were formed from 31 and 34 Squadron, SAAF and 178 Squadron RAF and were based at airfields in Foggia. Their first mission to Poland was on 13 August. They staged at Brindisi for loading as there were no supplies of packed containers at Foggia. This was later changed with stocks of packed containers being built up at the airfield. Eventually, an Anglo-Polish liaison unit with direct W/T communication back to Latiano was set up to Foggia which allowed for the briefing of crews. These organisational improvements meant that airfields as much as 150 miles from base could be used and although this put a considerable strain on RAF aircraft they were able to fly from their own airfield. Despite Poland being considered to be in the Soviet sphere of operation, SOE Section pushed on supporting the Poles and when the base in Brindisi requested permission to carry out 'token drops' they were approved, provided aircraft being available. Sixty tons of equipment was prepared for Warsaw and SOE was to inform Moscow of the impending drops. However, the first of these flights was called off because of bad weather. On 14 August, it was recorded that 28 aircraft took off for Warsaw with 12 reaching their objective, 12 having failed and 4 missing.[16]

\* \* \*

Events on the ground further complicated SOE policy towards Poland and in addition, there was no clarity coming from the COS. Chris Warner was to put into words the quandary facing SOE Polish Section when he said, two thirds of stores are being held in reserve to be used against the aggressor, but who was the aggressor, the Germans, the Russians or both? Although he probably did not know it, Warner's question was an astute summary of the complicated situation which had unfolding in occupied Poland. Meanwhile, Slessor maintained his position and refused to allow aircraft to continue flying to the Polish capital. When the Polish crews in Italy learned about his decision, morale all but collapsed. It was dented even further by information emanating from the conference at Teheran between the leaders of Britain, America and Russia where all resistance to Soviet policy regarding the removal of the Second Republic of Poland had evaporated. Seemingly, the betrayal of the Second Republic was a price worth paying for continued Russian military support on the eastern front. The conclusions reached at Teheran, which were later endorsed at Yalta, signalled the brutish fact that the Second Republic, for all intents and purposes, was lost which

14  TNA CAB 121/310: SOE Operations in Poland Vol. II, 317:
15  TNA CAB 121/310: SOE Operations in Poland Vol. II, 275B:
16  TNA CAB 121/310: SOE Operations in Poland Vol. II, 261A.

altered the situation significantly for: 1) it devalued Britain's obligations to the Polish ally, 2) it handed Poland over to the Soviets and 3) it ruled out the invasion of the European continent from the south and excluded Poland from Western planning. In these circumstances, which made it look as if Britain had totally betrayed the Poles, Slessor revoked his order on flights to Poland and Polish crew started to fly again.

\* \* \*

General Bor-Komorowski understood the technical difficulties pilots were facing in flying from bases some one thousand miles from Warsaw. But he failed to appreciate why flights could not take place from Soviet bases which were no more than fifty miles away. He was also aware of the bombing campaigns over Bucharest, Konigsberg and Ploesti by the RAF, all of which were further from English bases than was Warsaw. The commander of the Home Army was also perturbed by London continuously highlighted British losses during flights to Poland when Polish losses in the Battle of Britain, Tobruk, Monte Cassino and the Falaise Gap were never mentioned. Writing five years after the end of the war Bor-Komorowski estimated that all it would have taken for the Home Army to survive would have been a further five tons of ammunition dropped per night. At the beginning of the Warsaw Rising[17] the Poles were able to seize a large proportion of the centre of the city and to hold it for some time. However, in doing so their supplies of weapons and ammunition was woefully depleted and the subsequent history of the rising until final surrender on 2 October was one of carving up Polish held territory by the enemy. This meant that the size of the targets for drops gradually diminished the longer the rising continued. This handicapped some pilots, particularly those of the three squadrons of 205 Group, who were not trained in low level flying. Meanwhile, a telegram arrived in London from the Polish base in Italy. It said that the Poles were considering withdrawing their support for the Anglo-Polish treaty as the arrangement for mutual assistance appears to have been 'broken and abandoned.' SOE replied that laying down arms now would forfeit Britain's sympathy for Poland and promised to work at breakneck speed to assist the fighters in the Polish capital. After lobbying the Secretary State for Air, instructions were issued to increase the number of flights. Almost immediately, three aircraft were despatched to Warsaw. There followed a series of flights by Polish, British and South African crew, but due to murderous losses, approximately 17 percent, these were suspended only to be resumed immediately following pressure from London.[18] The news that flights would resume was announced in secretly distributed underground newspapers to people in the streets in Warsaw. Having read the headlines, the relieved population rejoiced and began chanting the names of Britain, America and the Polish Government in London in gratitude and anticipation. However, on

---

17   TNA HS4/157: Warsaw Rising: Reports from Poland. Foreign Office telegrams, Operations to Warsaw.
18   TNA HS/4/157: MJTP/PD/661 to Roberts. 8.8.44 Negotiations between Polish GHQ and COS during Warsaw Uprising 10.5.44. AD/M and MPCT 919 to Maryland (Italy).

the first night following the announcement no planes appeared over Warsaw. The following day the BBC broadcast a a coded message called 'Red Belt', to say that a special operations' flight was on its way. Bor-Komorowski climbed onto the roof of his secret HQ in Warsaw Old Town (*Stare Miasto*) and awaited the aircraft. Special observers were positioned around the Old Town square ready to give warning of the approaching aircraft. Eventually, in the distance, the rumble of aircraft engines could be heard and 15 women carrying hurricane lamps stepped out into the darkness and arranged themselves into the shape of a large cross in order to help the pilot locate the drop zone. Unfortunately, on hearing the aircraft approaching, German search lights sparkled into life and began scanning the skies. They swept left and right across the dark, cloudless sky until an aircraft was 'caught' in the beams. Once located, anti-aircraft guns opened up. As the roar increased and the planes approached the square, the women lit their hurricane lamps to guide the planes to their final target. This was done at the last moment so as not to attract the attention of the Germans patrolling the Old Town. A British aeroplane droned towards the square at roof top height and, as it reached the square, it dropped its load. According to Bor-Komorowski, another seven planes had followed. Unfortunately, some of the containers landed on German positions and were therefore lost.

\* \* \*

The Warsaw Uprising, lasted from 1 August to 2 October 1944. The number of RAF and SAAF drops over Warsaw during this time amounted to 38 in every 105 flights.[19] Proportionately, the American flights brought more success with 107 drops being made with 1,010 flights flying from the British Isles (see chapter 20). According to Alun Morgan, the reason given for the low number of RAF and SAAF missions was due to the fact that the Germans had installed a string of radar stations across Hungary making the route from Italy hazardous.[20] In spite of this development some supplies did get through, but the losses were very high which resulted in Slessor cancelling further operations. President Raczkiewicz, exiled in Britain, wrote to Churchill whilst Tabor contacted Gubbins protesting the decision. However, the protest fell on deaf ears for Slessor believed that under the prevailing circumstances any further attempts to supply Warsaw was futile. With the suspension of flights the situation in Warsaw became intolerable. SOE Polish Section cabled Moscow for immediate assistance and contacted the COS in the hope that there would be no repetition of events which occurred in September 1939 when Britain failed to help Poland during the German and Russian invasion of the country. This provocative act was designed to galvanise those in authority into action. General Tabor renewed his request for the resumption of flights and even suggested that Polish crews be used if the COS were worried about British losses over Europe. Gubbins responded by requesting maps of the drop zones which would help crews reach their targets

---

19  Garliński, *Poland, SOE and the Allies*, p. 237.
20  TNA HS4/148: Liaison with Poland by means of air.

in the Polish capital but this was considered to be no more than a delaying tactic. Meanwhile on 8 August the Home Army's Head Quarters cabled Captain Kolugin via London pleading for Russian support. Kalugin, who was Stalin's liaison officer with the Poles, wrote to Stalin informing him that despite a heroic stand by the Warsaw population there remains a need for automatic arms, ammunition, grenades and anti-tank weapons. The Varsovians waited for Russian help . The message also passed through SOE hands in Moscow. Threlfall, in Monopoli, reflected on the situation in Warsaw. He acknowledged the serious disquiet in Warsaw about the cessation of flights to the Polish capital and according to his assessment the laying down of arms by the fighters in Warsaw would result in confirming Russia's claim that the Poles do not want to fight which would have played right into the hands of the Lublin Committee.[21] Threlfall argued robustly that something had to be done to save the situation and recommended that flights be restarted forthwith. Even before he had received a response from London, Sir Charles Portal reported that the COS had been instructed by the Secretary of State for Air to telegraph Slessor in order to commence operations to Poland.

\* \* \*

General Ismay cabled Sosnkowski informing the Polish General that further flights were planned, weather permitting. Operations scheduled for the following night, however, were abandoned due to bad weather. Sosnkowski wrote to CIGS asking whether Polish crews held in reserve could be used solely for Polish operations and whether the Home Army could be afforded combatant status hence giving them protection under the Geneva Convention. During the night of the 12th, eleven sorties took place with seven successes. During the following consecutive days, from the 13th to 18th, 90 aircraft took off for Warsaw. The flights on 13 and 14 August, involved 28 and 26 aircraft respectively, with 13 and 10 successes. The operations on the first night were particularly fortunate, since a high proportion of the stores dropped were acknowledged as having reached the Home Army. But again, the losses were heavy with 11 aircraft reported as missing, making up 20 percent of the contingent, with nearly as many again seriously damaged and unserviceable. During the period 20 27 August, 32 missions took place, all flown by Polish crews.[22] These were followed on 1 September with seven flights taking place followed by 20 flights on the 19th by mixed crews.[23] The aircraft had to fly low over the city in order to pinpoint the drop zones, but given the heavy flak that the pilots had to endure, it soon became clear that the Germans had strengthened their defences in the Polish capital. On 15 August a conference was held at the HQ of the Balkan Air Force to discuss the situation. In attendance were Air Marshal Slessor, Air Vice Marshal Elliot, Brigadier Durrant (Commander of 205 Group), Group Captain Rankin (Commander 334 Wing) and

---

21　The title given to the communist Government of the People's Republic in waiting.
22　Garliński, *Poland, SOE and the Allies*, pp.208-209.
23　Garliński, *Poland, SOE and the Allies*, pp.208-209.

Lieutenant Colonel Threlfall. Air Marshal Slessor said that the losses were too heavy to bear and ruled that direct flights to Warsaw should cease but agreed that they could continue to the Kampinos Forest just outside the city. The Kampinos Forest was a dense woodland, 30 miles long and 10 miles wide, lying along the western bank of the Vistula characterised by marshes, bogs and the tributaries of two rivers – the Vistula and the Bzura.[24] This policy was tested on 15 and 16 August, but six out of 18 aircraft were lost. Air Vice Marshal Elloit, as the RAF officer responsible for sorties, explained that it was an operational risk which he could not ask the most courageous British, Polish or South African crews to run. He therefore ruled that flights, both to Warsaw and its vicinity, had to stop although, operations to the rest of Poland might continue as before.

\* \* \*

Ironically, the third stage of support for the Warsaw rising involved flights to the outskirts of the city by Polish aircrew.[25] During the period 2 to 18 August, 122 sorties took place. The success rate, however, was not impressive as only 52 percent completed their missions. Only 40 tons of materials was retrieved by the Home Army at a cost of 20 aircraft lost. Following these losses, SOE missions to Poland dwindled, compared to the number of sorties to other countries such as occupied Yugoslavia and France. The tonnage of materials delivered could be thought of as woeful. Up to 16–17 August SOE had delivered 56 tons of supplies including 1.3 million rounds of small arms ammunition, 54 light machine guns, 262 Sten guns, 4,700 grenades, 70 Piat anti-tank weapons and 1700 rounds of Piat ammunition. It was estimated that approximately 50 percent of this material ended up in Polish hands. Despite these disappointing statistics, the fact that the Poles were occupying up to four German divisions in Warsaw, it was thought that continuing with flights was well worth it. Nevertheless, not everyone agreed – Air Vice Marshal Elliot felt that the price being paid was too high and, in any case, he was convinced that such flights would do little to save Warsaw; however, he did believe that, rather than stopping flights altogether,, it would be helpful to concentrate on making drops in the vicinity of Warsaw, which would be safer. On hearing this suggestion, General Tabor contacted Gubbins in protest. He said that the only way to ensure that deliveries would help the fighters was to drop containers directly into the Polish capital. Meanwhile, Winston Churchill was not alarmed by the situation and expressed satisfaction with the help being offered to the Poles. The Foreign Office indicated, via the British Ambassador to Moscow, that there was concern in London that no news had been received from Moscow regarding Russian help for Warsaw, which was even more surprising given Stalin's promise to Mikołajczyk. Threlfall made it known that it was very difficult to explain to airmen why they should fly 850 miles on sorties when the Russians needed only to

---

24 Kochański, *The Eagle Unbowed, Poland and the Poles in the Second World War*, p. 73.
25 TNA HS4/157: Warsaw Rising: Reports from Poland; Foreign Office telegrams, Operations to Warsaw.

fly 20 miles. As the murderous losses continued to mount it was suggested that drops could be made from higher altitudes keeping aircraft out of the range of German anti-aircraft guns. One modification would have to be made if the containers were not to split open on hitting the ground from a greater height. Engineers suggested that a braking device would have to be attached to the parachute lines in order to slow the descent. A second modification could be the supplying of accurate bomb-sights for despatchers flying at high altitude so that the accuracy of drops was improved. Despite the promise that it would take three days to deliver these devices to bases no orders were placed, because there was still some doubt about their effectiveness and in any case, according to Keswick, such devices had not yet been approved for use.

* * *

On 16 August, Perkins met with Generals Tabor and Kopański. Prior to the meeting Perkins had decided that the time had come for plain speaking. He began by expressing his disquiet on the Polish approach to the rising and castigated the Polish High Command for not being honest with Bor-Komorowski who continued making unrealistic demands on SOE and hence the RAF. Perkins went as far as to accuse the Poles of making all kinds of promises to Bor-Komorowski in order to cover up their own poor judgement. This made Gubbins enquire whether a number of aircraft from bomber command could be diverted to missions over Warsaw. By this time the Poles had lost faith in the SOE and had decided to approach the Air Ministry directly. This demonstrated that by now the Poles perceived SOE as a mere transport agency with no influence regarding major policy decisions. This view was inadvertently endorsed by Selborne who instructed General Tabor that SOE Polish Section was only permitted to support sabotage and intelligence, so if General Sosnkowski wanted major military support for the Home Army, he should approach the COS. Selborne's advice was imprecise since the Poles had always been told that the correct line for communication always began with the SOE Polish Section. Despite this lapse, Selborne did his best for the Poles during the rising. On 11 August he wrote to Churchill[26] appealing for more help for Warsaw which, according to him, would not only help the Home Army, but redeem Britain's good name. He summed up the Polish cause in an insightful comment made to Sinclair[27] by saying that the 'Poles had put their shirt on Britain in 1939 and now Britain had a debt to repay.' It seemed at the time that the Poles had learned nothing from 1939. The Western allies proved themselves to be impotent then and so it was the case in 1944. In October Churchill travelled to Moscow to meet with Stalin to discuss the future of Poland. He had said, in confidence, that although the Polish soldier was dedicated and conscientious his leaders were unwise. At the meeting Churchill said to Stalin that he could keep Eastern Poland which he had forcibly annexed in 1939 and agreed that Britain would recognise the new border. He recommended that Stalin should invite Mikołajczyk to

26  TNA HS 4/154: Air19/816 Selborne to Sinclair 22.11.1944.
27  TNA: HS4/ 154.

Moscow to discuss the new arrangements and demonstrate that the relations between the West and Russia was not a complete wash out.

On 18 August General Maitland-Wilson ruled that only Polish aircraft of 1586 Flight might fly to Poland in future in view of the Italian resistance movement. Coming after the loss of 208 Group this was a severe blow to Polish hopes. But at least the Polish crews were allowed to fly to the out-skirts of Warsaw every night and from 20 to 27 August did so. Their drops depended on whether they could penetrate the flak gun fire over Warsaw, but if not, they were instructed to release their loads into the Kampinos Woods just outside the city. On two occasions, two out of a force of 6 aircraft were lost and others returned damaged by anti-aircraft fire. If Stalin had agreed to the use of Russian airfields for the refuelling of aircraft the outcome would have been significantly different. On 20 August Sosnkowski learnt that 6 Polish crews from 300 Squadron had been sent to supplement Flight 1568. This was in response to the withdrawal of 148 Squadron from operations to Poland. Also, what hampered proceedings is the fact that the Polish Government did not have direct communication with Moscow and the only thing it could do was to appeal to the British to put pressure on the Russians on their behalf. Stalin refused to listen even when the Americans sent a plea. Unfortunately, Stalin rebuffed Churchill stating that it was difficult to work with the Poles as they had not communicated with the Red Army Generals stationed on the Vistula regarding their intentions. On 22 August, Stalin wrote to Churchill that the only hope for Poland was if the Red Army occupied the whole country. He failed to mention landing American aircraft in Ukraine. Churchill invited Roosevelt to compose a letter to Stalin. The British Prime Minister even suggested dispatching aircraft to Poland without Soviet approval to see what the Russian would do. Roosevelt disapproved of the plan saying that Poland was in the Soviet sphere of operation and therefore Russian permission to fly was vital.

\* \* \*

Churchill and Roosevelt had lost patience with Moscow and began putting in place plans designed to force Stalin's hand. When the British COS suggested that the 15 American Airforce be used in the Warsaw theatre, the Americans answered that its range was insufficient. They also pointed out that there were insufficient fighter escort planes available which missions to Warsaw would require. However, the Americans were working on using 8 Airforce and aircraft which would fly at high altitude out of the range of German guns. The COS believed that such operations coupled to Soviet efforts would be sufficient in saving the Poles. They had planned a shuttle service to run between airbases in Western Russia and Warsaw. They presented their plans to Moscow which were rejected. Stalin said that the Russian Government cannot lend its hand to such a shuttle. In an explanation, which was shared with Churchill, the Soviets reported that they could not support a Polish insurrection which had little chance of success as the fighters on the ground lacked artillery, tanks and aviation. The Foreign Office instructed the British Ambassador to make it clear that such a position will have serious repercussions for Polish/Soviet and British/Soviet relations in the future. London could not fathom why, having encouraged the Poles to rise, Moscow was now punishing them for having done just that. The British pointed out that the Polish operation was not as badly planned as the Russians were making out. Of course it was not a matter of poor planning but more about Moscow's political objectives for post-war Poland. Moscow retorted that it did not have anything against giving the Poles support but objected to Russian airfields being used in such operations. Rather ominously Moscow clarified to the American ambassador that it did not want to be associated with the 'adventurers' in Warsaw. The ambassador requested to meet with Stalin over the matter but was turned down on the pretext that the Marshal was very busy. Molotov informed the American that the Soviet Government was very unlikely to reconsider its position. On the night of the 16 August Vyshinsky asked the United States Ambassador in Moscow to call and explaining that he wished to avoid any misunderstanding, read out the following statement:

> The Soviet Government cannot of course object to English or American aircraft dropping arms in the region of Warsaw, since this is an American and British affair. But they decidedly object to American or British aircraft, after dropping arms in the region of Warsaw, landing on Soviet territory, since the Soviet Government do not wish to associate themselves either directly or indirectly with the adventure in Warsaw.[28]

On the same day Churchill received the following message from Stalin:

> After the conversation with M. Mikołajczyk I gave orders that the command of the Red Army should drop arms intensively in the Warsaw sector. A parachutist liaison officer was also dropped, who, according to the report of the command, did not reach his objective as he was killed by the Germans. Further, having familiarised myself more closely with the Warsaw affair, I am convinced that the Warsaw action represents a reckless and terrible adventure which is costing the population large sacrifices. This would not have been if the Soviet command had been informed before the beginning of the Warsaw action and if the Poles had maintained contact with it. In the situation which has arisen the Soviet command has come to the conclusion that it must dissociate itself from the Warsaw adventure, as it cannot take either direct or indirect responsibility for the Warsaw action.

The Russian position, according to Laurence Rees[29], fitted a consistent pattern of behaviour, which Stalin had demonstrated time and time again. He mistrusted the Poles of the Second Republic and desired to see the Home Army disbanded and 'neutralised'.[30] On 1 October, Podoski contacted Pickles, to say that American drops

---

28   Winston Churchill, *The Second World War* (London: Pimlico, 2002), p. 818.
29   Laurence Rees, *Behind Closed Doors* (London: BBC Books, 2008), p. 288.
30   Rees, p. 288.

directed on Warsaw should be approved; however, the suggestion to drop equipment into the Kampinos Forest (*Puszcza Kampinoska*) near Warsaw should be avoided as the woods had been overrun by Germans Forces and atrocities were reported to have been observed.

\* \* \*

Preparations were started to send American bombers with fighter escorts to Warsaw. SOE Polish Section's role in the operations was to procure the materials the Poles had requested which the Americans would endeavour to deliver. The Polish Section worked closely with the Sixth Bureau so that the equipment the Poles wanted was made available. While the 'Great Armada' was being made ready, there was hope that the Russians would relent from refusing to play their part in helping Warsaw. In the meantime, stores continued to be collected. The Polish Section prepared 1,320 containers each packed with 2,976 Sten guns and 1,691,400 rounds of ammunition, 211 Bren guns with 584,000 rounds of ammunition, 110 Tank guns with 220 shells, 545 revolvers with 27,250 rounds, 2,490 grenades, 4,360 hand grenades and 17,523 pounds of plastic explosives. Included in the containers were 54,000 metres of detonating fuses, 8,700 metres of safety fuses, 22,000 detonators, 23,500 tins of meat, 2,016 tins of biscuits, 2,000 tins of margarine, 5,800 tins of milk rations and 12 containers of medical equipment. Then the news came that everyone was waiting for: Stalin announced on 10 September that the Russian government was ready to grant facilities for the American operation. It appeared that the planning of an American mission had forced Stalin's hand. In order to take advantage of Russian aid, Mikołajczyk asked the Foreign Office to explain to Moscow how contact could be made with the garrison commander in Warsaw and the location into which Soviet officers should be dropped. Stalin was informed that reception committees were always ready to receive drops in and around Warsaw. Meanwhile, Supreme Headquarters of the Allied Expeditionary Forces (SHAEF) anguished about what the Poles would do with the equipment provided by the Russians. They were convinced that the Home Army would use it against the Russians after the war in an attempt to resist the russification of Polish territory. To make sure the situation was clear SHAEF informed the Commander in Chief in Warsaw that the equipment delivered was only to be used against Nazi forces and that it was not to be stored for post-war operations. SHAEF reminded the US COS that Warsaw was a British problem and drops to Poland should only be organised through SOE Polish Section. The General also suggested to VCAS that the Italian base should be supplemented with Polish crews.

\* \* \*

Meanwhile, the War Cabinet passed the news of the Russian change of heart to the Foreign Office.[31] In the light of Stalin's announcement, SOE Polish Section and the

---

31   TNA CAB 1212/130: Vol II Doc 382.

Polish Sixth Bureau began making arrangements for daylight drops by the 8 USAAF. On September 12 Eisenhower approved a shuttle service to Warsaw.[32] The American authorities were willing and able and so prepared a flight plan. On the same day, Eisenhower telegraphed the Poles with what appeared to be a saving message. He informed them that Stalin had finally approved Americans using Soviet airfields and therefore significant drops for Warsaw were being prepared. Moreover, it was reported that Moscow had even approved some drops to be made by the Soviet Airforce. The flight plan for the American aircraft was based on route 2 over Denmark, which the RAF had previously used and abandoned. The only modification was that the Americans, having reached Warsaw, would fly on to the Ukrainian city of Poltava in the Soviet Union, where they would land and refuel before returning to Britain. On 14 September, Stalin enquired on the prevailing conditions in Warsaw, the areas of the capital which were in Polish hands and the quantity and nature of equipment he could contribute. The COS replied on 15 September, by writing that Warsaw was without electricity, water or gas. It was also pointed out to the Russians that the areas of Warsaw in Polish hands were difficult to delineate as the situation on the ground was in constant flux.[33] The food situation was described as critical, as was the situation regarding medicine. Disease was rife and the wounded lacked medical attention. The areas of Warsaw held by the Poles were listed as: Marymont, Żoliborz, Mokotów, Sielce and Belwederska. The Russians were asked to drop as much material as possible. The items requested were automatic machine guns with ammunition, grenades, explosives and engineering materials for demolition and the construction of road traps. Medical supplies were also added to the list. The message concluded that the airlift would be carried out by the USAAF with flights scheduled to operate during daylight hours dropping 130 tons of materials. This approximately amounted to 200 Brens, 100 anti-tank guns, 2,700 Stens, six and a half tons explosives, 40 tons of food and 2,000,000 rounds of ammunition.

On 22 August, SOE received a message from an unlikely source. The message came from an ex-POW called John Clark. His aircraft had been shot down over Luxemburg on the 10 May 1940 and he was kept captive by the Germans in occupied Poland. On managing to escape he joined the Home Army, where he was able to observe events first hand and managed to keep London informed by sending regular reports to SOE. The Foreign Office used his reports to verify the information emanating from the Home Army. Clark informed SOE that there should be no distinction made between the Home Army and the civilian population, as both were united and fighting heroically. On the 19th the Soviets made their first drop over Warsaw, releasing thousands of propaganda leaflets in the Polish language describing the rising as an unfortunate episode launched by a Polish clique of fascists in London. This was the term used by the Russians to describe the Polish High Command and the allied Polish Government of the Second Republic exiled in London . The leaflet recommended that all resistance fighters in Poland lay down their arms and cease

---

32  TNA CAB 1212/130: Vol II Doc 382.
33  TNA CAB 1212/130: Vol II Doc 393.

fighting, as Warsaw would be liberated by the Red Army. In a rather sinister way the Poles were also warned that the leaders of the rising would be punished for incitement, resulting in many deaths. The Russian action demonstrated Moscow's real attitude to the Home Army and to the allied Poles in the West. Polish military and political authorities of the Second Republic were nothing more than enemies of the Soviet Union. Nevertheless, Russia could not be seen as having abandoned the Home Army completely, although it was clear that it would annihilate it if it stood in the way of the formation of a People's Republic.[34] Early contacts between the Red Army and the Home Army soldiers were usually friendly, but as soon as the NKVD arrived, usually within hours, the Home Army soldiers were arrested, murdered, sent to the gulags or 'press ganged' into the Red Army. Ironically, some local units of the Home Army turned to local German forces for help, which was readily provided as a sop in the propaganda war. It was left to SOE Polish Section to continue supporting the Poles with hardware, despite the Foreign Office becoming progressively more pro-Soviet and anti-Polish. Threlfall had worked hard to persuade Slessor to support sorties to Warsaw by feeding him the best information and statistics he could garnish about the successes of Polish action. Slessor allocated an additional four aircraft of 1586 Flight, all that was available to him at the time, for Polish operations. Of the six aircraft Slessor could locate (one Liberator and five Halifax machines) two were unserviceable. At the same time from 11 complete crews, two had not yet completed their conversion training for Stirling aircraft, whilst two had little experience in flying to Poland and only one crew could fly the Liberator. The Poles estimated that it would take seven flights per night carrying 90 containers with ammunition and grenades to alleviate the situation in Warsaw. Warsaw fell at 8 p.m. on 2 October after 63 days of fighting. According to communists commentators the Warsaw Uprising had 'specific internal political objectives', which was to reinstate the Second Republic. This objective had little in common with the true interests of the Polish nation and therefore was not supported. The Soviet line was that the efforts of the insurgents were put into jeopardy by the political objectives of the scheme to liberate Warsaw before the arrival of Soviet Forces and the People's Polish Army. According to Moscow the rising was premature and could not be helped. Hence the plight of the Warsovians was sealed. The Warsaw airlift during the Uprising lasted from 4 August to 28 September 1944. All flights took off from bases in Italy and were conducted by Polish, British, Australian, Canadian and South African airmen. During the final days of the uprising USAAF flew some high altitude daylight missions from Britain using B17 aircraft. (see Capter 20).

\* \* \*

There is no mention of the Warsaw Uprising in Frank's wartime diary. The major concern on the home front was the impact of V1 flying bombs on southern England. For example:

---

34  TNA CAB 1212/130: Vol II Doc. 404.

Gerty and I set out at about 10.40 am on a most interesting journey of quite 70 miles, first by 90 bus to Richmond Station, then via Willsden and Watford to a point near Boxmoor Station where Eileen and her friend Joan joined us. We saw much Doodle Bug damage at South Acton. We heard no siren, however, until just after 1.30 pm when we were sitting on a number 301 producer-gas-propelled bus outside Warford Junction Station. The cause of this particular alert fortunately did not come near, and the All Clear sounded thirty minutes later when we were about two miles north of Kings Langley. Incidentally, there was a very bad D.B. incident at Watford about a week ago when, I understand, a D.B. brought down by A.A. fire, 'red hot and still carrying petrol', ploughed its way, engine still running, through 26 houses. There were some fifty deaths. After a very sorry cup of tea at wayside cyclists' halt, the four of us climbed a little way up to the south side of the valley, near Bourne End, admired apple orchards and the distant cornfields; watched the bombers risng from Bovington aerodrome, and for a short time did nothing in particular. We then hastened to Eileen's billet at Marlowes, Hemel Hempstead, and shortly after she left to go on duty we left too, for Berkhamstead, the most distant point of our excursion. By this time, 5.30pm, the blazing sunshine had made things more than hot, and as we sat in the top front seat of a number 353, Windsor bound bus, we were helpless as tomatoes in the hot sun. The bus journey south via Chesham, Amersham and Gerrards Cross was, I think, one of the finest bus journeys I have ever experienced near London. The Chiltern countryside is a very welcome change from the flatness of the Thames Valley.[35]

On 8 May, Frank reported that there were two alerts after dawn when three Doodle Bug's engines cut out as he lay in bed. He pondered over whether the machines were of the original design, which blew up after a few seconds after the engines had stopped or were they of the gliding type which fell a few miles away once the engine had shut down.[36]

---

35  Peter Minett, *Frank's Wartime Diary*, p. 560.
36  Minett, p. 560.

# 20

# The 'American Armada'

*The life of governments is like that of man. The latter has a right to kill in case of natural defence: the former have a right to wage war for their own preservation. In the case of natural defence, I have a right to kill, because my life is in respect to me what life of my antagonist is to him: in the same manner a state wages war because its preservation is like that of any other being. With individuals the right of natural defence does not imply a necessity of attacking. Instead of attacking they need only have recourse to proper tribunals. They cannot therefore exercise this right of defence but in sudden cases, when immediate death would be the consequence of waiting for the assistance of the law. But with states the right of natural defence carries along with it sometimes the necessity of attacking; as for instance when one nation sees that a continuance peace will enable another to destroy her, and that to attack that nation instantly is the only way to prevent her own destruction.*

Montesquieu, *Spirit of Law*, X, 2

The American mission to 'fighting Warsaw' (Operation Frantic VII) on 18 September 1944 was unique when compared to missions by SOE Polish Section and the RAF. Planned by the Sixth Bureau in London and executed by the United States Army Air Force (USAFF), its objective was to deliver equipment, arms and ammunition from high altitude flights during daylight hours. But why did the Americans choose to fly during the day when the British preferred difficult night time flying? The answer lay in the ability of American aircraft to fly at high altitude out of range of German AA fire. British aircraft were only able to fly at a lower altitude, making them more vulnerable to AA and therefore flew under the cover of darkness. This did not mean that night flying was free from risk far from it, as General Rayski had reported disdainfully to General Anders, the flights to Warsaw were nothing more than 'suicide missions'. According to his assessments, if it wasn't for the fact that Warsaw was the capital of the Second Republic, it would have been unlikely that any missions would have been authorised. But General Sosnkowski, being Commander in Chief, had a leaders perspective on warfare, where strategic objectives were more important than any individual suffering of airmen and so he ordered the airmen of Flight 1586 to continue flying to Warsaw at night even if this meant losing high numbers of aircraft and crew. With dangers prevalent over Warsaw the decision to continue flying to the city was a strategic necessity. Once it was decided by the Americans to send aircraft to Warsaw at high altitude, it become important to find a suitable aircraft for the task and they chose the B-17. Some of these were already based in Britain together with the P-51 'Mustang' and the P-47 'Thunderbolt' and could act as escorts for the B-17s. However, one difficulty was the fact that the B-17 could not fly the route Britain-Warsaw-Britain without a refuelling stop; this is where it was hoped the Russian would step in to help out. In autumn 1943 the Americans had already had permission to use Soviet airfields for bombing raids on Eastern Germany and the Romanian oilfields, so they envisaged that getting permission for operations to Poland would only be a formality. In February 1944 the Russians finally gave permission for landing and refuelling at Poltawie, Mirgorod and Piriatin in the Ukraine. The Americans began building temporary runways there out of prefabricated components airlifted from America and bases in Iran. They also built workshops and other ground facilities such as accommodation for approximately 2,500 personnel.

\* \* \*

By July 1944 American test flights from Britain to Poland had begun. The airfields in Russia could handle up to 360 bombers and 200 fighters at any one time pointing to the fact that things were ready for a huge mission to Poland. All that was needed was the go ahead from the American COS. This was received in early August 1944 and so General Kopański put in a formal request on behalf of the Poles to Lieutenant Palmer of the American Special Forces (OSS) in Britain. Similarly, General Sosnkowski met with General Spaatzen of the American Air Force to present his formal request for the run. The Americans replied on 8 August signalling that the American Air Force was ready to 'go.' Since the flights involved Polish airspace the Poles required final approval from Moscow, but given that they did not have diplomatic relations with the Russians, the British had to carry out the negotiation on the Poles behalf. On receiving approval, both the Americans and British began making extensive preparations. SOE Polish Section started to work closely with the Sixth Bureau compiling lists of equipment which the Poles had requested. It was up to the Polish Section to procure the material and pack it into containers ready for loading onto American aircraft. This was a difficult task for it did not have experience in handling such large quantities of equipment in such a short amount of time. Before the operations could commence, however, the containers had to be delivered to the airfield and loaded safely onto the aircraft. This took some time and each side blamed the other for any subsequent delays. On 13 September a message was sent stating that the airfield at Poltaw, Ukraine, was ready to receive aircraft. The message was received at 9.30 in the morning, but it was decided that it was too late to send the aircraft that day and so plans to fly were suspended for 24 hours. However, dispatch on the following day was equally impossible, as fog had enveloped southern England and the aircraft remained grounded for a further 24 hours. During the night, reconnaissance aircraft were sent up over the North Sea to report on the weather conditions. Although the reports were not the best, a brief break in atmospheric conditions over Southern England allowed for the despatch of the 3rd Division of Bombers. Unfortunately, the weather worsened over Denmark and the mission turned back. The aircraft waited fully loaded and fuelled at the aerodrome for the next two days. Reconnaissance aeroplanes continuously scanned the skies waiting for a window in atmospheric conditions. Eventually, it was decided to fly the mission on 18 September. Under the command of Flight Lieutenant Truesdella, aircraft took off from Horsham, Thorpe, Abbots and Tramlingham at 5.50. 110 B-17s climbed into the sky in waves and headed East towards Poland. A secret melody to the Home Army was broadcast by the BBC to inform it that the Americans were on their way. Over the North Sea the 'armada' rendezvoused with fighter aircraft which protected its flanks over the Baltic Sea. Three fighter aircraft had to return to England almost immediately suffering technical trouble. Over Bornhoch, the Americans were attacked by German fighters which were rebuffed. When the 'armada' reached the Polish coast and turned south towards Warsaw, the escorting fighters peeled away to fly back to England. As soon as this happened the Germans, realising that the B-17s no longer had fighter protection, sent up two Focke-Wulf 190s and eight Messerschmitt 109s to attack. American rear gunners reported they had done their job by shooting down five German aircraft, may be six and that the 'armada' was safe. The first heavy flak encountered was above Dąbrowy Lomianek, just before the drop zone. It was here that one of the 'Fortresses' was hit and lost. Only one member of the crew was able to parachute to the ground breaking his leg. On landing he was taken into German captivity and according to eye witnesses was taken straight for interrogation without first aid being administered. After interrogation the airman was taken to a nearby wood and shot. The Americans crossed into Polish airspace over Koszalin.

\* \* \*

When the 'armada' had reached the vicinity of the Polish capital, anti-aircraft fire intensified significantly. Nevertheless, in agreement with the plan the containers were pushed out of the aircraft over Warsaw. This was done from a height of four to six thousand metres at 13.30 hours. However, accurate drops were impossible to execute as heavy winds were battering the Polish city. The descent of each parachute lasted approximately seven minutes and by the time they reached the ground many had already been damaged by anti-aircraft guns or had drifted some distance away from the intended target. Some were hit by hot bullets, which ignited the silk of parachutes resulting in the containers thumping into the ground. Unfortunately, some were damaged on impact or burned. Nevertheless, the materials dropped included 3,000 machine guns, 7,000 grenades, seven tons of explosives and 2,000,000 pieces of ammunition. Apart from war materials, the Americans delivered humanitarian aid including food, first aid material and equipment. Unfortunately, many containers landed in areas out of reach of the Polish fighters. Many fell into German hands, on the eastern bank of the Vistula or into the river itself. The ones that fell into no-man's land were fought for with the occupying forces. After the drops were made the American aircraft flew on to the bases in Ukraine as arranged. One aircraft had to make an emergency landing on the East bank of the Vistula where the Russians had dug in. The crew was unharmed. Apart from the aircraft shot down over Dąbrowa where nine aircrew were lost, one other aircraft landed at the base severely damaged with the loss of one crew member.

\* \* \*

Meanwhile, the recovery of containers began immediately and included those which had landed in no-man's land. Unfortunately, unsightly ructions occurred between different Home Army units as they squabbled between themselves to snatch equipment and Officers found it difficult to calm the atmosphere. The American drops were received enthusiastically. It was the first time that operations had been observed during daylight by the Warsaw population and the size of them could do nothing but impress. It is difficult to assess the success of the mission, since it is difficult to ascertain how many of the containers dropped were recovered by the insurgents. A few days after the mission, General Bor-Komorowski sent a message to London, that 228 containers had been located and recovered. 32 had been fought over with the Germans and successfully rescued. 28 containers were damaged as their parachutes had tangled. The General also informed London that some containers of food had gone missing and he suspected that they had been pilfered by a starving civilian population. According to the Americans the mission was a success, even when compared to operations to occupied France. In the final analysis, 20 percent of the delivered equipment had made it into Polish hands. 20 percent was equivalent to 30 tons of arms, ammunition and other equipment which collectively amounted to approximately one third of the total material delivered to Warsaw to date. After completing their mission to Warsaw, the American aircraft proceeded to Poltava and Mirgorod to land for refuelling.

\* \* \*

During the period August to October 1944 a total of 306 missions had reached Warsaw, with 192 successful drops of which 107 were made by the Americans.[1] During the operations, out of 2,154 containers dropped, 1,284 were delivered by the Americans. Out of all the containers dropped 463 were recovered successfully.[2] The number of containers lost was disappointing, although if the Poles had held larger areas of territory the number would have been larger. Efforts were made to organise more operations by the Poles in the West even when Poland had been taken over by

---

1   Garliński, *Poland the SOE and the Allies*, p. 237.
2   Garliński, p. 237.

the Red Army but these were soon abandoned when Moscow disbanded the airfields in Ukraine. Stalin was not interested in facing a well-equipped Home Army on the approaches to Warsaw nor was Moscow keen to see the secret army snarling up the progress of the Soviet forces in their progress in securing Warsaw and the Second Republic for the communists. The grand total of drops during the uprising amounted to 370 tons, although 50 percent ended up in German hands.

# 21

# Surrender

*Wars can never cease so long as nations live under such widely differing conditions, so long as the value of individual life is in nation so variously computed, and so long as the animosities which divide them represent such powerful instinctual forces in the mind.*

Freud, *Thoughts on War and Death*, I

The third defence of Warsaw ended on 2 October 1944 when the isolated garrison, having undergone appalling suffering and with exhausted ammunition, surrendered to the German Forces while the Russians looked on from Warsaw's eastern province, Praga. Commander Bor-Komorowski, dressed in civilian clothes and trilby hat, was arrested and taken into German captivity. His men laid down their arms, throwing them into baskets whilst marching out of the Polish capital into Dulag 121 Holding Camp. The surrender was signed by Colonel Kazimierz Iranek-Osmecki, in Ozarow, on behalf of the commander. Meanwhile Warsaw was razed to the ground by the retreating Germans in some of the most vindictive operations of the Second World War. SOE missions from the Italian base together with those from England, cost 42 aircraft and 35 crews missing. 87 successful sorties had been achieved which delivered 151 tons of stores. This did not include the many other aircraft which were unserviceable when they returned to base nor the five others lost at the beginning of August on other operations to Poland. The fall of Warsaw disorientated the secret army central command, although some fragmented resistance continued led by area commanders. It was difficult to explain to the defenders of Warsaw why they had not received more consistant support from the allies, and it was even harder to explain to aircrews why they had had to risk their lives flying 1,000 miles to Warsaw when the Russians were only some 50 miles away. Finally, on the 14th, the first Russian help was sent out and thereafter several more sorties were made but by this time it was too little and too late to make any difference to the fate of the city. The number of Russian aircraft that took part is not known but drops were estimated to be 130 tons. It was not enough to stave off the final collapse of the Rising. According to Bor-Komorowski, Commander of the Home Army, the Russians sent out reconnaissance aircraft on 13 September, which dropped cans containing American fruit and rifle ammunition. These drops were made without parachutes or with parachutes which had previously failed to open, and so the tins smashed open on impact. He reports in his book, written some five years after the end of the war, that the ammunition was useless as Russian bullets 'did not fit our rifles.'[1] According to Churchill, the Russians wished to have the non-Communist Poles destroyed, whilst making it appear that they were coming to their rescue.

\* \* \*

This episode is interesting militarily as an attempt to supply a distant garrison by air points to the same lessons as Stalingrad, Tunis and Arnhem because it was an important period in the history of SOE Polish Section, as well as a tragic period in the history of Poland. The Home Army's military 'can do' mentality meant it soldiered on under resourced. With no military and political overarching plan and a lack of a cost-benefit analysis resulted in no decision being made on what blood should be spent to achieve objectives. The SOE Polish project has already given rise to much misunderstanding, falsehood recriminations which suggests that the Home Army should have been made aware that SOE flights would not fly to save Warsaw. Despite what was being said to the Polish government in London and as far as the Western allies were concerned the loss of the Second Republic was a price worth paying in return for Soviet military support in the east. This became clear for the Poles at the Yalta Conference in February 1944 where the Western Allies did little to prevent the succession of a Soviet sponsored government coming to power and the formation of the People's Democratic Republic in Poland. The authorities of the Second Republic of Poland, its government and military power exiled in the West, were eventually disbanded by London; although, a titular administration was set up by the enigmatic Tomasz Arciszewski in London, although he did not enjoy the favour of the British Government to the same extent as Mikołajczyk or Sikorski had done. Sir William Strong, Assistant Under Secretary of State for Europe, expressed robustly the mood in London by saying, that it would be far better if the Soviet Union dominated Eastern Europe than if Germany should dominate Europe. Stalin was in effect given carte blanche to do as he wished with Poland.

\* \* \*

The Warsaw insurgents felt betrayed and abandoned by their allies. As Perkins said, the Russians had been sufficiently close to the front line in Warsaw to be able to provide assistance to the Poles: but they did not think it politically expedient to do so and consequently the freedom fighters were crushed by the Germans. This was one of the last broadcasts from the heroic city picked up in London:

1   T. Bor-Komorowski, *The Secret Army*, p. 343.

This is the stark truth. We were treated worse than Hitler's satellites, worse than Italy, Romania, Finland. May God Who is just, pass judgement on the terrible injustice suffered by the Polish nation, and may He punish accordingly all those who are guilty. Your heroes are the soldiers whose only weapons against tanks, planes, and guns were their revolvers and bottles filled with petrol. Your heroes are the women who tended the wounded and carried messages under fire, who cooked in bombed and ruined cellars to feed children and adults, and who soothed and comforted the dying. Your heroes are the children who went on quietly playing among the smouldering ruins … Immortal, are the nation that can muster such universal heroism. For those who have died have conquered and those who live on will conquer, and again bear witness that Poland lives when the Poles live.

Gubbins, called for a register to be made of fifth columnists for use in a possible future war with the Soviet Union. It seemed that a new enemy of the West had emerged. Although Bor-Komorowski had been arrested by the Germans and taken into captivity, he was appointed as Commander in Chief of Polish Forces in absentia when President Raczkiewicz formally relieved Sosnkowski of his post.

As the Red Army was in the process of taking firm control of Poland it was inevitable that questions were going to be asked about the future of SOE's Polish Section. The conundrum facing SOE was whether to withdraw from Poland all together, leaving the field open to the communists, or continue delivering equipment for the 'Second Republic Poles' as a sign of solidarity knowing that this would not change a thing in Poland. All the Poles of the Second Republic could do under such circumstances was to continue passive resistance. Threlfall pushed for continued arial support and Tabor agreed; however, as Hungary and Romania were now under Soviet occupation, the route to Poland from Italy was problematical especially when Moscow refused permission for RAF aircraft to fly over Russian held territory. Consequently, the northern route would have to be reopened if support for Poland was to resume. Eventually, Nazi Germany surrendered and the war in Europe came to an end. Despite there being a good reason for the continuation of the war this time against the Soviet Union,[2] there was no enthusiasm amongst the Western liberal democracies for further conflict in defence of eastern Europe or of the Second Republic. This removed the need for the SOE base in Italy, which had been operating from Brindisi for exactly one year. The last flight to Poland took off in December 1944. 620 sorties were flown from the base of which 290 had been successful— a success rate of 47 percent. SOE had transported 152 men and 362 tons of stores. In total 48 four-engine aircraft had been lost during the 12 month period. The training school at Ostuni was closed in October.[3] In January 1945 the disbandment of the operational base was started. Much of the war material was transferred to Rome, with most of the American dollars held at the base being deposited into the British occupation zone in Germany. There was only

2   See 'Operation Unthinkable'.
3   TNA HS4/154: Liquidation of Force 139.

one more aspect of the work of Force 139 which had to be completed this being to extract Poles from the ranks of the German Forces in Greece and later, to organise and speed up the collection of Polish refugees and POWs. As the weather was closing in and flights had to be suspended, it was not until 26 December that Operation Freston was allowed to fly.

\* \* \*

By 1945 the Allied balance of power had altered yet again. Russia had succeeded in defeating the German Forces in the East on a number of significant fronts including Berlin, and was now the dominant military power in central and eastern Europe. This emboldened the Soviet government to return to the question of post war settlements. It was minded to 'keep' all the countries it had liberated from German occupation in its own sphere of interest, including Poland. What's more, it insisted that the governments of these countries be socialist if not communist. Polish communists agreed with the policy and they were prepared to go along with Moscow so long as they were put into power. Britain by now was spent, both militarily and economically and was relying on American support to win its arguments with Moscow; when this was not forthcoming Britain could do nothing but submit to Russian demands. The exiled Polish Government of the Second Republic in London was disenfranchised by both America and Britain in favour of the left wing government which would rule in the People's Democratic Republic of Poland. This act had shown that Britain with Amrica had thrown in the towel regarding the protection of the Second Republic. All the noble support of the SOE Polish Section failed to save the Second Republic, the country Britain had gone to war to defend. As the eastern front moved ever onwards towards Berlin repressions against opposition to communism in Poland increased. Between autumn 1944 and spring 1945 approximately 62,000 Poles were accused of belonging to prohibited organisations. 11,000 Varsovians were incarcerated in camps in Poland whilst 50,000 were forcibly deported to the Soviet Union, echoing events of 1940. Individuals who had evaded arrest enrolled in the new Polish socialist organisations either to submerge and hide themselves in the new order or to undermine communist rule from within. A popular choice was to join the new national army. Communist authorities, however, disapproved of using individuals with a history in conspiracy work as the basis of the new forces. It was expected that these individuals would find it hard to be loyal to their new officers. Surveys indicated that approximately 0.1 percent of recruits would show any loyalty to the new regime. Others chose to enlist in civilian security organisations such as the Citizen's Militia (MO) or the Security Bureau (UB). These recruits worked from within in order to undermine these communist institutions. For example, they encouraged desertion which obviously angered communist officers. In order to reduce the effect of the subversive recruits various strategies were employed for example, organising amnesties for the anonymous handing in of arms. Of course, more traditional methods such as purges were also employed.

\* \* \*

After 1945 the Government of the Second Republic of Poland, exiled throughout most of the War in London, became a vestigial administration. The Polish Prime Minister and President were disenfranchised, dismissed from official duties by Britain and were now no more than figureheads of a defunct organisation. At the same time the Polish Forces in the West, which had fought alongside the British were resettled in Britain as well as in other sympathetic countries. 200,000 fighting men and women were left to rebuild their lives either in the United Kingdom, Canada, the United States, Australia, New Zealand, Brazil, Argentina or Italy. Those who settled in Britain were provided with sanctuary and the means of making a living, perhaps as an atonement for failed promises. The place of the Second Republic, was taken over by an alien authority, the Polish Communist Party. This new communist Polish Government did not welcome back the soldiers who had fought alongside the western allies, calling them the forces of a 'spent bourgeois state.' Their contribution to the war was not even acknowledged by the British Government at the end of the war, in case this embarrassed Moscow. Even the weekly meetings between General Gubbins and staff of the Sixth Bureau descended into farce when the General departed to France unannounced, leaving the Warsaw Uprising near collapse. Losses in the Uprising amounted to: 18,000 members of the Home Army lost, 20,000 injured, and 15,000 taken prisoner. As far as the civilian population was concerned: 130,000 were lost, 550 were taken into captivity with 165,000 condemned to hard labour. 10,000 German troops lost their lives. According to Timothy Snyder (2001) the tragedy of Operation Tempest, was threefold: the Home Army lost men, women and its arms; the Government of the Second Republic saw its military strategy fail; and Poles lost their lives and freedom fighting for lands that Poland would not be able to regain in any event, since Churchill and Roosevelt had already ceded them to Stalin.[4] According to Stafford, Gubbins had always been too sympathetic to the Poles, which they had misinterpreted as Britain's unconditional support for the Home Army. Furthermore, the first successful SOE mission to Poland encouraged the Poles to believe that their country would be liberated by British and American Forces as part of Operation Overlord. This is certainly what the Poles would have preferred but as soon as it was clear that it would be the Red Army which would liberate Poland from German occupation, Polish anxiety increased. The Red Army was making such impressive progress from the east towards Berlin across Polish territory it was obvious that Polish authorities in London would have to accept that the front line of the Western Allies would not even reach the country let alone play a part in its liberation. Neither SOE nor the COS could bring themselves to convince the Poles that it would be the Red Army that would finally liberate Poland from German occupation. Soon 1,000,000 Russian boots would be marching on Polish soil, but this point was not emphasised strongly enough, fearing that it would bring out anti-Russian feelings in the Polish diaspora and disturb the existing consensus in the allied camp. Despite the fear that anti-Russian factions in the secret army would use some of the equipment being parachuted into Poland against the Russians, SOE continued flying in equipment only

4   Timothy Snyder, *Bloodlands* (London: The Bodley Head, 2010), p. 299.

adequate enough for low level resistance. This decision was a political decision made in order to keep the Russians on side, whilst at the same time trying hard to demonstrate that the Second Republic had not been betrayed. Colonel Mitkiewicz, Polish Liaison Officer to the COS, expressed great satisfaction that SOE was to continue supplying the Home Army as a vital component of the overall war effort perhaps not realising that decisions had already been taken to modulate the type of equipment being supplied. 'The Second Republic occupies', he wrote to the War Office, 'a central region and therefore has acquired a pre-eminent strategic position.' With adequate assistance the Home Army could participate in the fall of German European defences and could provide security against chaos from elements of the Wehrmacht dispersed throughout the region. 'In the light of recent developments', he continued, 'it has become essential to intensify the scale of flights to Poland, which demonstrates the complete desire for British planes to save Poland.' According to the Poles 500 SOE flights completed before April 1944 would have sufficed to keep the Home Army alive as a coordinated organisation. But it was not only a question of the number of flights, but also the type of equipment being delivered. The British General Staff agreed to 300 flights, whilst the Poles recommended the establishment of a special Polish squadron of 18 to 20 American B-24 bombers, although this suggestion was later rejected. The type of material delivered was only adequate for individual acts of sabotage and not for full scale military fighting. Following intervention from Washington, urging the British to possibly give the Poles some prospect of forming a Polish squadron in order to alleviate Polish disappointment, the Combined COS agreed to organise one squadron initially, followed by a second made up of US heavy bombers to operate from Britain under the command of the 8th Air Force. It was understood in America that these squadrons would coordinate action with Bomber Command.

\* \* \*

The Americans appreciated well what the value of such a move would be since they understood the vital concern of the Poles in the west regarding their Home Army. However, the Americans were also very clear that if this indeed was to be the case, Poland's future lay in cooperating with the Russians, something the Poles loyal to the Second Republic would be loathed to do. Those that insisted the Poles of the Second Republic should work with the Soviet Union misunderstood the Russian raison d'être. During an unofficial meeting between Tabor, Protasiewicz, and Grocholski, Perkins announced that the British COS would no longer offer advice regarding activities to occupied Poland as the country was now considered to be in the Russian sphere of operations. Tabor stated that it was impossible for the Poles in the West to approach the Russians on any matter whilst there was no official contact between the two countries. At the same time, the Germans were attempting to undermine Britain's decision to work closely with the Soviets in Poland by claiming that it was the Russians who had disarmed the Home Army and that the force was no more. The Germans also made it known that Mikołajczyk's trip to Moscow in search of an agreement with Stalin was a waste of time. The Germans warned that if Poland fell into Soviet hands, the Poles would never see their homeland again. The Germans were playing on historical and deep-rooted Polish fears regarding Russia.

\* \* \*

Unfortunately for Britain a large part of the Polish exiled diaspora, many originating from eastern Poland, was indeed anti-Russian and included many high-ranking officers in the Polish Forces who had fought under British command. Threlfall was so worried about the loss of solidarity amongst the Poles after Sikorski's death, that he insisted that anti-Russian feeling be eradicated as quickly as possible to avoid the spread of discontent. He was concerned that the morale of Polish troops would be irretrievably damaged and future Anglo-Polish relations would suffer hardship, particularly if Warsaw fell which it did on 2 October, 1944. These concerns resulted in Britain raising the profile of its support for Poland. Pickles furnished Keswick with a resume of operations to Warsaw[5] to demonstrate the extent of British help during the early stages of the uprising. Threlfall had worked hard to persuade Slessor to increase sorties to Warsaw by feeding him the best statistics that he could garner about the successes of clandestine action by the Poles. Slessor pointed to the allocation of a further six aircraft from 1586 Flight, all that was available to him at the time. Of the six aircraft Slessor could earmark (one Liberator and five Halifax aircraft) two were unserviceable. At the same time out of 11 complete crews, two had not completed their conversion training for Stirling aircraft, two had little experience in flying to Poland and only one crew could fly the Liberator. The Poles estimated that it would take seven flights per night carrying 90 containers with ammunition and grenades to alleviate the situation in Warsaw. On 16 September, Henry Threlfall, senior representative of SOE Polish Section in Italy, telegraphed London in praise of Slessor and Elliot for, as he put it, their splendid support through the Warsaw crisis. By now the Poles had approached every higher authority in Britain for help. Even SOE could not assist as decisions had passed on to another chain of command beyond its influence. However, Keswick suggested to Perkins that one more action could be attempted, before admitting failure in Poland. The exploit which Perkins could try was to get Mikołajczyk to support Selborne's appeal for the Mediterranean Airforce to lay on a large scale daylight drop in Poland using long range US aircraft.

5   TNA HS4/157: Operations to Warsaw.

## 22

# Death of the Second Polish Republic

By 1944 Stalin had decided on the future geopolitical make up of post-war Europe, which included Poland being made part of the new Soviet empire. This meant, according to Stalin, that the Polish Government of the Second Republic in London would have to be disbanded and replaced by a new administration. This was eventually done when the British Government removed its recognition of the Government of the Second Republic and transferred its allegiance to the puppet government of the People's Democratic Government Moscow had established. This was the price the West had to pay in exchange for Soviet military support against the Germans; although eventually this move would precipitate the Cold War. Help from America had not been forthcoming either since it was not sure whether it would require Soviet help in in the far east.[1] Stalin's plan had been particularly troublesome for Britain, because London was the champion of the Second Republic even to the extent of arming the Second Republic's Forces who had been fighting alongside the British under British command from the beginning of the war to the end. Given London's position, all that could be done was to accept Stalin's plans and in doing so betray the Government of the Second Republic and to resettle the Polish Forces which had fought under British command in the West. This was done in 1946. In order to save face, the British Government began laying the blame for the betrayal on the Poles themselves calling them intransigent and unrealistic when they refused to accept Stalin's plans. It was their fault that there were no diplomatic relations with the Russians during the war. It was their fault that the Warsaw Rising[2] had failed and that there was no understanding between the Home Army and the Red Army in the field. It was their fault that they did not want to understand that Britain was unable to help

1  See 'Operation Unthinkable'.
2  TNA HS4/157: Warsaw Rising: Reports from Poland. Foreign Office telegrams, Operations to Warsaw.

the insurgents in Warsaw with SOE drops. It was their intransigence that prevented negotiations taking place between the representatives of the Second Republic and Stalin and it was their fault that they did not accept Churchill's advice to sacrifice one half of the Republic for some kind of power sharing agreement with Moscow. Churchill only managed to persuade one ex-member of the Polish Government in London to travel to the Soviet capital and then to Warsaw as part of a power sharing exercise. Initially Mikołajczyk was welcomed by the communist regime in Poland, for it was hoped that his presence would give the communist administration some continuity and credibility. But no sooner had Mikołaczyk settled in, there was a change of heart and he was hounded out of the country.

\* \* \*

All that was left to be done by Britain was to tidy up the upheaval that Stalin's political aims for the Polish ally had caused. What should be done with the Polish Government of the Second Republic exiled in London? And what should be done with approximately 250,000 Polish servicemen and women in the West, who had fought during the war under British command and then refused to stand down in protest against the Yalta agreement. This was a difficult dilemma for Churchill and later Attlee, for it meant that a decision had to be made; whether to betray Britain's Polish ally or betray the Russian ally. The line of least resistance was, of course, to betray the Poles of the Second Republic which Churchill did at the Yalta Conference.

\* \* \*

On the 26th, SOE received information on the Moscow meeting. Despite Churchill's cajoling, Mikołajczyk was hesitant about accepting Stalin's insistence to keep Eastern Poland[3] and promised to discuss the issue with the Polish Cabinet on his return to London. The Polish Prime Minister's view was that the eastern borderlands could be sacrificed if Stalin guaranteed the existence of the remainder of the Second Republic. Although Mikołajczyk was sure that this would be the only realistic compromise for post-war agreements, the Polish Cabinet in London decided that this solution was unacceptable. They did not agree to the loss of Eastern Poland and did not believe that Stalin would remove the Red Army from Polish territory after the war. Mikołajczyk wanted to give Stalin the benefit of the doubt which was so unpopular amongst his retinue that he felt he had no options but to resign over the matter which he did on 25 November, 1944. Meanwhile the Red Army continued to fight its way Westward towards Germany and Berlin, whilst Moscow and London accepted an approximation of the Curzon Line as the new post war Polish/Soviet border. SOE learnt of Mikołajczyk's resignation on the 25th. His position was taken over by the little-known Jan Kwapiński. The British expected him to be malleable in Stalin's hands but fearing that he would be more anti-Soviet than Mikoajczyk, insisted that

---

3   Also known as Kresy to the Poles

the new administration surrender its secret ciphers and cease all secret transmissions to Poland. The Poles were also warned that all SOE drops to the territories liberated from German occupation would be curtailed. Perkins saw Colonel Utnik of the Sixth Bureau and Siedak of the Polish Ministry of the Interior on the 30th to discuss Britain's new position regarding ciphers, couriers and 'bag traffic'.

\* \* \*

As some predicted, the unpopular Kwapiński was unable to form a government; consequently, a new administration was brought into being on 1 December. Arciszewski became the new Prime Minister in exile, but he too had showed himself to be anti-Soviet consequently the British Government began to distance itself from his administration. Perkins believed that the British attitude towards Polish ciphers was intended to demonstrate its disapproval of Arciszewski and his policies. However, in order to ensure that Britain did not appear to be indifferent to the forced Russian takeover of Poland, Eden suggested to Churchill that the RAF undertake a humanitarian airlift to Poland, stationing in Russia. Such a move, he argued, would at least demonstrate that attempts had been made to help the Polish population. The Poles were troubled by this suggestion, as it meant that support for Poland depended on Russian approval. The COS, instructed SOE to maintain close contact with the Home Army and the Polish Government in London. On 14 December Selborne wrote to Sinclair at the Air Ministry regarding a letter he had received form SHAEF.[4] The letter informed Selborne that it had been agreed to remove 138 Squadron from special duties. SOE made it known that it had views on the matter and Selborne wrote to Churchill to block the move. Selborne's opinion was that if this was allowed to happen it would appear that Britain had contravened the 1939 Anglo-Polish Pact. For the first time Churchill had responded with an offer of a meeting, rather than with an offer of immediate support. This was taken as a sign that Churchill's interest in the Home Army had waned. Britain's Prime Minister had come to the conclusion that a bomber squadron was more useful in supporting the European invasion than the Polish Home Army. Opinions regarding Poland and its territory, were seemingly in constant flux. Pickles noted on 20 December, that the British Prime Minister was getting fed up with the Poles and appeared to agree with Moscow that Russia was justified in claiming Polish territory east of the Curzon Line. As the influence of the Polish Government in London waned, the influence of the Lublin Committee[5] grew. It determined what the relationship between the Poles and Moscow should be while Britain stepped aside and allowed this situation to proceed. On Boxing Day 1944, the ban on flights to Poland was lifted. Two drops went ahead with the second, Operation Freston, delivering the British Military mission to Warsaw. The 301 Squadron's Liberator was piloted by Edmund Ladro, navigated by Roman Chmiel

4  Supreme Headquarters Allied Expeditionary Force.
5  A communist administration established with Moscow's support and expected to be installed as the new government of the People's Republic of Poland after the war.

and inserted: Colonel D.T. Hudson, Major P. Solly Flood, Major P. Kemp, Sergeant D. Galbraith and Captain A. Pospieszalski. By this time the British had accepted the establishment of the Soviet controlled People's Republic of Poland.

\* \* \*

By the end of the year Moscow had ordained the Lublin Committee as the new Polish Government in waiting, whilst on 1 January the Polish Government of the Second Republic exiled in London was disenfranchised by the Western Allies. This was the ultimate betrayal, although the administration continued working as a titular authority in London. Averell Harriman, the American Ambassador to Moscow justified the action with the following statement:

> I don't know what the Poles in Poland think. We know very well what the Polish government in London thinks. It is predominantly a group of aristocrats looking to the Americans and the British to restore their position, landed properties and feudalistic system of the period before and after the last war. They have a basic suspicion of the Soviets and don't like Communism., which latter opinion I share with them. They think the future of Poland (the Second Republic) lies in Great Britain and the United States fighting Russia to protect Poland. I don't see that we have any interest in that kind of thing.[6]

On 7 January 1945 SOE Polish Section informed the Poles that there could not be any further drops into Poland. With no further aerial support for the Home Army, a liquidation committee for the Polish Section was established in London. Those on the committee were Lieutenant Colonel Utnik, Lieutenant Colonel Hancza, Captain Podoski, and Captain Szanser of the Sixth Bureau. SOE was represented by Lieutenant Colonel Perkins, Threlfall and Major Pickles. The Home Army was wound up officially on 19 January 1945, whilst the Sixth Bureau was closed in January 1946. At the same time the Polish administration was prevented from transmitting to Poland in case the messages that were being sent contradicted Yalta agreements. Meanwhile, the Polish Workers' Party (Polska Partia Robotnicza) now in power in Poland, decided, with Russian help, to eliminate members of the Home Army. These Soviet inspired operations were sometimes more bestial than the German atrocities. The situation in Poland was now very dangerous for the special forces which had been transferred from Britain in the name of the government of the Second Republic as there were no more SOE flights available to return them back to safety. Nevertheless, the difficulty was what to do with the Poles in the West who had fought under British command and felt they could not return to a sovietised homeland. Threlfall thought the only answer was to re-settle them outside the Russian sphere of interest. According to him there were four options: let them settle in Britain, in the Commonwealth, in America or in a catholic country in South America. Meanwhile,

---

6   Victor Sebestyen, *1946 The Making of the Modern World* (London: Macmillan, 2014), p. 174.

in May 1946, 700,000 Russians were taught the Polish language in order to be sent into Poland to rig the post war elections in favour of the communist Polish Workers' Party. Little cooperation was evident between the Red Army and the Polish citizens on the territory east of the Curzon Line. These areas were ruthlessly sovietised by NKVD action which saw thousands of Poles being forcibly moved to the territories of the new People's Republic in the west. As the war drew to a close and with allegedly Churchill saying privately, 'I'm sick of the bloody Poles,' Britain eventually turned her back on the authorities of the Second Republic exiled in London and it did not stand in the way of the Soviet Union gathering up Polish territory into her sphere of interest. However, SOE continued flying supplies to the Polish people for it feared that stopping supplies would appear that Poland had been betrayed. Supplies delivered was done on a humanitarian basis rather than for any military reason. The Russians called for the cessation of SOE flights and on 6 January the Foreign Office questioned whether flights to Poland should continue. Sargent's opinion was to curtail all flights whilst Keswick and Perkins argued that they should continue. The material which was delivered included medicine, clothing, money and small arms for personal protection against German punitive action. Meanwhile, the new communist leadership in Poland declared the Home Army as illegal and any action in its name as treason. On January 19, General Okulicki released Home Army soldiers from their oath and disbanded them saying there seemed little point in carrying out further operations in Poland. With no further ado the Polish Section of SOE was wound up. Meantime, the Lublin Committee, dissolved the civilian underground state, which was the representative of the Second Republic, murdering many civil servants and Home Army soldiers. According to communist historians the Polish contribution to the final victory over Nazism was achieved by tens of thousands of Polish peasants and labourers aided by the Soviet Army. In these accounts the contribution made by the Home Army and the SOE Polish Section was described as 'insignificant.' According to them, it was the communist resistance fighters and the Polish Forces under Soviet command which were the key in the pursuit of freedom.

# 23

# Postscript

The Second Republic of Poland, allied to Britain since 1939, had been defeated by the dual invasion of Nazi Germany and the Soviet Union in the first two months 0t the Second World War. The Republic's territory was bisected by the victors and the country was wiped off the European map. The Republic's military and political authorities escaped to their allies, first to France and then to Britain when France fell. Whilst doing so they left behind on Polish territory a well organised and extensive secret army which eventually became known as the Home Army. Britain's SOE Polish Section was authorised to procure armaments and to train Polish Special Forces and to then parachute them in the occupied country. In June 1941, Nazi Germany betrayed her Soviet ally by invading Russia. During the early days of the invasion Moscow realised that the Red Army was not in a position to hold the rampant Germans and so sought new alliances in the West. Churchill, blinded by the huge potential of the Red Army, ignored earlier Soviet war crimes (many committed on Polish and Ukrainian citizens) and gladly accommodated Soviet advances and signed a pact with Moscow. This change in the Soviet Union's fortune would have been of little significance for the Poles, if it was not for the fact that Russian intentions after the war were to replace the Second Polish Republic with a communist People's Republic. Throughout the war Britain had been supporting the Second Republic but its commitment wavered just as soon as Soviet power came over to the Western allied side. As the huge Red Army was considered to be crucial for the balance of power in Europe, SOE Polish Section was told to scale back on its help for the Second Republic and instead carry out its missions in such a way as not to antagonize Moscow.[1] Consequently, by 1944, the equipment and armaments that were parachuted into Poland by the RAF, were only sufficient for low scale resistance against German targets. This is well demonstrated when the tonnage of material that was dropped in to Poland is compared to that delivered to other European countries: Yugoslavia 16,469 tons, France 11,333 tons, Italy 5,907 tons, Greece 4,205 tons, Albania 1,205

---

1   Walker, *Poland Alone*, p. 146.

tons, Denmark 700 tons and Poland 600 tons. As the military fortunes in the east had swung in Russia's favour in 1943, Britain had to decide which one of her allies to betray, Russia or the Second Republic of Poland. The dilemma was how to nurture Russia's fighting power, whilst at the same time ensure that it did not appear that the Second Republic had been betrayed. The war was being won and the Second Republic of Poland was becoming inconsequential.[2] In the final analysis therefore, the British decided to follow the line of least resistance which saw SOE operations being scaled back and stopped. This led to the dismantling of the Second Republic, leaving the field open to the new Soviet sponsored People's Republic in 1945. Stalin calculated that his victories in the east had provided him with the excuse and window of opportunity he needed to try to correct the punitive settlement imposed on Russia two decades ago at the treaty of Riga after the Russo-Polish war of 1918-1921. As well as removing the recognition of the allied Government exiled in London, Britain also took it upon itself to stand down the Polish Republican Forces that had fought in the West under British operational command throughout the war. The Home Army was finally annihilated by the NKVD fighting in association with the communist People's Army in fratricidal conflict, which amounted to no more than a Polish civil war.[3] The dismantling of the Second Republic's forces in the west, who refused to return home, took approximately five years to complete. Having attempted to dispose of these forces by dispersing them to countries which had signalled that they would be prepared to take a number of the displaced men and women, Britain was left with resettling most of them in this country.[4] This included personnel who had been trained by the SOE but had not yet been deployed. As a result they were left with an important decision to make, whether to return to a People's Republic or stay in the west as exiles and seek British naturalisation. Most chose to remain. The British Government would have preferred it if they had returned to Poland, albeit to a communist state. Ironically, the government of the new People's Republic did not want these men to return as they were the representatives of the bourgeois Second Republic. After some discussion Attlee's government agreed to their resettlement in Britain. This decision was not welcomed by everyone in the country, particularly not the trade unions and the professional associations and many people in the street. The unions feared that the Poles would compete for jobs with British troops after demobilisation. Others lamented that they would be rivals for health services, housing and retraining. Apart from such social issues there were legal matters that the British Government had to contend with too, the most important being that the members of the Sixth Bureau and the Silent and Invisible special forces, belonged to a foreign army. As such the British Government had no jurisdiction over them, meaning that no court in the land could prosecute any misdemeanours or transgressions. In order

---

2 Michael Peszke, British Special Operations Executive Archives and Poland, *The Polish Review*, Vol. XLII, No 4, 1997:431-446
3 Anita, Prażmowska, *Civil War in Poland, 1942-1948*, p. 121.
4 See Wiesław Rogalski, *The Polish Resettlement Corps 1946-1949: Britain's Polish Forces* (Warwick: Helion and Company, 2019).

to rectify the situation two things needed to happen. Firstly, the Poles would have to be enrolled into the British Army, thus placing them under British military law, and so allowing for their discharge. Secondly they would have to be given certain civil rights under the law of this country. These privileges were also offered to members of the Home Army who had been released from German captivity when the war ended. The legislative framework for this was the Polish Resettlement Act of 1947 and allowed for the creation of the Polish Resettlement Programme, Britain's first mass immigration programme. All that was left to be done at war's end was to dismantle all the symbols and vestiges of the Second Republic and replace them with new communist emblems. The Government of the Second Republic, exiled in London, was disenfranchised in July 1945 when Britain transferred its allegiance to the new communist administration in Warsaw. The members of the exiled Polish government were given favoured status to settle in Britain, as well as in other friendly countries such as Australia, Canada and the United States.

\* \* \*

On the 2 May 1945 Frank sat in his armchair listening to the New World Symphony. He had learned yesterday that Hitler was dead and today he pondered the fact that German forces in Italy had surrendered unconditionally. On Saturday 5 May he noted in his diary that German forces had also surrendered to General Montgomery in Holland, Denmark and northwest Germany. In response to a telephone order, two hundredweight of coal was delivered to his home. As from the first of the month, people were limited to receiving 34 hundredweight in any one year. Frank's diary entry notes that numerous UNRAA[5] vehicles were passing through Staines and heading south-west. He continues, 'The much-mentioned V.E. Day approaches tardily, and I, for one, am somewhat tired of hearing about it: what with the official code words 'Waterloo' and 'Apple'; telephone amendment to instruction 'Waterloo', and reference to the ultimate 'Obliteration', especially as, 'I regard with considerable misgiving the deadlock on the Polish Question. I think there is much more in this than a question of Polish rights.'[6] The 7 May was a warm sunny day. Frank describes in his diary how people were putting up flags whilst awaiting the V.E. day announcement. On finishing his duty at work, he collected his evening newspaper and returned home in the normal way. At 7 pm whilst cutting the grass he heard V.E. Day being announced and that the 8 May 'will be a public holiday.' [7]

\* \* \*

---

5   United Nations Relief and Rehabilitation Administration.
6   Peter Minett (ed), *Frank's Wartime Diary*, p. 634.
7   Minett, p. 636.

Total figures for aid to Russia were published on 11 May 1944.[8] In the two and a half years from October 1941 to March 1944, Britain sent 5,031 tanks and 6,778 aircraft to Russia. Churchill added, 'We have also sent over £80,000,000 worth of raw material, foodstuffs, machinery, industrial plant, medical supplies and comforts.' These supplies were fought through to Russia along the Arctic route under the general direction of successive Commander in Chiefs of the Home Fleet. Almost all losses of warships fell on the Royal Navy. In merchant shipping, on the other hand, the Allied nations, and particularly merchant ships of the USA, bore the heaviest losses. Churchill continued informing the House that many brave men had fallen into icy water, 'but our Russian Allies have had some of the help and comforts they needed and deserved'. He reassured the House, that he was not boasting 'in the slightest' about British effort as compared to other allies, nor was he making any counter claims against the heroism and glorious military exploits of the Soviet armies. The British Prime Minister then referred to a list of items despatched to Soviet Russia from 1 October 1941 to 31 March 1944:

Military Supplies: Armaments and Military Stores

Tanks: Since October 1941, 5,031 tanks have been supplied, of which 1,223 were Canadian built;

Vehicles (lorries and ambulances inclusive): 4,020;

Bren carriers and starters and charges, 2,463 (including 1,348 from Canada); motor cycles, 1,706.

Weapons: 800 P.I.A.T, with ammunition, 103 Thompson sub-machine guns, 636 two-pounder anti-tank guns, 96 six-pounder anti-tank guns, 3,200 boys anti-tank rifles, 2,487 Bren guns 581, 7.92 mm Besa guns.

Ammunition: 85,000 rounds P.I.A.T., 19,346, 000 rounds, 45 machine guns, 2,591,100 rounds two- pounder anti-gun, 409,000 rounds six-pounder anti-tank gun, 1,761,000 rounds .55 Boys anti-tank rifle, 75,134,000 rounds 7.92 mm tank gun Besa.

GL. Equipment: (A) Mark 3 302 sets; (B) Mark 3, 15 sets British, 29 sets Canadian.

Cable: 30,227 miles telephone cable.

---

8  *The Daily Telegraph*, 11.5.1944

Naval Supplies: nine minesweeping trawlers, three motor minesweepers, 102 ASDICS, 3,006 mines, 50 Vickers 130 mm guns, 603 anti-aircraft machine guns, 40 submarine batteries.

Aircraft: 6,778 aircraft, including 2,672 aircraft sent from USA.

Raw Materials, Foodstuffs, Machinery and Industrial Plant;

Raw Materials, The Greater part of these supplies have been brought from Empire sources. Over the last two and a half years the following was sent: 30,000 tons of aluminium from Canada (£3,038,000), 2,000 tons of aluminium from the United Kingdom, (£720,000), 27,000 tons of copper from Canada (£1,431.000), 10,000 tons of copper from the United Kingdom (£620,000), $4,672,000 worth of industrial diamonds, mainly from South African production, 80,000 tons of jute from India (£3,687,000), 81,423 tons of rubber from the Far East and Ceylon, (£9,911,000), 8,550 tons of sisal from British East Africa, (£194,000), 3,300 tons of tin from Malaya and the United Kingdom, (£7,774,000), 29,610 tons of wool from Australia and New Zealand (£5,521,000). The total value of these and other raw materials £39, 115,000.

Foodstuffs: Tea from Ceylon and India; cocoa beans, palm oil and palm kernels from West Africa; ground nuts from India; coconut oil from Ceylon; pepper and spices from India, Ceylon and British West Indies. Total value of all foodstuffs, £7,223,000.

Machine tools, Industrial Plant, and Machinery:
Machine tools: £20,218,000;
Power Plant: £4,250,000;
Electrical Equipment, £3,314,000;
Miscellaneous; industrial equipment, £1,980,000;
Telephone Equipment, food processing plant, textile machinery, port and salvage equipment, £3,019,000

Total £20,781,000

Grand Total of civilian stores made available to Russia £77,186,000

Medical Supplies and Comforts:

Since October 1941, £3,047,000 sent through charities; £2,500,000 grant for clothing.[9]

---

9  *The Daily Telegraph*, 11.5.1944

## Closing Remarks

In the prologue the following question was posed; there may be a number of reasons why the SOE's Polish Section has been ignored in literature, one being the relegation by the COS of Polish resistance effort to a secondary tier of importance especially as the war continued and the view that the support provided by SOE Polish Section to Polish resistance fighters was disappointing with some even arguing that it did more harm than good. Is this true? Are we now in a position to attempt a response? It will be recalled that the mission statement of the Polish Section describes its objectives as follows: To equip the Poles with resources required for day-to-day sabotage on German communication and installations; to assist the Poles in their planning for a general uprising, to assist planning for intensified sabotage campaigns by maximum increase in guerrilla activity to be timed to take place in support of Overlord, the invasion of western Europe by the allies. Perkins described his role as; to assist the Poles in their various subversive activities with the conviction that a successful military and civil revolt executed at the appropriate time will have a significant impact on the Republic's predicament. According to Garliński, 600.9 tons of materials were dropped in Poland throughout SOE's operations. Most of this was small scale ordnance suitable for low scale sabotage. Although this amount does not compare favourably with other theatres of resistance, such as France and Yugoslavia a significant amount of damage was perpetrated on the German occupying forces using this equipment. Many kilometres of rail tracks were destroyed alongside many rail bridges. Sabotage of factories and Nazi installations was also noteworthy. On the question of assisting the Poles in their planning for a general uprising, it is clear that this objective was not achieved. Moreover, this planning was discouraged, not only through the lack of assistance offered by the SOE but a refusal to deliver the appropriate ordnance for an uprising. This was done so not to antagonize the Soviet Union. Regarding assisting in planning for the intensification of sabotage campaigns to be timed to take place in support of Overlord, again this objective was not realised. It could not have been achieved if we remember that the Poles were discouraged from rising and no advice was given about its timing. The decision when to begin the rising was left solely to the High Command of the Home Army with the view that it would be the only command best placed for the decision. The Warsaw Rising started on the 1 June 1944 and Overlord started on the 6 June 1944. Finally, Perkins' objective to assist the Poles in their various subversive activities with the conviction that a successful military revolt executed at the appropriate time will have a significant impact on the Second Republic's predicament was also a failure for in the final analysis the Home Army's activity had little impact on the Republic's final predicament. It is possible to see how SOE raised expectations in Poland about the survival of the Second Republic in the war. What with encouraging Polish Forces to fight on in the west for the survival of the Second Republic of Poland, why was it that the Republic was lost? It is not recommended to answer one question with another question therefore, this work seems to support the view that in the final analysis SOE Polish Section failed to achieve all of its stated objectives as the Second Polish Republic was lost and the reason for its failure is that it ran up to political limits. After the war Dalton became Chancellor of the Exchequer in Clement Attlee's Labour government. He died 13 February, 1962 aged 74. Roundel Palmer-Lord Selborne, was made a member of the Order of the Companions of Honour and in 1948 Master of the Worshipful Company of Mercers. He was also appointed the chairmen of the National Provincial Bank from 1951 to 1953. At the time he was also chairman of Boots and Company an office he held until 1964. He died 3 September 1971 aged 84. Frank Nelson retired in 1942 due to ill health. He married Jean in 1911, daughter of Colonel Patrick Montgomerie. When she died in 1942 he married Dorothy Moira Carling. He died in Oxford on 11 August 1966. Charles Hambro returned to the City, assuming responsibility for companies associated with Hambros Bank. He became Chairman of Hambros Bank on the death of his uncle, Olaf Hambro in 1961. Colin Gubbins retired from the army in 1946 and became the managing director of a carpet and textile manufacturer. He also co-founded the Special Forces Club. Not a lot is known about Perkins only that he worked in the Mediterranean region after the war.

\* \* \*

Frank's diary entry for Tuesday 8 May 1945, VE Day:

> Off duty (otherwise would have been Late Supervising: 2.30 to 10.10pm). Towards 4pm Michael and I went up to Town. Though the train was crowded no-one was at all concerned, indeed in our corridor we even had mouth organ music and singing. There was every indication en route that the celebrations would last well into the evening, for there were great heaps of debris, etc., in almost every other street. Against one such heap I saw a gibbet. It was beautifully sunny as we walked along York Road and over the temporary bridge which starts at the north end of the County Hall and from that approach the plane trees along the Embankment looked lovely. At 4.40 pm we caught a glimpse of Mr Churchill as he left Parliament in his car. The crowd gave him a very warm reception. We threaded our way across to the Abbey where a service had just finished and hundreds of people were moving about. I was very glad to see scarcely any signs of war damage there. We paused and looked down at the Unknown Soldier's grave and then went out via the cloisters into the sunlight again. After sitting down for a minute or two opposite Westminster Hall we then fought through a thick crowd outside the Ministry of Health (even the buildings opposite had people perched on their roofs) in Whitehall, where Mr. Churchill, I think, was expected to appear on the balcony, and soon reached Trafalgar Square. There were no buses running hereabouts. Passing along the Mall we than made for the edge of the water in St James Park, where a further rest seemed very desirable – this time punctuated with sandwiches etc. It was so hot that some people – 3 New Zealand soldiers among them – took off their shoes and socks and dangled their feet in the lake. The constant stream of people seemed to be quite satisfied to move quietly along – the general

reaction, I thought, being restrained contentment. Our next move was into the crowd outside Buckingham Palace, where, after waiting about 20 minutes we saw the Royal Family appear on the balcony. There was much whole hearted enthusiasm. Then we walked to Victoria Underground, passing a barrel organ being playfully operated by some sailors and Wrens whilst the owner went around with his cap, enroute for Blackfriars and St Paul's. Not far from the cathedral we paused for a grape fruit at 8d a glass (trade price 2 1/2d) – tea was not to be had anywhere. We stayed in St Paul's for a short service at 8pm (special St Paul's Watch Service) and then returned by Embankment tram – old fashioned now but somehow like an old friend – to Westminster Bridge. The constant stream of people over the bridge was most interesting and there was quite a bit of hilarity. The floodlighting did not properly begin until nearly 10.30 pm when we started on a lightning tour of the nearest floodlit buildings: the County Hall, Big Ben, the Ministry of Health, the Shell-Mex building — finishing our tour in Trafalgar Square, which provided a most memorable scene. People had climbed to all accessible positions. The Admiralty Arch and the National Gallery shone brilliantly, and a quick succession of at least 40 rockets soared as high as Nelson's Column. A firework which went off with a particular loud bang near the portico of the National Gallery disturbed dozens of pigeons which circled a little way and returned to their resting place inside the portico. Just after 10.50 pm we very reluctantly had to leave it all to catch the 11.24 pm from Waterloo. All the seats in the train were taken 20 minutes before departure time and so we had to stand until half way home. But it was worth it. Incidentally we saw dozens and dozens of bonfires on either side of the railway as we passed through built-up areas, and later, dozens and dozens of searchlights waving round and round. The final contribution, as we walked from Staines station, was a cheerful succession of electrical illuminations in the doorways and over windows of ordinary folk's houses.[10]

10  Peter Minett, *Frank's Wartime Diary*, p. 638-639.

# Appendix I
# Maps

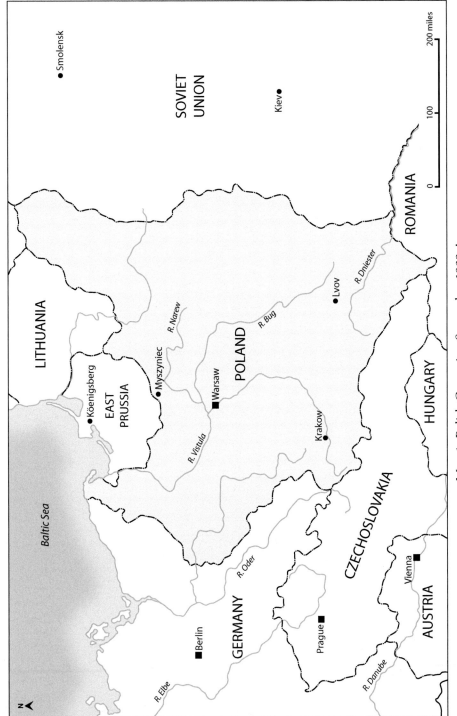

Map 1 Polish Campaign September 1939 A.

APPENDIX I 205

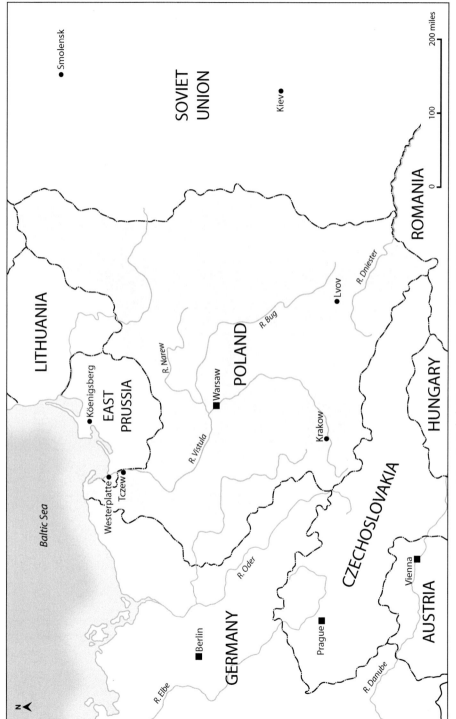

Map 2 Polish Campaign September 1939 B.

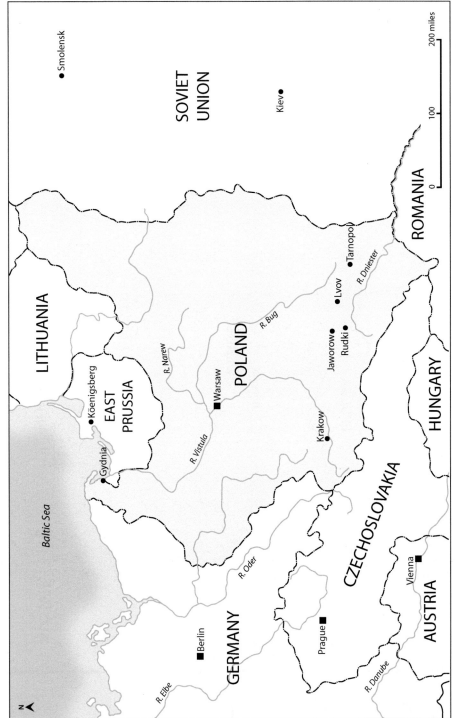

Map 3 Polish Campaign September 1939 C.

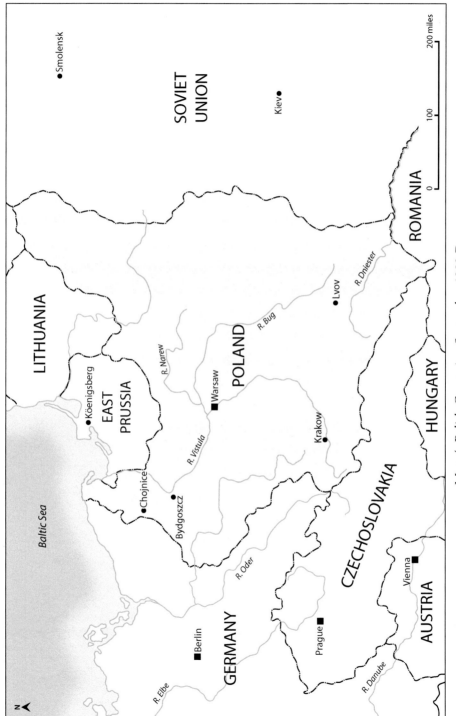

Map 4 Polish Campaign September 1939 D.

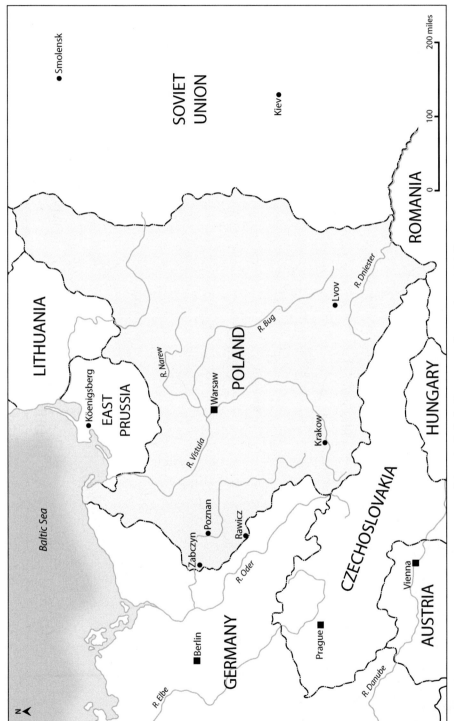

Map 5. Polish Campaign September 1939 E.

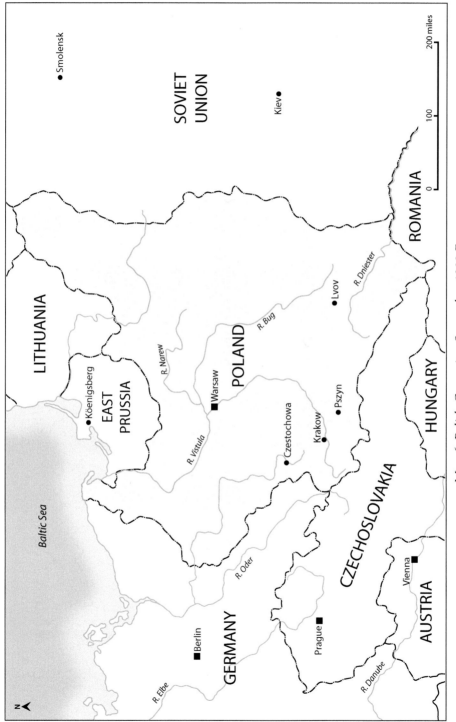

Map 6 Polish Campaign September 1939 F.

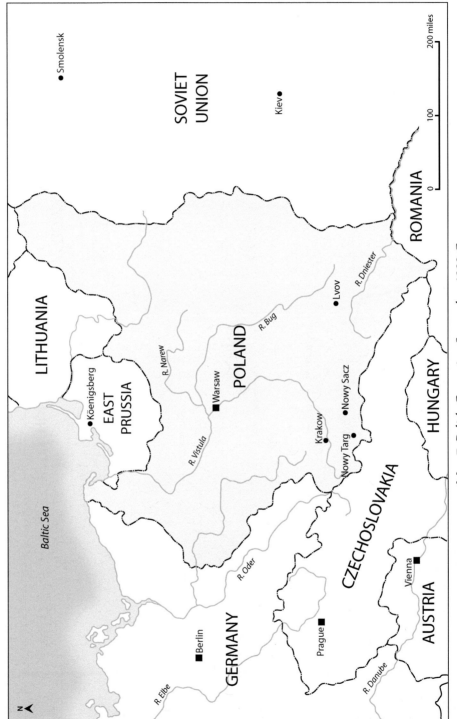

Map 7  Polish Campaign September 1939 G.

APPENDIX I 211

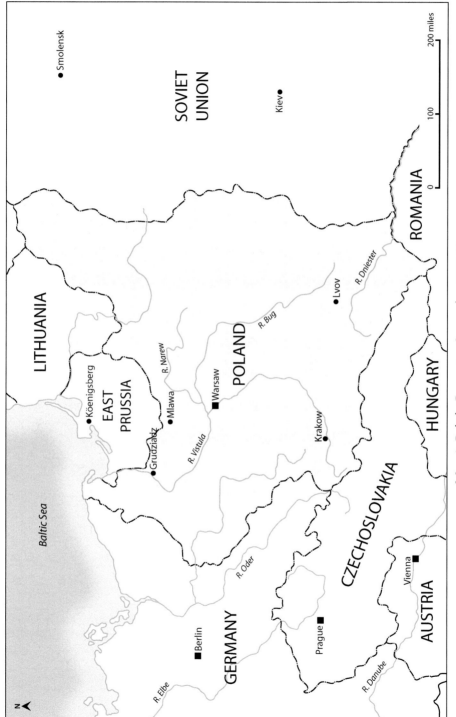

Map 8 Polish Campaign September 1939 H.

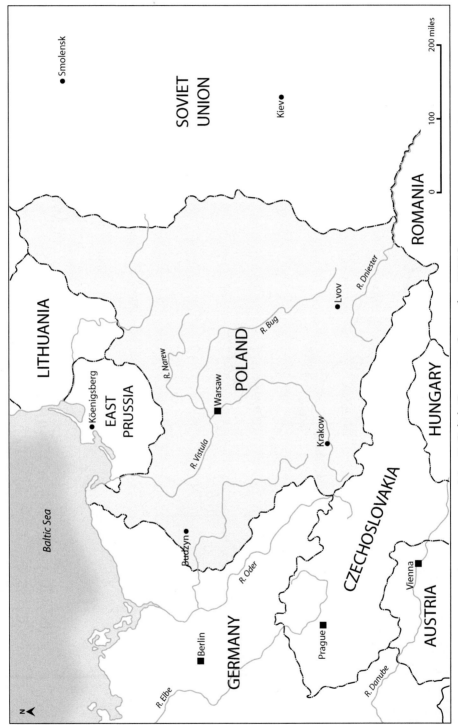

Map 9  Polish Campaign September 1939 I.

APPENDIX I 213

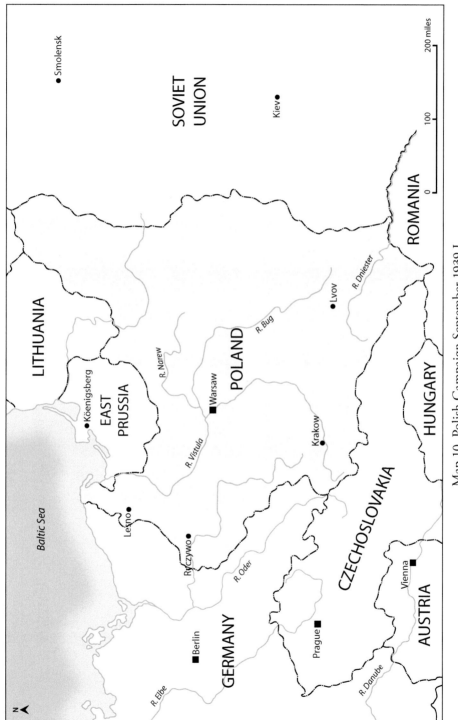

Map 10 Polish Campaign September 1939 J.

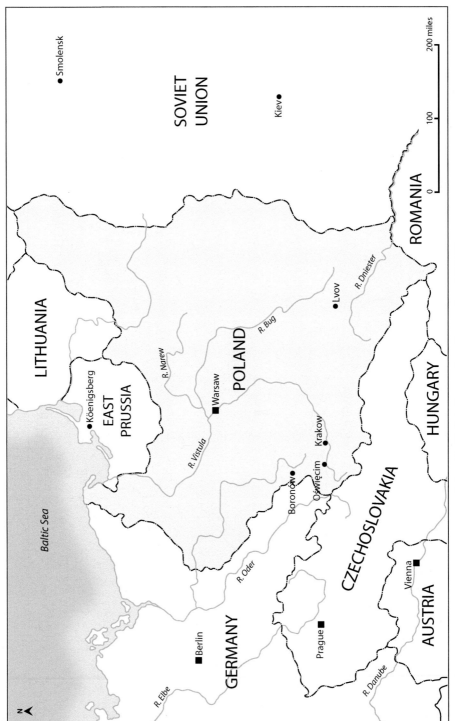

Map 11  Polish Campaign September 1939 K.

APPENDIX I 215

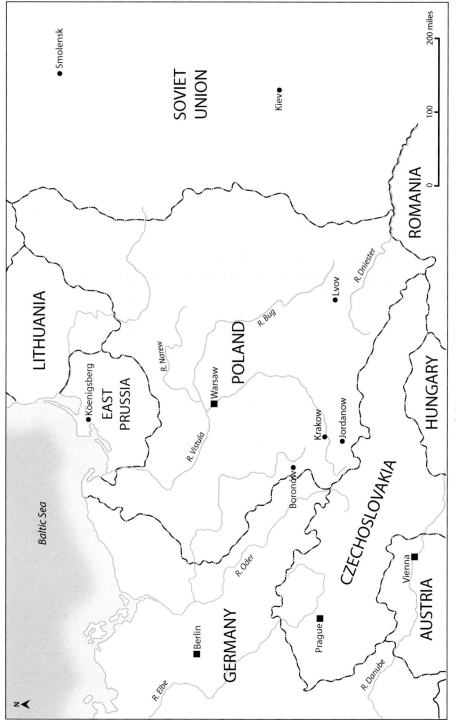

Map 12  Polish Campaign September 1939 L.

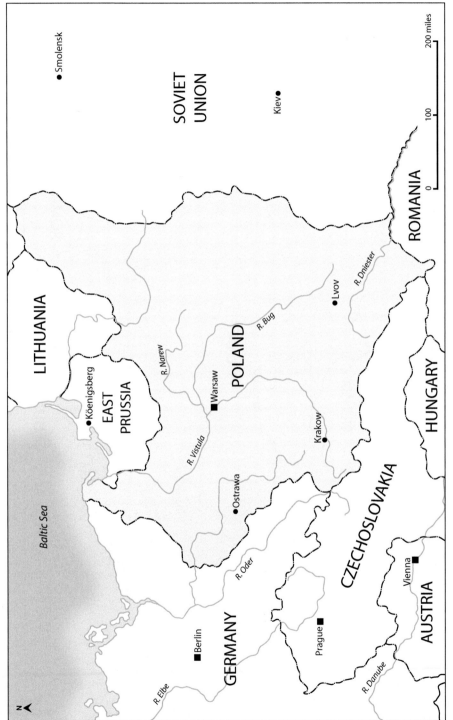

Map 13 Polish Campaign September 1939 M.

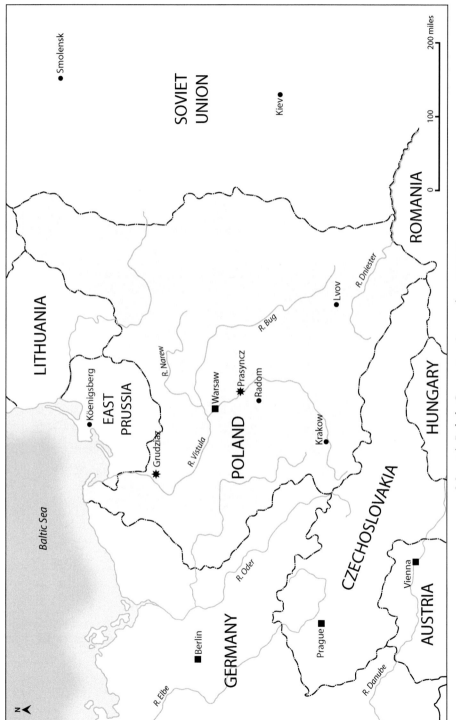

Map 14 Polish Campaign September 1939 N.

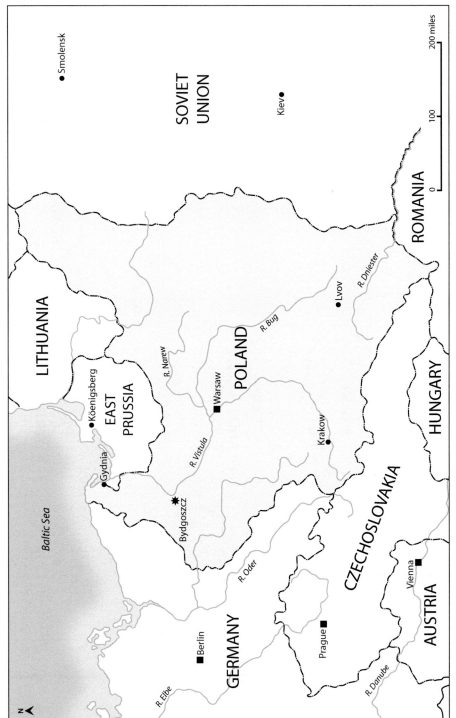

Map 15  Polish Campaign September 1939 O.

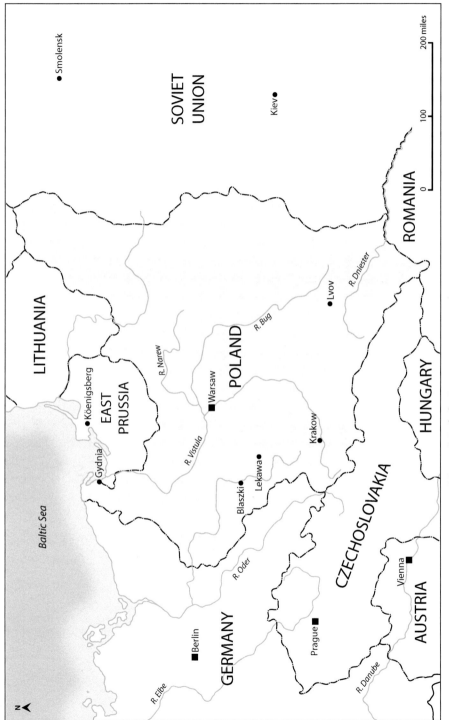

Map 16 Polish Campaign September 1939 P.

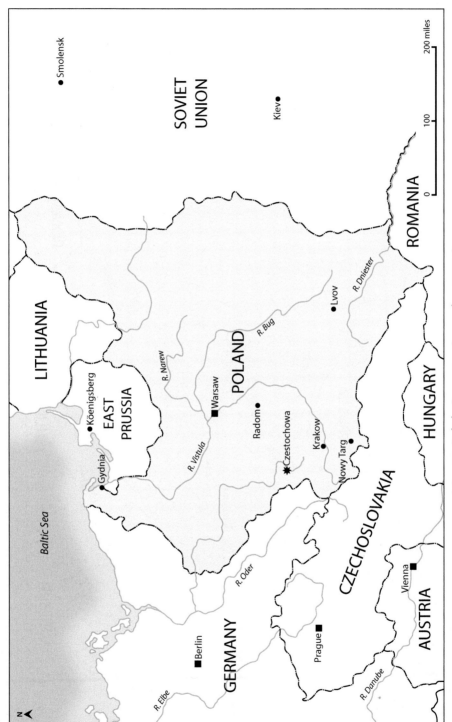

Map 17 Polish Campaign September 1939 Q.

APPENDIX I 221

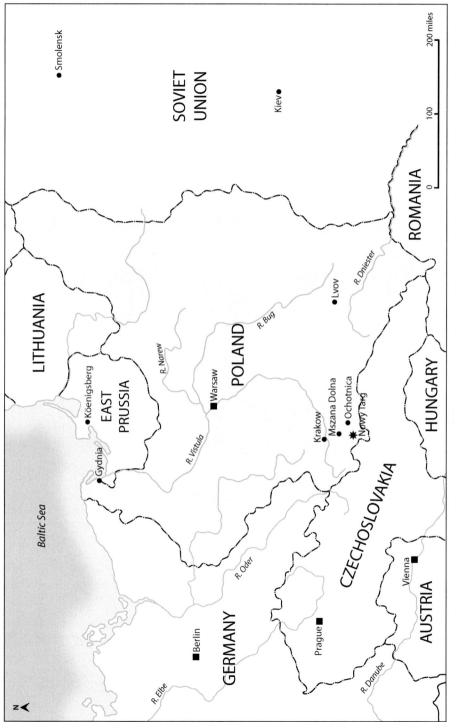

Map 18 Polish Campaign September 1939 R.

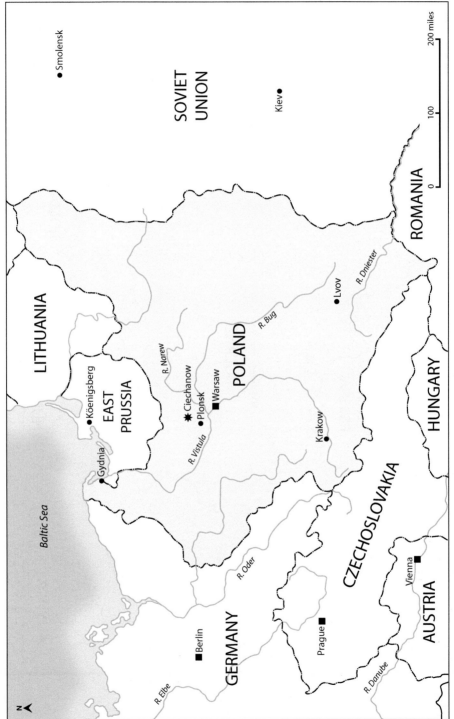

Map 19  Polish Campaign September 1939 S.

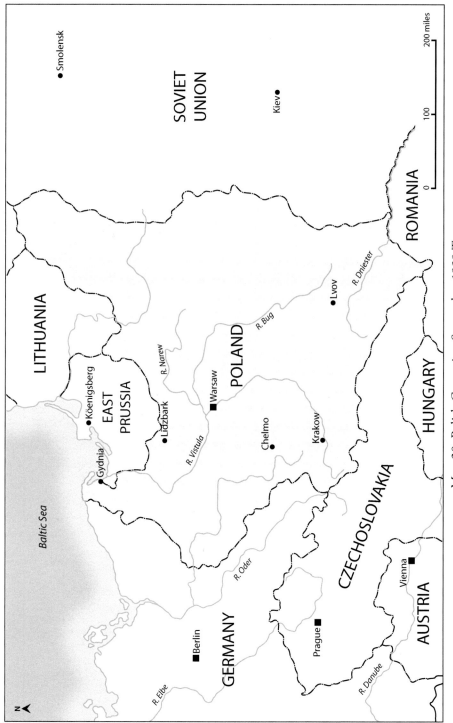

Map 20 Polish Campaign September 1939 T.

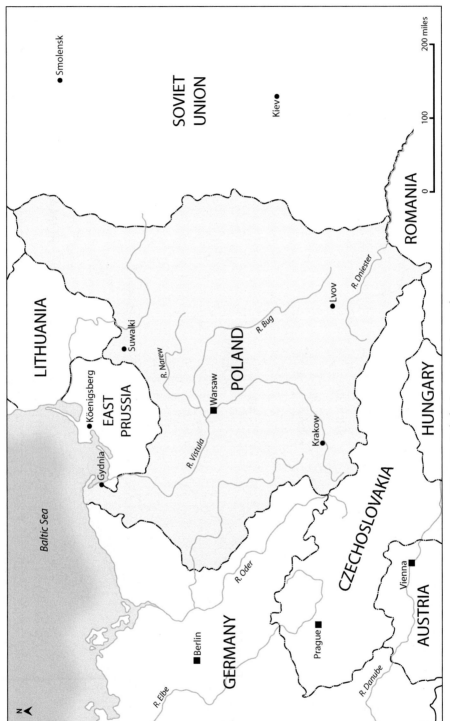

Map 21  Polish Campaign September 1939 U.

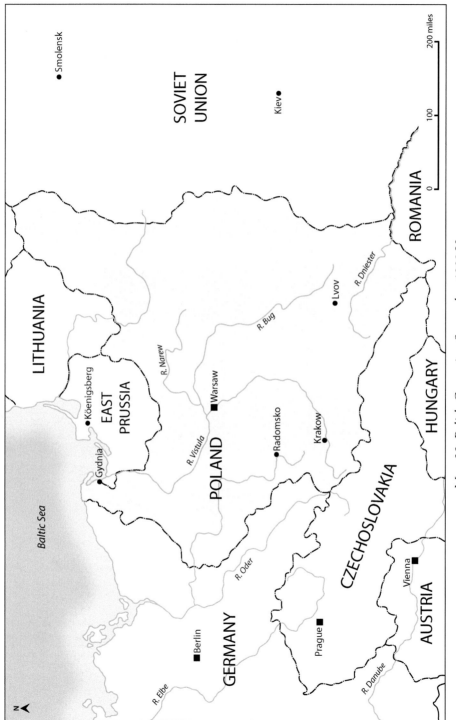

Map 22 Polish Campaign September 1939 V.

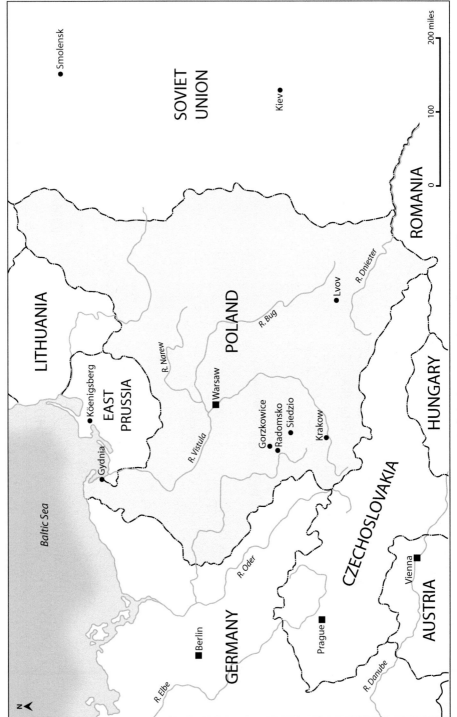

Map 23  Polish Campaign September 1939 W.

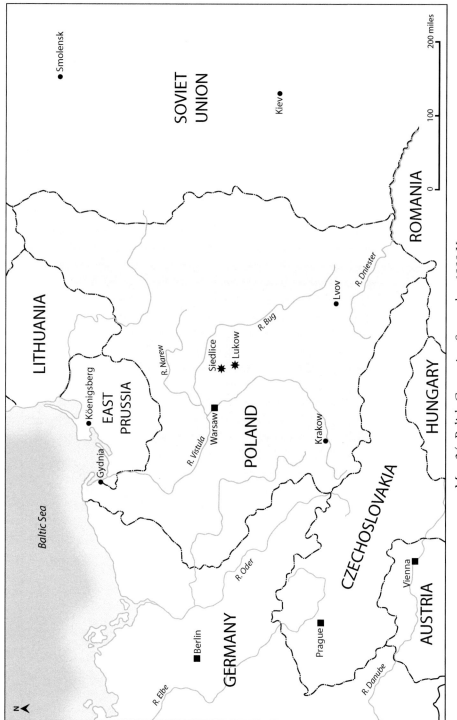

Map 24 Polish Campaign September 1939 X.

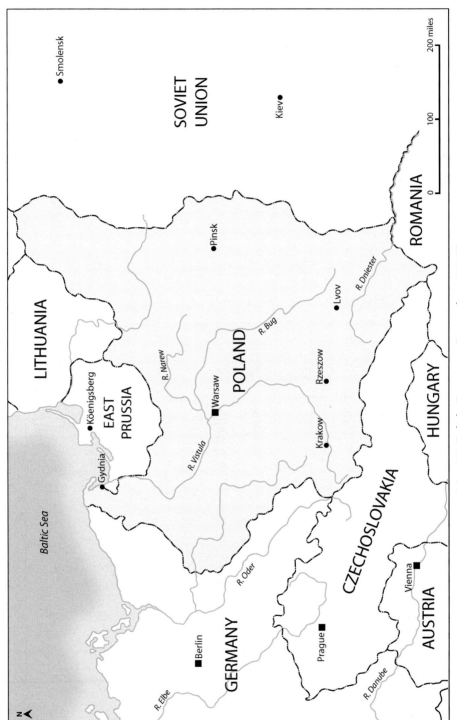

Map 25  Polish Campaign September 1939 Y.

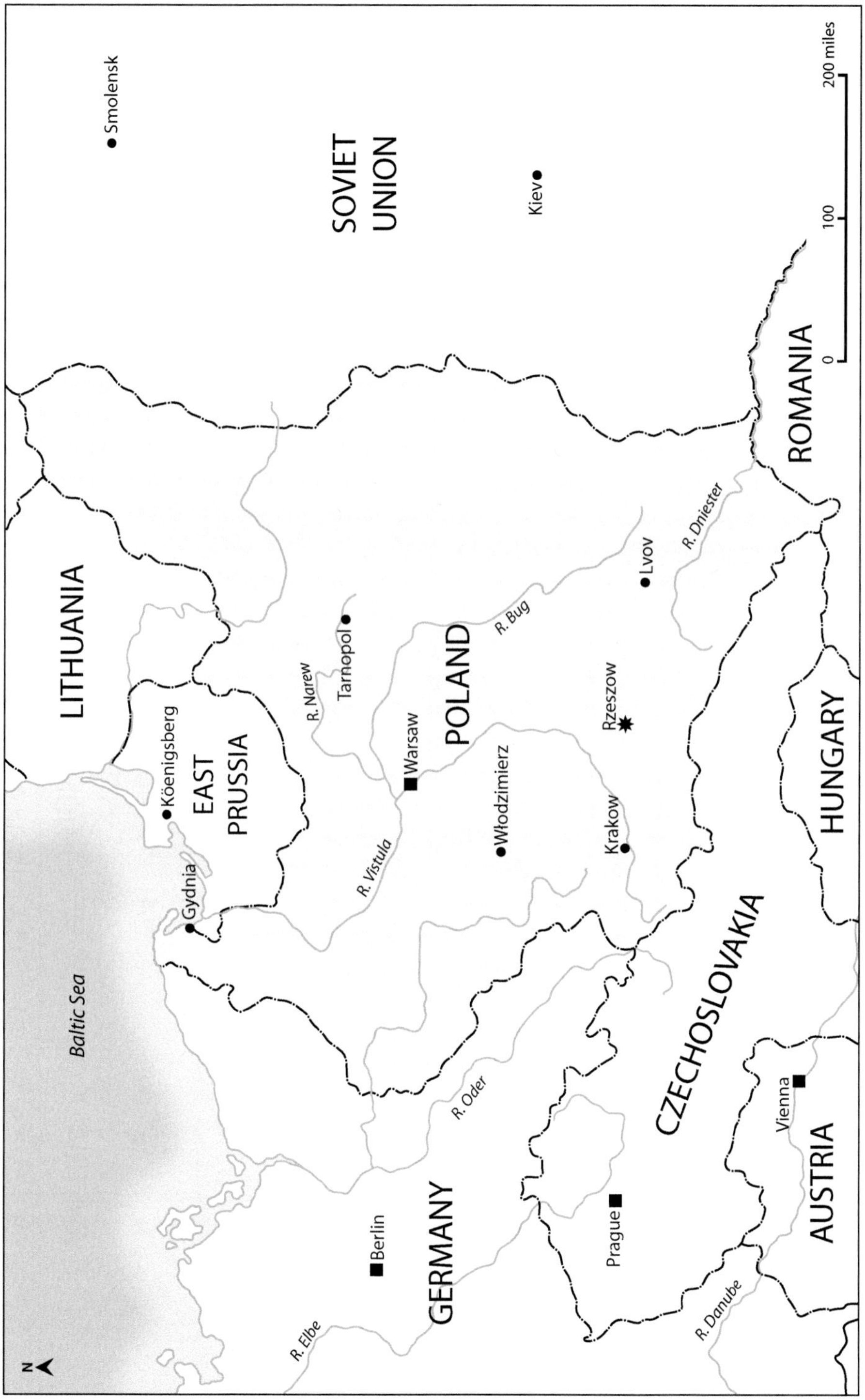

Map 26 Polish Campaign September 1939 Z.

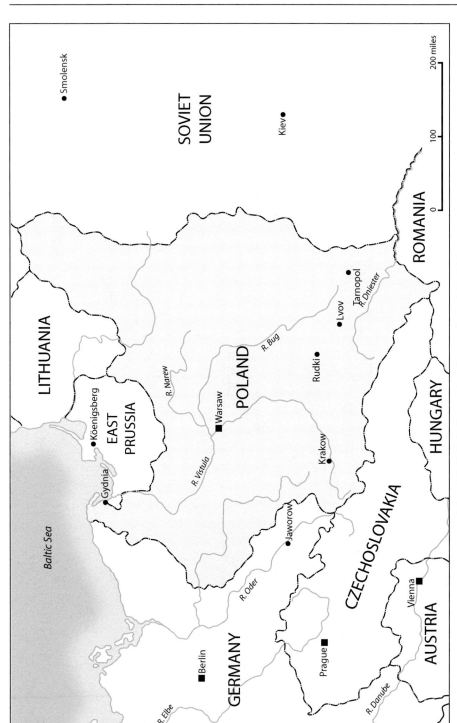

Map 27 Polish Campaign September 1939 A(a).

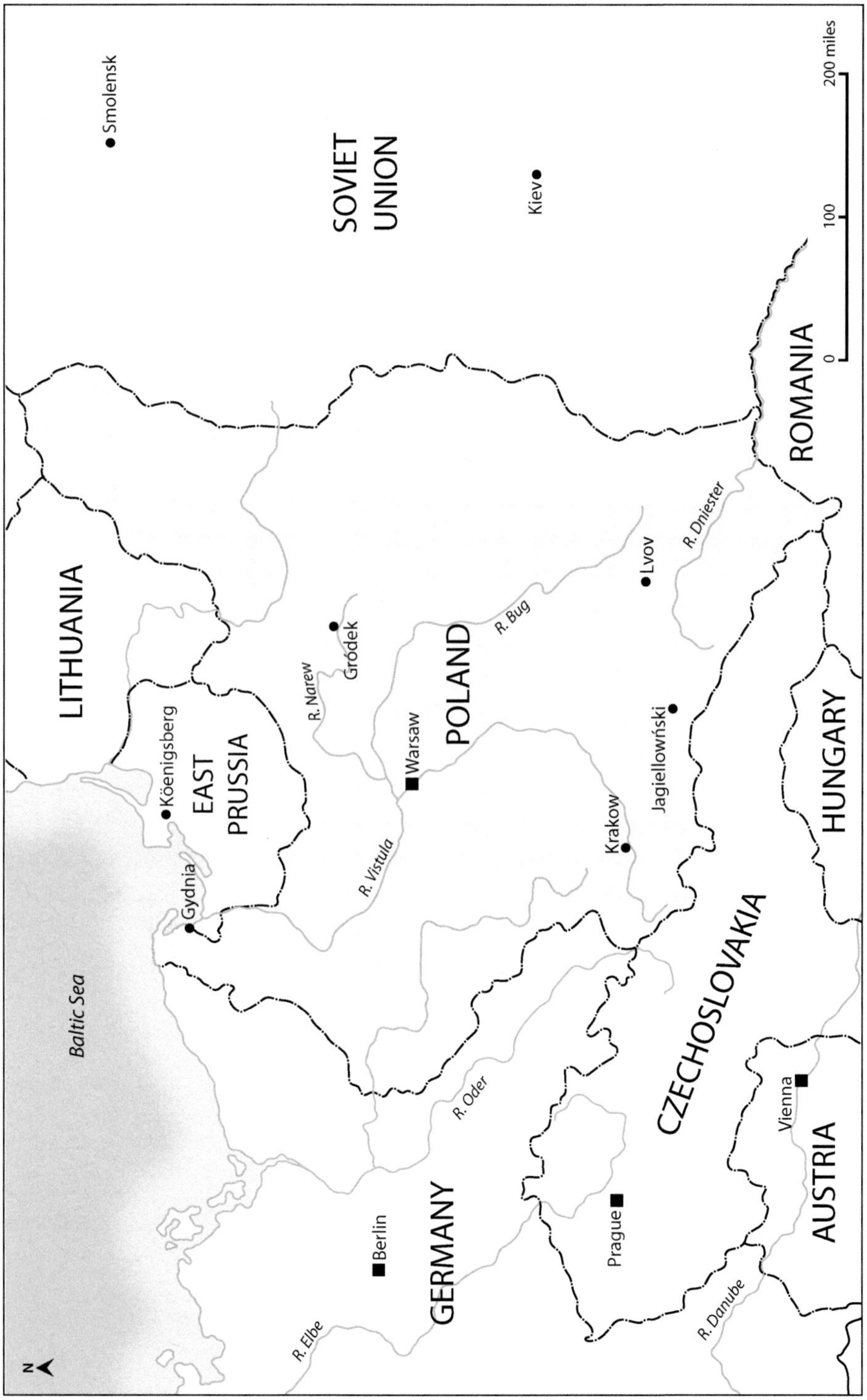

Map 28  Polish Campaign September 1939 B(b).

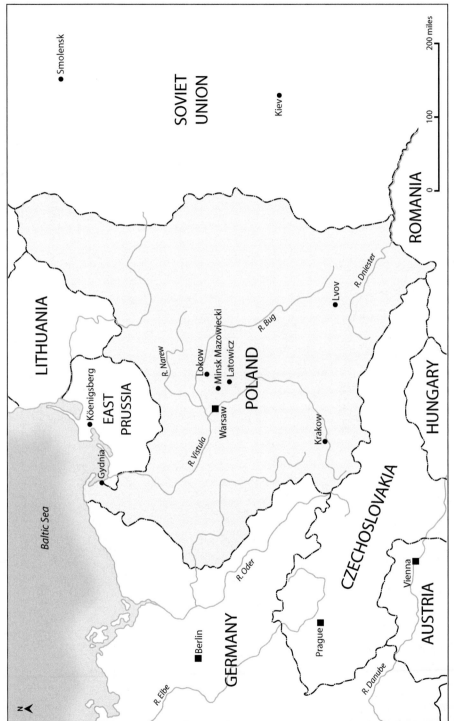

Map 29 Polish Campaign September 1939 C(c).

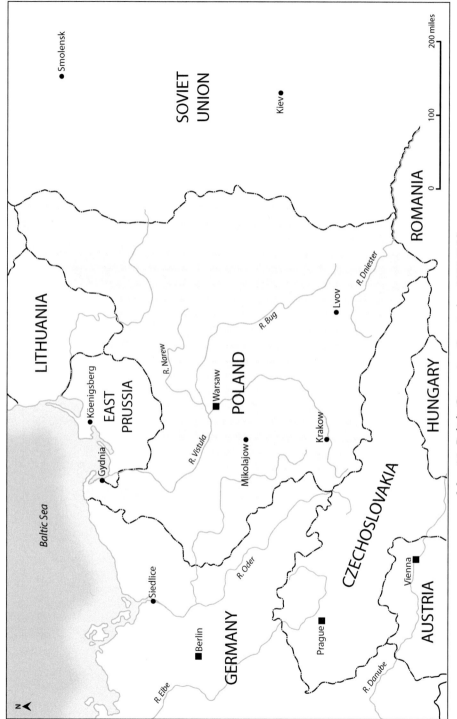

Map 30 Polish Campaign September 1939 D(d).

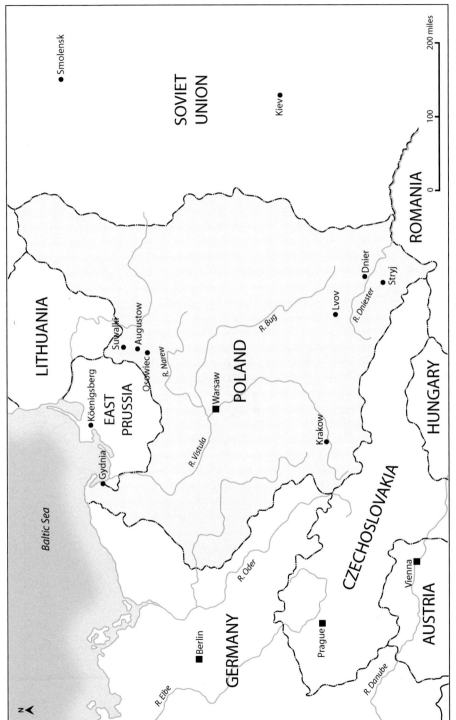

Map 31  Polish Campaign September 1939 E(e).

APPENDIX I 235

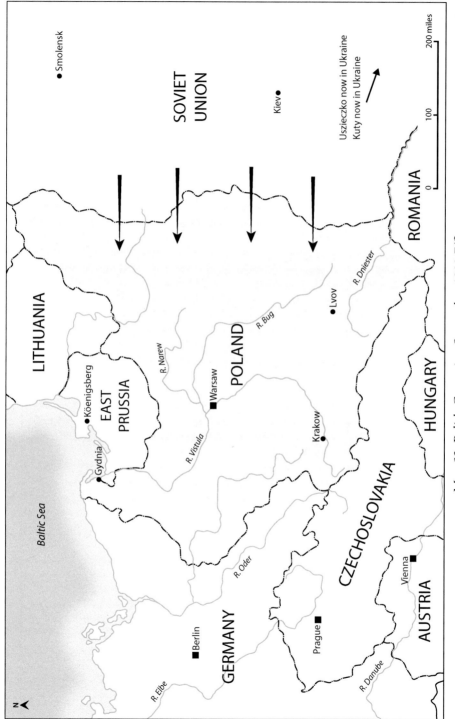

Map 32 Polish Campaign September 1939 F(f).

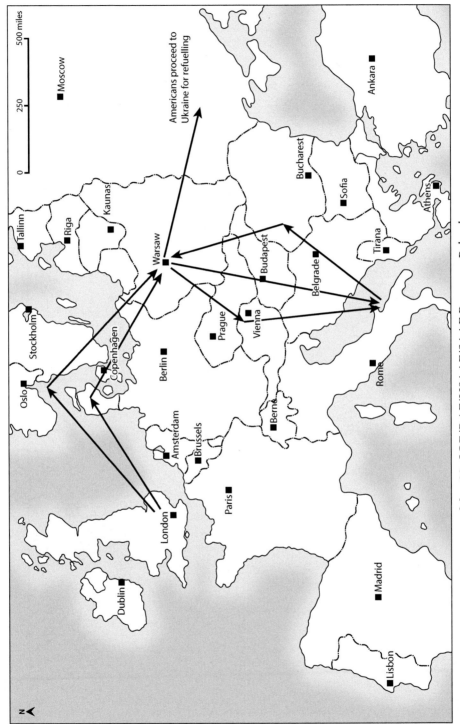

Map 33 SOE/RAF/USAAF/SAAF Routes to Poland.

# Appendix II
# Aircraft Employed in Operations to Poland (not to scale)

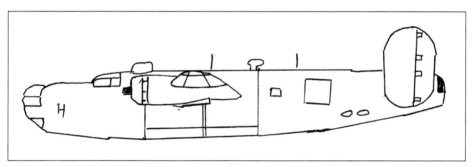

Boeing B-17 Flying Fortress Four-engine heavy bomber. (Developed 1930)

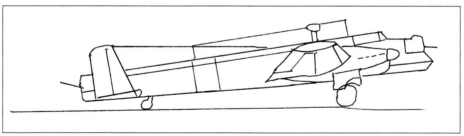

Armstrong Whitworth Whitley Twin-engine medium bomber. (First flight March 1936)

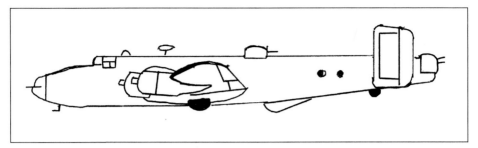

Hadley Page Halifax Four-engine heavy bomber. (First flight October 1939)

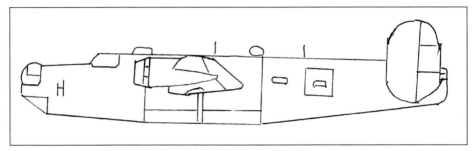

Consolidated Liberator four-engine heavy bomber. (First flight December 1939)

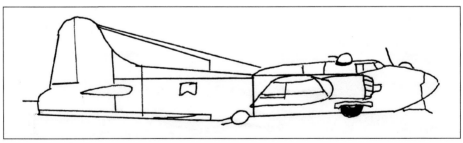

Douglas C-47 Dakota Military Transport Aircraft. (First flight December 1941)

# Appendix III

# List of Polish Special Forces Dropped into Poland (pseudonyms inclusive)

Adrian Florian 'Liberator'
Bałuk Stefan 'Starba'
Bator Ignacy 'Opór'
Bazała Leon 'Striwiąż'
Bąkiewicz Zbigniew 'Zabawka'
Benedyk Tadeusz 'Zahata'
Benrad Adam 'Drukarz'
Bernaczyk Kazimierz 'Rango'
Bętkowski Jacek 'Topór'
Biały Jan 'Kadłub'
Bichniewicz Jerzy 'Błękitny'
Bidziński Niemir 'Ziege Karol'
Biedrzycki Stanisław 'Opera'
Bielski Romuald 'Bej'
Bienias Jan 'Osterba'
Bieżuński Jan 'Orzyc'
Bilski Kazimierz 'Rum'
Bogusławski Prus Andrzej 'Pancerz'
Boryczka Adam 'Brona'
Borys Adam 'Pług'
Burdziński Tadeusz 'Malina'
Busłowicz Michał 'Bociek'
Buyno Jerzy 'Gżegżółka'
Bystrzycki Przemysław 'Grzbiet'
Bzdawka Bernard 'Siekiera'
Cetys Teodor 'Wiking'
Chmieloch Ryszard 'Błyskawica'
Chmielowski Antoni 'Wołk'

Chyliński Eugeniusz 'Frez'
Cieplik Franciszek 'Hatrak'
Czaykowski Andrzej 'Garda'
Czepczak-Górecki Bronisław 'Zwijak'
Czerwiński Kazimierz 'Bryzga'
Człapka Kazimierz 'Pionek'
Czuma Józef 'Skryty'
Dąbrowski Adam 'Puti'
Dekutowski Hieronim 'Zapora'
Dmowski Stanisław 'Podlasiak'
Dziadosz Rudolf 'Zasaniec'
Dzikielewski Feliks 'Oliw'
Eckhardt Mieczysław 'Bocian'
Emir-Hassan Jerzy 'Turek 2'
Farenholc Oskar 'Sum'
Fijałka Michał 'Kawa'
Flont Władysław 'Grandziarz' or 'Grandziarzon'
Fortuna Ludwik 'Siła'
Fuhrman Kazimierz 'Zaczep'
Gałecki Adolf 'Maszop'
Garczyński Marian 'Skała'
Gaworski Tadeusz 'Lawa'
Gilowski Stanisław 'Gotur'
Godzik Władysław 'Skrzat'
Golarz-Teleszyński Marian 'Góral 2'
Gołębiowski Marian 'Ster'
Gołuński Norbert 'Bombram'

Górski Jan 'Chomik'
Górski Stefan 'Brzeg'
Grodzicki Krzysztof 'Jabłoń'
Gromnicki Zygmunt 'Gula'
Grun Bronisław 'Szyb'
Grycz Jan 'Dziadzio'
Harasymowicz Stanisław 'Lalka'
Hauptman Władysław 'Gapa'
Heczko-Kalinowski Gustwa 'Skorpion'
Hencel Stanisław 'Pik'
Hoffman Wojciech 'Bugaj'
Hörl Jan 'Frog'
Iglewski Antoni 'Ponar' or 'Vanadi'
Ignaszak Stefan 'Drozd'
Ipohorski-Lenkiewicz Wiesław 'Zagroda'
Iranek-Osmecki Kazimierz 'Heller' or 'Makary'
Iszkowski Jerzy 'Orczyk'
Jabłoński Bolesław 'Kalia'
Jachciński Henryk 'Kret'
Jackiewicz Bolesław 'Łabędź'
Jagileski Stanisław 'Gacek'
Jakubowski Ewaryst 'Brat'
Jankowski Stanisław 'Burek'
Januszkiewicz Henryk 'Spokojny'
Jarosz Janusz 'Szermierz'
Jasieński Stefan 'Alfa' or 'Urban'
Jastrzębski Antoni 'Ugór'
Jaworski Tadeusz 'Gont'
Jaworski Tadeusz Stanisław 'Bławat'
Jeziorański Zdzisław, Nowak Jan 'Zych'
Jokiel Jan 'Ligota'
Jurecki Marian Aleksander Józef 'Orawa'
Jurkiewicz Longin 'Mysz'
Kalenkiewicz Maciej 'Kotwicz'
Kamieński Jan 'Cozas'
Kamiński Bronisław 'Golf'
Kaszyński Eugeniusz 'Nurt'
Kazimierczak Stanisław 'Ksiądz'
Kiwer Edward 'Biegaj'
Klimowicz Władysław 'Tama'
Klimowski Tadeusz 'Klon'
Klinicki Maksymilian 'Wierzba 2'
Klocek-Niewęgłowski Włodzimierz 'Garłuch'
Kobyliński Tadeusz 'Hiena'
Kobyliński Wacław 'Dziad'
Kochański Jan 'Jarema'
Kochański Władysław 'Bomba'
Kolasiński Stanisław 'Ulewa'
Konik Bronisław 'Sikora'
Konstanty Ignacy 'Szmaragd'
Kontrym Bolesław 'Żmudzin'
Kopisto Wacław 'Kra'
Koprowski Franciszek 'Dąb'
Kossakowski Tadeusz 'Krystynek'
Kostuch Tomasz 'Bryła'
Kotorowicz Stanisław 'Kron'
Kowalik Edward 'Ciupuś''
Kowalski Jerzy 'Baba'
Kowalski Ryszard 'Benga'
Kozłowski Julian 'Cichy'
Kożuchowski Henryk 'Hora'
Krajewski Henryk 'Trzaska' or 'Wicher'
Krasiński Adam 'Szczur'
Krizar Leopold 'Czeremosz'
Krokay Walenty 'Siwy'
Kryszczukajtis Mirosław 'Szary'
Krzymowski Stanisław 'Kostka'
Kuczyński Marian 'Zwrotnica'
Kujawiński Stanisław 'Wodnik'
Kułakowski Aleksander 'Rywal'
Kwarciński Mieczysław 'Ziut'
Kwiatkowski Bohdan 'Lewar'
Lech Jan 'Granit'
Lech Włodzimierz 'Powiślak'
Leśkiewicz Marian 'Wygoda'
Lewandowski ALeksander 'Wiechlina'
Lewko Kazimierz 'Palec'
Lewkowicz Bronisław 'Kurs'
Linowski Artur 'Karp'
Lipiński Wojciech 'Lawina'
Luszowicz Zdzisław 'Szakal'
Łada Lech 'Żagiew'
Łagoda Hieronim 'Lak'
Łakomy Albin 'Twornik'
Łastowski Zenon 'Łobuz'
Łojkiewicz Adolf 'Ryś'
Łopianowski Narcyz 'Sarna'
Łoś Ezechiel 'Ikwa'

Mackus Adma 'Prosty'
Majewicz Stefan 'Hruby'
Majorkiewicz Felicjan 'Iron'
Makagonow Aleksander 'Wschód'
Makarenko Anatol 'Tłok'
Maksyś Władysław 'Azot'
Malik Franciszek 'Piorun 2'
Marecki Władysław 'Żabik 2'
Marek Jan 'Walka'
Marynowski Edmund 'Sejm'
Matula Zbigniew 'Radomyśl'
Matysko Jan 'Oskard'
Mazur Stanisław 'Limba'
Messing Janusz 'Bekas'
Mich Stefan 'Jerz'
Michałczewski Wincenty 'Mir'
Miciek Władysław 'Młot'
Milewicz Zygmunt 'Róg'
Mostowiec Marian 'Lis'
Motylewicz Piotr 'Grab' or 'Krzemień'
Mrazek Zbigniew 'Aminius'
Nadolczak Bruno 'Piast'
Nakoniecznikoff-Klukowski Przemysław 'Kruk 2'
Niedzielski Rafał 'Mocny'
Niemczycki Jerzy 'Janczar'
Niepla Kazimierz 'Kawka'
Nosek Antoni 'Kajtuś'
Nowacki Józef 'Horyń'
Nowak Piotr 'Oko'
Nowakowski Michał 'Harpun'
Nowobilski Tadeusz 'Dzwon'
Nowodworski Cezary 'Głód'
Nuszkiewicz Ryszard 'Powolny'
Odrowąż-Szukewicz Bolesław 'Bystrzec'
Okulicki Leopold 'Niedźwiadek' lub 'Kobra'
Olszewski Stanisław 'Bar'
Ossowski Stanisław 'Jastrzębiec 2'
Ostrowiński Henryk 'Smyk'
Osuchowski Kazimierz 'Rosomak'
Paczkowski Alfred 'Wania'
Parada Michał 'Mapa'
Parczewski Jan 'Kraska'
Pentz Karol 'Skała 2'

Perekładowski Fliks 'Przyjaciel 2'
Peszke Zdzisław 'Kaszmir'
Pękala-Górski Mieczysław 'Bosak'
Piasecki Zbigniew 'Orlik'
Piątkowski Bohdan 'Mak'
Pic Witold 'Cholewa'
Piekarski Aleksander 'Turkuć'
Pieniak Czesław 'Bór'
Pijanowski Wacław 'Dym'
Pich Adolf 'Góra' lub 'Dolina'
Piotrowski Edward 'Mema'
Piotrowski Julian 'Rewera 2'
Piwnik Jan 'Ponury'
Pluta Wilhelm 'Pion'
Pokładecki Marian 'Zoli'
Pokultinis Alfred 'Fon'
Policiewicz Zygmunt 'Świerk'
Poliszuk Jarosław 'Arab'
Polończyk Bolesław 'Kryształ'
Pospieszalski Antoni 'Curie'
Poznański Jan 'Pływak'
Prądzyński Janusz 'Trzy'
Przetocki Jacek 'Oset'
Przybylik Stefan 'Gruch'
Psykała Mieczysław 'Kalwadosik'
Pukacki Franciszek 'Gzyms'
Rachwał Bronisław 'Glin'
Raczkowski Stanisław 'Bułany'
Raszplewicz Kazimierz 'Tatar 2'
Ratajski Leszek 'Żal'
Riedl Adam 'Rodak'
Rogowski Jan 'Czarka'
Romaszkan Roman 'Tatar'
Rossiński Czesław 'Kozioł'
Rostek Jan 'Dan'
Rostworowski Jan 'Mat'
Różycki Jan 'Busik'
Rudkowski Roman 'Rudy'
Runge Tadeusz 'Osa'
Rybka Franciszek 'Kula'
Rydzewski Lech 'Grom'
Rzepka Kazimierz 'Ognik'
Sawicki Zygmunt 'Samulik'
Scheller-Czarny Edwin 'Fordon'
Seeman Tadeusz 'Garbus'

Serafin Jan 'Czerchawa'
Serafiński Fryderyk 'Drabina'
Sędziak Stanisław 'Warta'
Siakiewicz Władysław 'Mruk'
Sikorski Zenon 'Pożar'
Skowron Marian 'Olcha 2'
Skowroński Ryszard 'Lechita'
Skowroński Stanisław 'Widelec'
Skrochowski Jan Kanty 'Ostroga'
Skwierczyński Leopold 'Aktor'
Smela Jan 'Wir'
Smolski Kazimierz 'Sosna'
Sokołowski Jerzy 'Mira'
Sokołowski Tadeusz 'Trop'
Sokół Tadeusz 'Bug 2'
Sołtys Stanisław 'Sowa'
Specylak Zbigniew 'Tur'
Spychalski Józef 'Grudzień' or 'Luty'
Sroczyński Zdzisław 'Kompresor'
Starzyński Leszek 'Malewa'
Starzyński Tadeusz 'Ślepowron'
Stocki Tadeusz 'Ćma'
Stołyhwo Olgierd 'Stewa'
Stpiczyński Aleksander 'Klara'
Straszyński Zdzisław 'Meteor'
Strumpf Witold 'Sud'
Szczepański Mieczysław 'Dębina'
Szewczyk Piotr 'Czer'
Szpakowicz Wiesław 'Pak'
Szternal Kazimierz 'Zryw'
Sztrom Jerzy 'Pilnik'
Szubiński Władysław 'Dach'
Szwiec Waldemar 'Robot'
Szydłowski Adam 'Poleszuk'
Szymański Feliks 'Boga'
Ściegienny Wincenty 'Las'
Śliwa Kazimierz 'Strażak'
Śmietanko Władysław 'Cypr'
Śmigielski Tadeusz 'Ślad'
Świątkowski Andrzej 'Amurat'
Tajchman Michał 'Mikita'
Tarnawski Aleksander 'Upłaz'
Tomaszewski Tadeusz 'Wąwóz'
Trojanowski Czesław 'Litwos'
Trondowski Stanisław 'Grzmot 2'
Trybus Adam 'Gaj'
Twardy zbigniew 'Trzask'
Uklański Witold 'Herold'
Ulm Zygmunt 'Szybki'
Walter Jan 'Cyrkiel'
Waruszyński Zbigniew 'Dewjtis 2'
Wątróbski Józf 'Jelito'
Whitehead Alfred 'Dolina 2'
Wiącek Jan 'Kanarek'
Wiechuła Bernard 'Maruda'
Wiechuła Ludwik 'Jeleń'
Wierzejewski Tomasz 'Zgoda 2'
Wilczewski Michał 'Uszka'
Wilczkiewicz Zbigniew 'Kij'
Winiarski Zdzisław 'Przemynik'
Winter Stanisław 'Przemytnik'
Wiszniwski Otton 'Topola'
Wiszniowski Roman 'Harcerz'
Wiśniewski Władysław 'Wróbel'
Witkowski Ludwik 'Kosa'
Wolniak Bogusław 'Mięta'
Woźniak Jan 'Kwaśny'
Zabielski Józef 'Żbik'
Zachmost Henryk 'Zorza'
Zając Józef 'Kolanko'
Zalewski Janusz 'Chinek'
Zaorski Wacław 'Ryba'
Zapotoczny Stanisław 'Płomień'
Zarembiński Wiktor 'Zrąb'
Zawacka Elżbieta 'Zo'
Zawadzki Alfred 'Kos'
Zub-Zdanowicz Leonard 'Dor'
Zyga Ryszard 'Lelum'
Żaak Franciszek 'Mamka'
Żabierek Lech 'Wulkan'
Żakowicz Józef 'Tabu'
Żelechowski Tadeusz 'Ring'
Żelkowski Bronisław 'Dąbrowa'
Żórawski Bogusław 'Mistral'
Żychiewicz Antoni 'Przerwa'

Source: <www.elitadywersji.org> (accessed 28 August 2019)

# Appendix IV

# Details of RAF Flights to Poland Procured by SOE

| | Date | Code Name | Aircraft Type | Course set for |
|---|---|---|---|---|
| Saturday/Sunday | 15/16 Feb 1941 | Adolphus | Whitley | Dębowiec |
| Friday/Saturday | 7/8 Nov 1941 | Ruction | Halifax | Lyszkowice |
| Saturday/Sunday | 27/28 Dec 1941 | Jacket | Halifax | Brzozów Stary |
| Tuesday/Wednesday | 6/7 Jan 1942 | Shirt | Halifax | Stefanówka |
| Tuesday/Wednesday | 3/4 Mar 1942 | Collar | Halifax | Wyszków |
| Friday/Saturday | 27/28 Mar 1942 | Boot | Halifax | Przyszowa |
| Monday/Tuesday | 30/31 Mar | Belt | Halifax | Podstoliska |
| Monday/Tuesday | 30/31 Mar 1942 | Legging | Halifax | Barycz |
| Wednesday/Thursday | 8/9 Apr 1942 | Cravat | Halifax | Drzewicz |
| Tuesday/Wednesday | 1/2 Sept 1942 | Chickenpox | Halifax | Stanisławów |
| Tuesday/Wednesday | 1/2 Sept 1942 | Smallpox | Halifax | Bogatki |
| Thursday/Friday | 3/4 Sept 1942 | Rheumatism | Halifax | Lyszkowice |
| Thursday/Friday | 3/4 Sept 1942 | Measles | Halifax | Stachlew |
| Thursday/Friday | 1/2 October 1942 | Chisel | Halifax | Lupiny |
| Thursday/Friday | 1/2 October 1942 | Hammer | Halifax | Głosków |
| Thursday/Friday | 1/2 October 1942 | Gimlet | Halifax | Tyczyn |
| Friday/Saturday | 2/3 October 1942 | Lathe | Halifax | Mokobody |
| Thursday/Friday | 29/30 Oct 1942 | Pliers | Halifax | Shot Down |
| Monday/Tuesday | 25/26 Jan 1943 | Brace | Halifax | Białobrzeg |
| Monday/Tuesday | 25/26 Jan 1943 | Screwdriver | Halifax | Łowicz |
| Tuesday/Wednesday | 26/27 Jan 1943 | Gauge | Halifax | Promnik |
| Tuesday/Wednesday | 16/17 Feb 1943 | Vice | Halifax | Minska |
| Tuesday/Wednesday | 16/17 Feb 1943 | Saw | Halifax | Sulejów |

| | | | | |
|---|---|---|---|---|
| Tuesday/Wednesday | 16/17 Feb 1943 | Rasp | Halifax | Sulejów |
| Wednesday/Thursday | 17/18 Feb 1943 | Wall | Halifax | Żelechów. |
| Wednesday/Thursday | 17/18 Feb 1943 | Floor | Halifax | Lapec |
| Friday/Saturday | 19/20 Feb 1943 | Spokeshave | Halifax | Radzice |
| Saturday/Sunday | 20/21 Feb 1943 | Rivet | Halifax | Naklo |
| Saturday/Sunday | 20/21 Feb 1943 | File | Halifax | Kotlice |
| Saturday/Sunday | 13/14 Mar 1943 | Window | Halifax | Bystrznowice |
| Saturday/Sunday | 13/14 Mar 1943 | Tile | Halifax | Kielc |
| Saturday/Sunday | 13/14 Mar 1943 | Stock | Halifax | Karpisk |
| Saturday/Sunday | 13/14 Mar 1943 | Brick | Halifax | Konskich |
| Saturday/Sunday | 13/14 Mar 1943 | Door | Halifax | Zwolenia |
| Sunday/Monday | 14/15 Mar 1943 | Step | Halifax | Ksiazenice |
| Tuesday/Wednesday | 16/17 Mar 1943 | Attic | Halifax | Stachlew |
| Friday/Saturday | 19/20 Mar 1943 | Beam | Halifax | Wielka Dabrowka |
| Wednesday/Thursday | 24/25 Mar 1943 | Cellar | Halifax | Helenow |
| Thursday/Friday | 9/10 Sept 1943 | Neon 4 | Halifax | unsuccessful |
| Tuesday/Wednesday | 14/15 Sept 1943 | Neon 7 | Halifax | Lucznica |
| Tuesday/Wednesday | 14/15 Sept 1943 | Neon 10 | Halifax | Lucnicza |
| Tuesday/Wednesday | 14/15 Sept 1943 | Neon 8 | Halifax | Tluszcza |
| Tuesday/Wednesday | 14/15 Sept 1943 | Neon 6 | Halifax | Nieporet |
| Thursday/Friday | 16/17 Sept 1943 | Neon 1 | Halifax | Wyszkowa |
| Thursday/Friday | 16/17 Sept 1943 | Neon 3 | Halifax | Tluszcza |
| Thursday/Friday | 16/17 Sept 1943 | Neon 2 | Halifax | Milenia |
| Tuesday/Wednesday | 21/22 Sept 1943 | Neon 5 | Halifax | Unrecorded |
| Wednesday/Thursday | 14/15 Sept 1943 | Neon 9 | Halifax | Shot Down |
| Monday/Tuesday | 18/19 Oct 1943 | Oxygen | Halifax | Nieborow |
| Monday/Tuesday | 3/4 Apr 1944 | Weller 5 | Halifax | Malcanow |
| Saturday/Sunday | 8/9 Apr 1944 | Weller 4 | Halifax | Cisow |
| Saturday/Sunday | 8/9 Apr 1944 | Weller 6 | Halifax | Zamozna Wola |
| Saturday/Sunday | 8/9 Apr 1944 | Weller 7 | Liberator | Dobieszyna |
| Sunday/Monday | 9/10 Apr 1944 | Weller 2 | Liberator | Kolakow |
| Sunday/Monday | 9/10 Apr 1944 | Weller 1 | Halifax | Nieporet |
| Wednesday/Thursday | 12/13 Apr 1944 | Weller 3 | Halifax | Zalesia (unsuccessful) |
| Wednesday/Thursday | 12/13 Apr 1944 | Weller 14 | Halifax | Belzyce |
| Friday/Saturday | 14/15 Apr 1944 | Weller 11 | Halifax | Koniusze |
| Saturday/Sunday | 15/16 Apr 1944 | Wildhorn 1 | Dakota | Matczyn |
| Sunday/Monday | 16/17 Apr 1944 | Weller 10 | Halifax | Kazimierza |
| Sunday/Monday | 16/17 Apr 1944 | Weller 12 | Halifax | Baniocha |
| Sunday/Monday | 16/17 Apr 1944 | Weller 15 | Halifax | Krawcowizna |

| | | | | |
|---|---|---|---|---|
| Thursday/Friday | 27/28 Apr 1944 | Weller 21 | Liberator | Bystrzyca |
| Sunday/Monday | 30 Apr/1 May 44 | Weller 16 | Liberator | Przybyszew |
| Thursday/Friday | 4/5 May 1944 | Weller 17 | Halifax | Kazimierza |
| Thursday/Friday | 4/5 May 1944 | Weller 26 | Liberator | Wola Galezowska |
| Wednesday/Thursday | 10/11 May 1944 | Weller 27 | Liberator | Zerechowa |
| Friday/Saturday | 19/20 May 1944 | Weller 18 | Liberator | Bronowicze |
| Sunday/Monday | 21/22 May 1944 | Weller 29 | Liberator | Wierzbno |
| Wednesday/Thursday | 24/25 May 1944 | Weller 23 | Halifax | Bochenski |
| Monday/Tuesday | 29/30 May 1944 | Wildhorn 2 | Dakota | Jadowniki Mokre |
| Tuesday/Wednesday | 30/31 May 1944 | Weller 30 | Halifax | Babrowka |
| Tuesday/Wednesday | 25/26 June 1944 | Wildhorn 3 | Dakota | Jadowniki Mokre |
| Sunday/Monday | 30/31 June 1944 | Jacek 1 | Liberator | Podkowa Leśna |
| Thursday | 21 Sept 1944 | Przemek 1 | Liberator | Czaryż |
| Monday | 16 Oct 1944 | Wacek 1 | Liberator | Kolonia Żerechowa |
| Monday | 16 Oct 1944 | Poldek 1 | Liberator | Kolonia Żerechowa |
| Saturday | 18 Nov 1944 | Kazik 1 | Liberator | Osowiec |
| Wednesday | 22 Nov 1944 | Kazik 2 | Liberator | Mogielnica |
| Tuesday | 25 Dec 1944 | Staszek 2 | Liberator | Szczawa |
| Tuesday | 26 Dec 1944 | Freston | Liberator | Żarki |

# Appendix V
# Drop sites in occupied Poland

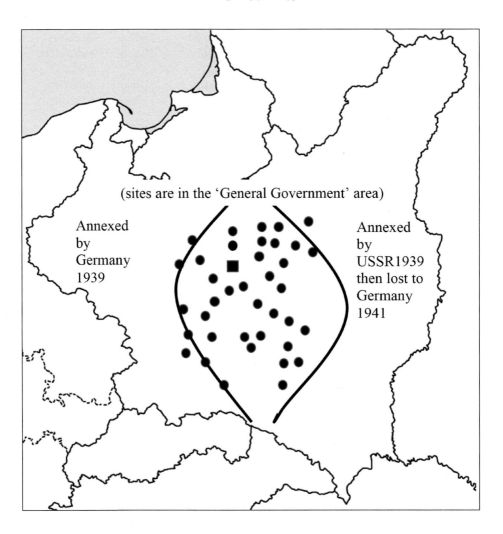

# Appendix VI
# SOE locations employed by Poles

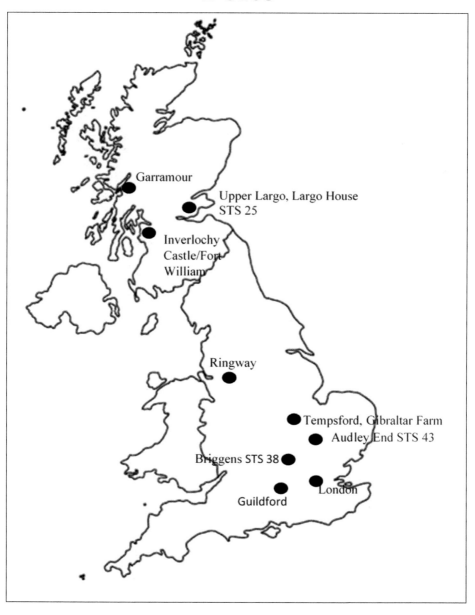

# Bibliography

## Archival Sources

*The National Archives of the United Kingdom (Kew)*
TNA HS4/147 Polish Secret Army, Polish planning for the reoccupation of Poland.
TNA HS4/148 Liaison with Poland by means of air
TNA HS4/ 154, Air19/816 Selborne to Sinclair 22.11.1944
TNA HS4/154 Liquidation of Force 139
TNA HS4/156 Warsaw Rising; War effort to Poland
TNA HS4/157, MJTP/PD/661 to Roberts. 8.8.44 Negotiations between Polish GHQ and COS during Warsaw Uprising 10.5.44. AD/M and MPCT 919 to Maryland (Italy)
TNA HS4/157 Operations to Warsaw
TNA HS4/157 Warsaw Rising: Reports from Poland. Foreign Office telegrams, Operations to Warsaw
TNA HS4/157 Warsaw Rising: Reports Poland. Foreign Office telegrams, Operations to Warsaw
TNA HS4/163 Sabotage and Guerrilla Warfare in Poland.
TNA HS4/166 1942-1944 The Use of Diplomatic Bags
TNA HS4/171 Planning and policy: operations to Warsaw, FINCHAM
TNA HS4/171 Planning and Policy: operations to Warsaw
TNA HS4/177 Results and Reports, equipment dropped
TNA HS4/180. 1943-1945 Wildhorn and Wildhorn VI air landing: planning and policy
TNA HS4/180 Wildhorn and Wildhorn VIV: air landing operations to Poland from N. Africa and Italy
TNA HS4/183 Wildhorn III pick up operations for special passengers to come to the UK from Poland
TNA HS4/184 Colonel Threlfall's report on air operations from Mediterranean theatre; training school at Latiano
TNA HS4/186 Polish military wireless research unit Stanmore, Anglo-Polish wireless meetings
TNA CAB121/310, SOE Operations in Poland Vol. II, 261B.
TNA CAB121/310, SOE Operations in Poland Vol. II, 321
TNA CAB121/310, SOE Operations in Poland Vol. II, 317
TNA CAB121/310, SOE Operations in Poland Vol. II, 275B

TNA CAB121/310, SOE Operations in Poland Vol. II, 261A.
TNA CAB 1212/130 Vol II Doc 382
TNA CAB 1212/130 Vol II Doc 393
TNA CAB 1212/130 Vol II Doc 404

**Printed Sources**

Brodecki, B, Wawer, Z, Kondracki' T., *Polacy na Frontach II Wojny Swiatowej*, Bellona, Warszawa 2005
Andrew, Christopher, *The Defence of the Realm*, Penguin Books, London 2009
Bellamy, Chris, *Absolute War*, Macmillan Publishers, London 2007
Berthon, Simon, *Allies at War*, Carrol and Graf Publishers, New York 2001
Bielecki, Zugmunt, Dębowski Ryszard, *In Defence of Independence, September 1939*, Interpress Publishers, Warsaw 1972
Bor-Komorowski, T, *The Home Army*, Publisher Victor Gollancz, London 1950
Bullock, Alan, *Hitler and Stalin*, Fontana Press, London 1993
Ciechanowski, Jan, *The Warsaw Rising of 1944*, Cambridge University Press, Cambridge 2002
Clarke, Alan, *Barbarossa*, Hutchinson, London 1995
Conway, M, and Gotovitch, J, *Europe in Exile*, Berghahn, New York 2001
Corrigan, Gordon, *Blood, Sweat and Arrogance*, Phoenix, London 2007
Davies, Norman, *Rising '44*, Macmillan Publishers, London 2003
Davies, Norman, *Europe*, Pimlico, London 1997
Davies, Norman, *Europe at War*, Macmillan, London 2008
Deighton, Len, *Blood, Tears and Folly*, Vintage Books, London 2007
Deighton Len, *Blitzkrieg*, William Collins, London 1979
Escott, B., *The Heroines of SOE*, The History Press, London
Fenby, Jonathan, *Alliance*, Simon and Schuster, London 2006
Fennel, Jonathan, *Fighting the People's War*, Cambridge University Press, Cambridge 2019
Foot, M.R.D., *SOE 1940-1946*, The Bodley Head, London 2014
Garliński, Jozef, *Poland, SOE and the Allies*, George Allen and Unwin, London 1969
Garliński, Jozef, *Poland in the Second World War*, Macmillan, London 1985
Goławski, Michał, *Polska Moja Ojczyzna*, Nakladem Ksiegarnia Polskiej Orbic Polonia, Londyn 1961
Gorodetsky, Gabriel, Editor, *The Maisky Diaries,* Yale University Press, London 2015
Gretzyngier, Robert, *Poles in the Defence of Britain*, Grub Street, London 2001
Hastings, Max, *Finest Years*, Harper Collins, London 2009
Juchniewicz, Mieczysław, *Poles in the European Resistance Movement 1939-1945*, Interpress Publishers, Warsaw 1972
Karski, *Jan: Story of a Secret State*, Penguin Books, London 2010
Kochański, Halik, *The Eagle Unbowed, Poland and the Poles in the Second World War*, London: Allen Layne, London 2012.

Koonz, Claudia, *The Nazi Conscience*, Cambridge University Press, London 2003
Kosgodan, Kenneth, *No Greater Ally*, Osprey Oxford 2009
Leslie, R. F. (ed.), *History of Poland since 1863*, Cambridge University Press, Cambridge 1995
Lett, Brian, *Mastermind: Sir Colin Gubbins*, Pen and Sword, Barnsley 2016
McGilvray, Evan, *A Military Government in Exile*, Helion, Solihull 2010
Minett, Peter (ed.), *Frank's Wartime Diary*, Self-published 2014
Milton Giles, *Churchill's Ministry of Ungentlemanly Warfare*, John Murray, London 2017
Moorhouse Roger, *First to Fight*, The Bodley Head, London 2019
Olson, Lynne, and Cloud, Stanley, *For Your Freedom and Ours*, Arrow Books, London 2004
Overy, Richard, *Why the Allies Won*, Pimlico, London 2006
Piotrowski, T, (ed.), *The Polish Deportees of World War Two*, McFarland and Co. Inc., London 2004
Plokhy, S. M., *Yalta*, Penguin Books, London 2010
Prażmowska, A. J., *Britain and Poland 1939-1943*, Cambridge University Press, Cambridge 1995
Prażmowska, A. J., *Civil War in Poland 1942-1948*, Palgrave, Macmillan, Basingstoke, 2004
Rees, Laurence, *Behind Closed Doors*, BBC Books, London 2009
Richie, Alexandra, Warsaw 1944, William Collins, London 2013
Roberts, Andrew, *The Storm of War*, Allen Lane, London 2009
Sebestyen, Victor, *1946: The Making of the Modern World*, Macmillan, London 2014
Schen, Peijian, *The Age of Appeasement*, Sutton Publishers, London 1999
Shachtman, Tom, *The Phony War, 1939-1940*, Harper Collins, New York 1982
Snyder, Timothy, *Bloodlands*, Vintage Books, London 2010
Stella-Sawicki, M, Galiński J., Mucha, J. (eds.), *First to Fight*, Polish Ex-Combatants Association of Great Britain, London 2009
Sword, Keith, *Sikorski*, Orbis Books, London 1990
The National Archives, *SOE Manuel*, William Collins, London 2014
Terlecki, Olgierd, *Poles in the Italian Campaign, 1943-1945*, Interpress Publishers, 1972
Thorne, J. O. and Collocott, T. C. (eds.), *Chamber's Biographical Dictionary*, Chambers, Edinburgh 1985
Valentine, Ian, Station 43: *Audley End House and SOE's Polish Section*, Sutton Publishing, Stroud, 2004
Walker, Jonoathan, *Poland Alone*, History Press, Stroud, 2008
Weinberg, Gerhard, *A World at Arms*, Cambridge University Press, Cambridge 1994
Wheal, E. and Pope, S., *The Second World War*, Macmillan, London 1995
Williamson, D. G., *Poland Betrayed*, Pen and Sword, Barnsley 2009
Zamoyski, A., *Warsaw 1920*, Harper Press, London 2008
Zamoyski, A., *The Forgotten Few*, The Polish Airforce in the Second World War, John Murray, London 1995

Zaluski, Zbigniew, *Poles on the Fronts of the Second World War*, Interpress Publishers Warsaw, 1969

## Journals and Conference Papers

Second International Military History Conference, Conference Papers, *The Polish Heritage Society*, 11 June 2016

Szołdrska Halszka, Zrzuty, *AK Pamięć i tożsamość, Biuletyn Informacyjny*, Listopad 2014, pp. 44-48

Tochman Krzysztof, Ptaszki i Kociaki, *Kombatant* Nr. 2 (242)2011, pp. 15-21

## Electronic Sources

*Cichociemni elita dywersji* <www.elitadywersji.org>

# Index

Air Ministry, 73, 93, 96, 99, 102, 109, 113–14, 116, 119–20, 128, 130, 132, 156
Alexandria, 26–27

B-17 Flying Fortress, 179–80
B-24 Liberator, 102, 114, 117, 122, 145
Baltic Sea, 18, 93, 95, 97, 116, 128, 180, 204–35
Berlin, 18–19, 45, 92, 95, 125–26, 150–51, 156–57, 161, 186–87, 191, 204–36
Bor-Komorowski (General Tadeusz Komorowski), 126, 131, 141, 156, 160–61, 164–65, 167-68, 171, 181, 184–85, 249
Bucharest, 26–27, 45, 49, 167, 236

C-47 Dakota, 89, 143–46
Canada, 43, 187, 197–99
Chamberlain, Neville, 18, 108–9
Churchill, Winston, 19, 53–54, 64–67, 76, 104–5, 107–8, 125, 150, 153–54, 162–65, 171–73, 191–92, 194–95, 198, 201
Cichociemni, 80, 90–91, 115
Czechoslovakia, 18, 22, 32, 88, 138, 204–35
Czestochowa, 37–38, 209, 220

Dalton, Hugh, 66, 73, 77, 91, 99, 103, 112–14, 151–52
Danzig, 18, 29–30, 36
Dniester, 204–35

Eisenhower, General Dwight, 150, 175

Foreign Office, 59, 61, 63–64, 135–36, 148, 153, 167, 170, 172, 174–76, 190, 194, 248

Germany, 18–19, 21, 23, 28, 30–31, 49, 51, 57–59, 92–94, 96, 102–3, 107, 184–85, 204–35
Górski, Captain J., 78, 80–81
Gubbins, Brigadier Colin, 20–22, 25–27, 29, 46–48, 52–53, 68, 101, 103, 110, 112–14, 116, 120, 122, 132–33, 185

Hambro, Charles, 67, 119, 201,
Hitler, Adolf 17–21, 27, 64, 66, 89, 197, 249
Home Army, 51–53, 60, 74–78, 85–87, 96–97, 99–100, 112–13, 125–26, 128, 131–33, 135–36, 138–40, 142–49, 151–52, 155–58, 160–65, 169–71, 173–76, 181, 187–88, 192–97
Hungary, 22, 51, 73, 88, 137–38, 168, 185, 204–35

Italy, 25, 88, 91–92, 137–41, 143–45, 150–51, 153, 164, 166–67, 185, 187, 189, 195, 197, 248

Kiev, 204–35
Klauber, Captain G.L., 71–72, 139
Köenigsberg, 204–35
Krakow, 204–35

Lublin, 41, 144
Lwów, 41, 43–44, 47, 81

MI5, 63–64, 83
Mikolajczyk, Stanislaw, 61, 74, 112, 147, 153, 158, 170–71, 173–74, 184, 189, 191

Nelson Frank, 67, 119, 201-2

Oddzial Lacznikowy Komendanta Glownego AK przy Naczelnym Wodzu, 71–72
Operation Barbarossa, 19, 103
Operation Boot, 114
Operation Collar, 114
Operation Freston, 186, 192
Operation Jacket, 109, 113
Operation Overlord, 158, 200
Operation Shirt, 109, 113–14
Operation Unthinkable, 185, 190
Operation Weller, 141

People's Republic of Poland (PRP), 49, 107, 192–93
Perkins, Captain Harold, 25, 70-72, 77, 109-11, 114, 117-18, 132-33, 153, 156, 158, 164-65, 171, 184, 188-89, 192-94, 200-1
Polish Diaspora, 107–8, 131, 134, 152, 187
Polish Second Republic, 87, 105, 108
Polish Underground Army, 52, 82, 148
Prague, 204–36

Radom, 33, 38, 40, 42, 217, 220
Red Army, 44, 104–6, 108, 125–26, 131, 134, 155–58, 161–62, 165, 172–73, 176, 185, 187, 190–91, 194–95
Romania, 21–23, 25–26, 41, 45, 47–48, 51, 73–74, 185
Rudnicki, Lieutenant-Colonel T., 112–14, 117–18

Second Polish Republic, 17–19, 27–29, 49, 53, 57–61, 74, 77–78, 80–81, 105–8, 126–27, 134, 146–48, 154–58, 166, 175–76, 184–88, 190–91, 193–97, 200
Selborne, Earl of, 114, 118–20, 129–31, 133, 151, 163, 165, 171, 192, 248
Slessor, Air Marshal Sir John, 162, 164–66, 168–70, 176, 189
Śmigly-Rydz, Marshal Edward, 42–43, 45
Sikorski, General Eugeniusz, 51–61, 74,, 77–78, 81, 91–93, 102, 107–8, 110, 112–13, 116, 122–23, 126-27, 135, 144, 148

Silesian Front, 37–39, 41
Sinclair, Sir Archibald, 92–93, 112–13, 120, 171, 192, 248
Sixth Bureau, 70–73, 75–78, 81–82, 86–87, 92, 94, 96–97, 99–101, 112, 117–18, 123, 125, 128, 138–40, 192–93
Smolensk, 204–35
Smoleński, Colonel Józef, 21, 56, 72, 103, 111–12, 117
Sosnkowski, General Kazimierz, 61, 112, 128–32, 153, 169
Soviet Union, 19–20, 25, 49–52, 58–61, 64, 68., 93, 103–8, 130, 133–34, 136, 151–52, 175–76, 184–86, 188, 192, 195, 198-99
Stalin, Józef, 49, 59, 93, 103-4, 106-8, 111, 126, 131, 134, 136, 146–47, 150, 161-65, 169, 171-75, 182, 184, 187, 189-91, 196
Supreme Headquarters of the Allied Expeditionary Forces (SHAEF), 174
Sweet-Escott, Bickham, 70–71, 77

Tabor, General Tatar, 132, 147, 168, 170–71
Threlfall, Henry, 139, 142, 169–70, 176, 185, 189, 193
Truszkowski, Major R., 71–72, 126, 132, 138

Ukraine, 19, 22, 172, 179, 181–82, 235–36
Union of Armed Struggle (UAS), 21, 43, 52
United States of America, 74, 78–79, 108, 111, 122, 125, 150, 166–67, 179, 186-88, 190, 193, 197

Vienna, 204–36
Vistula, 61, 170, 172, 181

War Office, 22–23, 25–26, 64–65, 69, 76–77, 79, 112, 118, 128–30, 136, 156
Warsaw Uprising (1944), 59–60, 89, 126, 140, 167–68, 170, 176, 187, 190, 200
Westerplatte, 30, 36, 205
Wiart, General Sir Adrian Carton de, 24–25, 27. 30, 48
Wildhorn Operations, 143, 145-147, 149